READING LUKE-ACTS

READING LUKE-ACTS

DYNAMICS OF BIBLICAL NARRATIVE

William S. Kurz, S. J.

Westminster/John Knox Press
Louisville, Kentucky

Book design by Susan E. Jackson

First edition

This book is printed on acid-free paper that meets the American National Standards Institute Z39.48 standard. ∞

Published by Westminster/John Knox Press
Louisville, Kentucky

PRINTED IN THE UNITED STATES OF AMERICA

9 8 7 6 5 4 3 2 1

Library of Congress Cataloging-in-Publication Data

Kurz, William S., 1939–
    Reading Luke–Acts : dynamics of Biblical narrative / William S. Kurz.
        p.   cm.
    Includes bibliographical references and index.

    ISBN-0-664-25441-1 (pbk. : alk. paper)

    1. Bible. N.T. Luke—Criticism. Narrative.   2. Bible. N.T. Acts—Criticism. Narrative.   3. Narration in the Bible.   I. Title.
BS2589.K87   1993
226.4′066—dc20   93-18125

Contents

Abbreviations

Abbreviations are primarily based on those in the style sheets of the *Journal of Biblical Literature* and *Catholic Biblical Quarterly*. Unless indicated otherwise, texts and translations of Greek and Latin authors are taken from the Loeb Classical Library (LCL).

Ag. Ap. = Josephus, *Against Apion*

Apuleius *Met.* = Apuleius, *Metamorphoses*

Aristotle, *Poetics* = Aristotle, *The Poetics*

AsSeign = *Assemblées du Seigneur*

BAGD = Bauer, Arndt, Gingrich, Danker, *A Greek-English Lexicon of the New Testament and Other Early Christian Literature*

Beginnings = *Beginnings of Christianity*

Bel = Josephus, *Jewish War*

Bib = *Biblica*

BTB = *Biblical Theology Bulletin*

CBQ = *Catholic Biblical Quarterly*

Dionysius, *Roman Antiquities* = Dionysius of Halicarnassus, *Roman Antiquities*

ETL = *Ephemerides theologicae lovanienses*

EvT = *Evangelische Theologie*

Herm. Vis. = *Visions of Hermas*

Herodotus = Herodotus of Halicarnassus, first Greek historian

IDB = Interpreter's Dictionary of the Bible

IDBSup = Interpreter's Dictionary of the Bible Supplement

JBL = Journal of Biblical Literature

Jos. Ant = Josephus, Jewish Antiquities

Jos. Ag. Ap. = Josephus, Against Apion

Jos., Vit. = Josephus, Vita (or Life)

JSJ = Journal for the Study of Judaism in the Persian, Hellenistic and Roman Periods

LCL = Loeb Classical Library

Lucian, Hist. = Lucian, How to Write History

Nestle-Aland[26] = Nestle-Aland Novum Testamentum Graece, 26th ed.

NovT = Novum Testamentum

NTS = New Testament Studies

Plato, Phaedo = Plato of Athens, Phaedo

Pliny Ep. = Pliny the Younger, Letters

Ps.-Clem. Recog. = Pseudo-Clement, Recognitiones

RevExp = Review and Expositor

SBL = Society of Biblical Literature

SBLSP = Society of Biblical Literature Seminar Papers

SBLDS = Society of Biblical Literature Dissertation Series

SecCent = Second Century

TCGNT = Metzger, Textual Commentary of the Greek New Testament

TS = Theological Studies

TynBul = Tyndale Bulletin

UBSGNT[3] = United Bible Society Greek New Testament, 3d ed.

WTJ = Westminster Theological Journal

ZNW = Zeitschrift für die neutestamentliche Wissenschaft

Preface

The original seeds that resulted in the full flowering of this monograph were sown in spring 1986, during my first sabbatical at the Library of Congress and the Catholic University of America library in Washington, D.C. There began my fascination with the new application of literary-critical narrative approaches to biblical writings, primarily then the Hebrew Scriptures. The pioneers in these narrative approaches to the Bible were either themselves secular literary critics or heavily reliant on them, and they pointed me toward many literary, philosophical, and historiographical serials and sections of libraries that I had not been used to consulting in my exegetical research. That semester I was able to read widely and deeply, follow leads, and gather materials and bibliography for my own later publication. While I was absorbing this material and writing exploratory articles using these methods, invitations and contracts to publish another monograph and some essays intervened before I could begin the actual work on the present book. During that time I was also able to test the methods that undergird this book in both graduate and undergraduate courses. All of that gave these new seeds an opportunity to mature and gave me the opportunity to weed out undesirable offshoots.

As is true of many practitioners of narrative biblical criticism, my initial interest was partially fed by pastoral and theological concerns about the need to "put Humpty Dumpty back together again" after the disintegrating and alienating effects of some historical criticism of the Bible. From my earliest forays into narrative criticism, I had become aware of deconstruction and other literary approaches that would not address my concern for some unity in the church's scripture. Therefore I looked also to a second movement in biblical criticism, the pioneer efforts in the so-called "canonical criticism."

My search for canonical approaches to make scripture more usable by faith communities continues. In my judgment, these canonical efforts have not led to methods as plainly teachable as have the literary studies of narrative. For example, I continue to try in my Marquette graduate courses to enlist students with diverse theological specialties to try to elaborate actual methods of achieving the canonical concerns so eloquently voiced but not so frequently incorporated in actual exegesis and hermeneutics of biblical texts. Though not as fully developed as narrative methods, these more tentative canonical approaches have contributed to *Reading Luke-Acts: Dynamics of Biblical Narrative.*

I am grateful to the Marquette University Theology Department and to the Marquette Jesuit Community for enabling the sabbatical leaves of 1985–86 and 1990–91, which respectively facilitated the initial research and the final manuscript of this book. I have profited much from and deeply appreciate the editorial expertise of Westminster's Associate Editorial Director, Dr. Cynthia Thompson, who encouraged this project from the time it was "just a glint in its father's eye," and Danielle Alexander, Carl Helmich, Sandra Jull, and Katy Monk in the copyediting division. At Marquette, I benefited from early editing aid from Edmund Miller (English) and research assistance from Robert Helmer (Theology). My brother and sister-in-law Andrew and Janet Kurz generously contributed the computer system on which this was written, and my family, Jesuit community, Servants of Yahweh prayer community, Marquette colleagues, and many friends provided the personal support needed to finish such a long-range project. To all of them I am deeply thankful.

1 Introduction: Reading Luke-Acts as Biblical Narrative

This book approaches the Gospel of Luke and Acts of the Apostles as a unified two-volume narrative, Luke-Acts, whose unity is a composite result of diverse sources. It treats Luke-Acts as a scriptural narrative, that is, as a part of the Christian Bible and as the kind of narrative common in the Greek Bible of the Jews, the Septuagint, which provided inspiration and models for many of the Lukan narratives. While going beyond the more usual historical-critical approaches to scripture, it builds on them. Narrative criticism or focus on narrative concentrates on the story line, narrators, points of view, implied commentary, and process of reading that make Luke and Acts a narrative as distinguished from a treatise, letter, speech, or even a collection of unrelated stories. The special emphasis on Lukan narrators highlights the Lukan point of view on the events recounted, both as subsuming traditional materials and sources and as adding a distinctive voice to the harmony of the New Testament.

The biblical focus features the contributions of Luke-Acts to the Christian Bible, considered as a major source of Christian life and theology. Just as a purely historical focus fails to do justice to the nature of the text as part of Christian revelation, so would a merely literary focus, or even a combination of historical and literary approaches, fail to deal specifically with Luke and Acts as scripture. Canonical concerns restore emphasis on the unity of the Lukan narrative, which some deconstructionist literary modes can overshadow as much as the more dichotomizing forms of historical source criticism. Canonical concerns broaden the context of a purely literary criticism to include the place of Luke and Acts within the whole Christian Bible and traditions of interpretation, which are the contexts within which most ordinary Christians read Luke's Gospel and Acts.

1

Since Luke and Acts are traditional community narratives, which differ in significant ways from the more individualistic contemporary novels on which most literary theories are predicated, this work selects and emphasizes only those current methods and approaches of literary criticism that seem appropriate for the Lukan narrative. It will not stress other methods that seem to alienate Luke-Acts from the biblical tradition in which it participates, or from the religious and historical realities to which it claims to refer, or from the religious context of the readers for whom it was intended. Biblical critics have been rebuked for not fully plunging into the latest trends of literary criticism.[1] But my objective is not to be au courant with the latest approaches to a contemporary fiction that is often nihilistic; my concern is to make a discerning application of those methods that seem helpful for the kind of ancient traditional literature with a strong oral substratum that appears in the Gospels and Acts.[2]

The book's structure first emphasizes the characteristics, methods, and questions appropriate to narrative in general, such as implied authors and readers (chap. 2) and plotting and gaps (chap. 3). The following chapters of applications (4–8) dwell chiefly on the narrator, who is the key to the focus and perspective of the narrative as a whole. All narrative comes through the narrator's point of view to a far greater extent than most people realize. It is through the narrator that readers have access to the narrative's plot, characters, theology, or ideology, and so on. The same event told by two different narrators, or from two different narratorial points of view, will result in two quite different narratives. This can be illustrated by the experiment of retelling an incident of conflict between Jesus and the Pharisees from the point of view of a Pharisee.

The final application in chapter 9, implicit commentary, is also closely related to the narrator. The kinds of implicit commentary treated, misunderstanding and irony (following Culpepper's approach), are filtered through the narrator and the narrator's point of view.[3] In a narrative, misunderstanding and irony depend utterly on the stance of the narrator in recounting an incident.

VALUES OF NARRATIVE CRITICISM

Some forms of narrative criticism seem especially promising for getting beyond current impasses among scripture scholars. Narrative analysis applies to narratives of all genres, whether their primary objective is historical or fictional.[4] It can therefore be applied to Luke and Acts without first solving the dispute over what genre(s) they are. Narrative criticism studies how all narratives work and uncovers what in a narrative is conventional and how it refers to events it describes. It can thus explain resemblances between earlier and later biblical narratives, such as similarities in Luke-Acts to stories in the Christian Greek Old Testament. It studies the plot of any narrative, including history, with a beginning, middle, and end. It examines what kinds of narrators tell the story, to whom and from what point of view they tell it, and what gaps are left for readers to fill in. It explains implicit commentary in narrative through use of irony, symbolism, and misunderstanding of characters. Narrative criticism describes what kind of readers are implied by the text and what the author reveals about himself or herself in the text.[5]

Thus, narrative analysis can throw new light on the following issues and passages that have continued to elude consensus among Lukan interpreters: the prologues of Luke and Acts; the role of Theophilus (Luke 1:3, Acts 1:1); the kinds of narrators, including the notoriously difficult "we" narrator first appearing in Acts 16:10; the function and discrepancies of the three versions of Paul's conversion narrative in Acts 9, 22, and 26; the ending of Acts and overlap between the end of Luke and beginning of Acts; various points of view and standards of judging characters and actions; the use of irony and misunderstanding as implicit commentary; the kind of author and reader implied by the narrative itself (to limit and ground historical conjectures about authors and communities); and the significance of Luke and Acts for later Christians beyond "what the author intended."

HISTORICAL CRITICISM AND ITS LIMITS

The increasing prominence of scriptural narrative criticism is in great part due to intensifying dissatisfaction with approaching the Bible exclusively through historical criticism. In fact, many authors have referred to a contemporary crisis for historical criticism of the Bible.[6] Several even refer to a paradigm shift for biblical study. Just as the historical paradigm of the Enlightenment completely replaced the dogmatic-allegorical paradigm of medieval biblical approaches, so now there appear to be signs of a movement beyond the historical paradigm to some new paradigm or paradigms.[7] The evolution within historical criticism, which has been going on for some time, seems now to be heading beyond mere evolution to quite new viewpoints and approaches.[8] As each phase of historical-critical methodology reached the limits of its usefulness, a new phase would evolve, building on the previous one. Thus the methods evolved from source to form to redaction to composition criticism, but all were governed strictly by the historical paradigm and answered historical questions.

Several recent methodological variations have continued this evolution, straining perhaps but still not bursting the historical perspective. These include the revised historical methods of varieties of biblical theology, as well as sociological and anthropological interpretation.[9] One type of canonical criticism studied how, after individual works were composed, later generations of believers appropriated and incorporated those works into a larger biblical corpus.[10] Another form dealt with the final canonical text and context of books as parts of scripture.[11] Not even these canonical approaches escaped the overall historical perspective. They seemed rather to deal with a later phase in the works' histories: either the process of canonization or the time of the final canonized text. They still did not focus on how these texts are read in the twentieth century.

In the meantime, there were parallel movements of hermeneutics to try to deal with contemporary application of scripture, especially the Bultmannian and post-Bultmannian approaches.[12] These could not quite overcome a kind of schizophrenia between theologians and biblical scholars: hermeneutics remained more akin to systematic theologizing than to exegesis. Many exegetes virtually ignored hermeneutics, with its philosophical terminology, to pursue their historical and textual interests.

This kind of schizophrenia evolved into a double-vision approach, with some writers distinguishing exegesis in the university from exegesis in the church.[13] Reconciling dogmatics and exegesis remained a problem: some theologians tried to elaborate a dogmatic-historical exegesis. Questions arose over whether the Bible is to be exegeted as historical source or as scripture.[14]

Early versions of literary approaches remained under the overarching historical paradigm. They appeared to be a way to focus more holistically on the text, which would continue to be studied within its ancient settings and genres.[15] But as dissatisfaction with historical criticism's limits grew, literary criticism as practiced on contemporary literature began to attract increased attention from biblicists.[16]

Diverse currents have fed into the dissatisfaction with and apparently imminent breakdown of the historical paradigm in biblical studies. These have ranged from the frustration of both dogmatic theologians and Christian believers in dealing with a text that historical criticism alienated from the present and fixed in the irrecoverable past, to charismatic and Pentecostal dissatisfaction with historicist reductionism that would deny the miraculous elements of scripture, to economic and feminist liberation theologies' discontent with a supposedly uncommitted objective approach to scripture.[17]

The combination of all these factors has led to a severe strain on the overarching historical paradigm that has had virtually absolute dominion over biblical studies since the Enlightenment breakdown of the dogmatic-allegorical paradigms.

LITERARY-CRITICAL CORRECTIVES

As scholars look for correctives and supplements for the shortcomings of historical criticism, contemporary literary criticism appears to offer many advantages. One is its ability to examine any narrative as narrative, regardless of its individual genre. The continuing vigorous debates about the genre(s) of Luke and Acts are complicated by differences between ancient and contemporary historiographical, biographical, and fictional genres. For example, ancient history was always written for a general audience, never solely for academic historians, as today.[18] Therefore historians had to tell an interesting tale, and they sometimes mixed genres (like history and fiction with speeches added) that contemporaries would keep distinct. Ancient history diverges from contemporary historiography especially in the extent to which it employs kinds of "omniscient" narration (usually reserved for fiction today) that use the writer's imagination to fill in gaps in the historical sources.[19] Consequently, ancient historians would describe conversations for which they had no witnesses, reconstruct speeches they did not hear, and report inner motivations and thoughts. It is possible to analyze in significant detail how Luke-Acts works as narrative without getting grounded on the shoals of Lukan genre debates.

This book will apply literary criticism especially to passages in Luke and Acts that have caused interpreters problems. The title, *Reading Luke-Acts: Dynamics of Biblical Narrative,* indicates a focus on reading the Gospel of Luke and the Acts of the Apostles together as a two-volume narrative, Luke-Acts.[20] It implies special emphasis on how readers respond to Luke and Acts in the act of reading. It promises analysis of how the narrative genre of Luke and Acts, as well as their canonical status as parts of the Bible, affect their interpretation. Some of these questions go beyond those normally asked by historical-critical methodologies and deal with the meaning of Luke and Acts not only for the original author and intended audience but for the church through the ages and for contemporary readers. They do not ignore but build on insights from historical criticism.

Such questions treat Luke-Acts as a two-volume biblical work, the purpose of which reaches beyond some original first-century community or communities. The author of Luke-Acts (henceforth often simply

"Luke") gives clear evidence of designing these books to be continuations of the biblical narratives inherited from Judaism in what Christians call the Greek Old Testament.[21] As such, they were intended to become part of the Christian Bible and faith heritage of future as well as living generations. To read them as biblical includes reading them from a faith stance within the church, not solely from a historical or academic perspective.

This combination of literary and canonical approaches promises to break an impasse reached in the more historical approaches. By asking different questions, we can avoid some of the dead ends of previous Lukan debates. By focusing on passages, we can keep our treatment of Luke and Acts concrete and grounded in the Lukan text and not just an exercise in theory. By stressing problematic passages rather than obvious ones, we can best demonstrate within the limits of a single book the fruitfulness of narrative approaches for elucidating the meaning of Luke and Acts, especially where other methods have exhausted their usefulness. Readers can apply similar methods to the less problematic sections.

We turn now to characteristics of and methodological approaches toward narrative in general, implied authors and readers (chapter 2) and plotting and gaps (chapter 3), before their applications in the narratives of Luke and Acts (chapters 4–9).

1

Methodological
Considerations
of Narrative

2 Implied Authors and Readers

IMPLIED AUTHOR VS. LUKE

An important contribution of narrative criticism to understanding biblical texts is the concept of implied authors (and the corresponding implied readers).[1] Historical criticism seems to have exhausted the plausible alternatives in its attempts to identify the actual authors and readers of New Testament documents, with an unsatisfying maze of incompatible hypotheses and counterhypotheses as a result. This is especially true of Luke-Acts. Scholars have come to a satisfactory consensus that the same hand wrote both the Third Gospel and Acts, but there persists some dissent against reading both books as a single, two-volume work.[2] Attempts to establish the identity of that single author of Luke and Acts exhibit far less unanimity, with hypotheses ranging from a second-century writer who had never met Paul to a companion of Paul on some of his later travels.[3]

The search for the community to which Luke-Acts is addressed seems to have uncovered even less hard data for a definitive solution.[4] Since Luke-Acts is a narrative (with its own concerns and laws that are unaffected by its intended readership) and not a letter (directed to specific addressees and to their situation), the evidence for its designated recipients is at best indirect. The solutions suggested seem to have no stronger evidential weight than educated guesses.

The concepts of implied authors and readers skirt these impasses. Since they have firm footing in the text itself, the evidence for them is more reliable and less controversial. Instead of trying to determine the actual author and readers of these narratives, these concepts ask what kind of author with what point of view is implied by the intentionality of the text itself (and what aspects of himself or herself the actual author chooses to reveal) and what the text's assorted perspectives can indicate about the kinds of readers for whom the narrative was envisaged.[5]

In addition to the textual signals about both the author and original readers that the narrative implies, the fact that Luke and Acts belong to the Christian canon suggests a wider expected range of readers than the original implied readers and relativizes the importance of the original circumstances for which form criticism searches. As canonical, Luke and Acts are now meant to address a far wider range of audiences and situations than their original writer could have imagined. Although contemporary concerns about which readers consult Luke and Acts may sometimes be analogous to those of the originally envisaged addressees, they go far beyond them. Reading Luke and Acts as part of the Christian Bible brings to the reading process the long history of their interpretation in the Christian churches, as well as contemporary Christian readings of Luke and Acts.[6]

PERSONAE PROJECTED BY THE REAL AUTHOR IN THE TEXT

In any writing, actual authors reveal only select aspects of their personalities. This is most clearly exemplified in letters, in which the same writer will reveal one persona to a possible employer, another to her parents, a third to her pastor, and another to her closest friend. Such selectivity concerning the author's persona that is revealed by a document also applies to narratives. The persona a given author chooses to reveal will vary from one narrative to the next, especially if he or she elects to write different genres of narratives.[7] Thus, C. S. Lewis reveals in his Narnia chronicles for children an implied author different from that in his space trilogy for adults.

Histor *sifting evidence and arranging a narrative*

The first aspect of his persona the author reveals, in the Lukan prologue, is that of a *histor*, a careful historical investigator who collects and sifts evidence and orders it into a unified narrative.[8] By beginning his narrative with an elegant, subordinated complex sentence in good literary Greek, he portrays himself as educated. He discloses his historiographical claims by using such technical expressions of historiographical prologues as "compile a narrative," "eyewitnesses," "handed down," "I too have decided," "investigating," "accurately," "orderly sequence," and "certainty" (Luke 1:1–4, RNAB). He implies his artistic or professional status by addressing his narrative to a patron, "most excellent Theophilus," as does his contemporary, the Jewish historian and apologist Josephus, at the beginning of both volumes of his *Against Apion*.[9]

Christian apologist continuing the biblical history

The writer also reveals that the implied author of Luke-Acts is an insider or Christian. His repeated use of the first-person plural—"events fulfilled among us," "handed them down to us"—establishes himself as a member of the Christian community whom these events concern.[10]

The unusual expression, "events that have been fulfilled [πεπλη-ροφορημένων] among us" (Luke 1:1, RNAB), admits possible connotations of fulfillment of biblical promises and prophecies, thus suggesting that the narrative belongs to the tradition of the scriptures of the Jews as well as to the tradition of Greek professional writing.[11] That Luke-Acts belongs to this biblical narrative tradition is confirmed after the prologue, when the narrator shifts to a type of biblicist Greek from Luke 1:5 throughout the rest of the infancy narrative. His imitation of the style of biblical narratives like Samuel-Kings and 1–2 Maccabees suggests that this narrative continues that biblical tradition.

The apologetic thrust of Luke-Acts receives its first strong indication at the end of the prologue: "so that you may realize the certainty [ἀσφάλειαν] of the teachings you have received" (1:4, RNAB). What Theophilus has heard orally (perhaps through his catechesis), this written narrative intends to confirm. The prologue does not specify whether this is primarily the confirmation of free-floating oral traditions and episodes by ordered written narrative, or confirmation that what "happened among us" is adequately grounded in the fulfillment of biblical promises and prophecies.[12] It could refer to both.

The writer reveals himself as an apologist vis-à-vis Judaism by the strong emphasis in Luke 1–2 (the introduction) on the Jewish piety of the parents of John and Jesus and of the seers Symeon and Anna who prophesy about Jesus, as well as by the major emphasis throughout Acts on Paul's Jewish piety and obedience to biblical law.[13] The stress on Paul's Roman citizenship and on Jesus' and Paul's innocence of any violation of Roman law conveys a balancing apologetic concern vis-à-vis the Roman empire.[14]

Master of Hellenistic and biblical styles

A corollary to these first two aspects of the Lukan persona revealed in Luke-Acts is his self-presentation as a master of both Hellenistic and biblical styles of Greek. The abrupt transition from an extended complex sentence in elegant literary Greek (Luke 1:1–4) to the biblical paratactic style (Luke 1:5–2:52), of which the lack of subordination ("and . . . and . . . and") and many foreign names would sound barbarous to Hellenistic readers, seems too deliberately conspicuous to be overlooked. The contrast calls attention to the author's style. The elegant Greek of the prologue provides his warrant as an educated, professional writer. The barbarous but biblical Greek of the rest of his introduction suggests a purpose that combines Hellenistic historiographical concerns with a narrative in the biblical tradition and style. It also acts as a defense against the dismissal of the Gospel by educated Hellenists because of what they would consider its barbaric style (see the patristic comments about the uncultivated style of the Gospels).[15]

Travel companion on Paul's later journeys

As the chapter on "we" narrators will show, the use of a first-person character narrator in sections from Acts 16:10 to 28:16 makes narrative claims that the implied author was a companion on some of Paul's later journeys. This implies that he was an eyewitness to the events he narrates in the first person, which naturally would make his account more vivid and authoritative. His claims for authority, however, are more moderate than those of most of his contemporaries who use first-person narrators, such as Josephus. Whereas Josephus and others normally use the first-person singular, the writer of Acts only uses the first-person plural. Whereas most first-person narrators are involved in the events they recount, the "we" narrator in Acts stays with a group in the background, seldom contributing to events (only as part of a gathering of Christians briefly trying to dissuade Paul in Acts 21).[16] In the events narrated with "we," the implied author of Acts claims only limited participation and occasional companionship on Paul's journeys. As will be shown, the emphasis seems more on providing a vivid account than on stressing the historical authority of an eyewitness.[17]

IMPLIED READERS VS. "LUKE'S COMMUNITY"

The same kinds of problems that are encountered in determining an actual author bedevil historical-critical attempts to pinpoint the original readers of Luke-Acts. Once a writing is made public, the writer can no longer control or even predict who will read it. One can search Luke-Acts for clues about the intended audience, but the result is only the implied readers of the text. It is a further step, for which the text itself can provide no evidence, to argue that a particular community is its actual original recipients and readers.

Even regarding the readers *implied* by Luke-Acts, the narrative provides few unambiguous clues beyond the named addressee Theophilus. It is not then surprising that historical-critical speculations about the actual community to which Luke-Acts is addressed have found no consensus. Most critics have argued for a Gentile Christian community, fewer for a Jewish Christian community.[18] Some regard Luke-Acts as an apologetic addressed to non-Christian Romans, others as a defense of Paul against

Jewish or Jewish-Christian charges of apostasy.[19] Concerning the geographical location of the Lukan community, the narrative likewise contains little hard evidence on which to base a definite answer.[20] Acts includes depictions of Christianity in Jerusalem, Syrian Antioch, Philippi, Corinth, Ephesus, Rome, and so on. But that is because the narrated events are located in those cities, not because the original readers are located there. Might not Luke-Acts have even been intended for more than one community, as an "ecumenical" narrative for the whole church, supplanting earlier Gospels belonging originally to one or another local church?[21]

CLUES IN LUKE-ACTS TO THE IMPLIED READERS

Since implied readers are in some sense properties of the narrative, we can expect to find clues in Luke-Acts for describing them. In fact, the evidence for implied readers is the same evidence that has been thoroughly discussed by historical critics in search of the Lukan community and readers and by redaction critics regarding special Lukan emphases that point to the setting of his readers.

We can start with the indicators about the identity of Lukan readers that Fitzmyer has gathered. The Gospel of Luke exhibits fewer purely Jewish preoccupations than its apparent source material (e.g., compared to what it has in common with Mark and Matthew). Both Luke and Acts have a Greco-Roman preface. Several times the Gospel uses Judea as generic for the whole of Palestine rather than for a district distinct from Galilee and Samaria. Both volumes accentuate outreach to Gentiles. Luke-Acts exhibits a marked concern to relate Gentile Christianity to Israel as the restored people of God (rather than new Israel, as in Matthew).[22] The Gospel also features imperial dating in Luke 3:1–2, but in a manner that imitates the dating of the prophecy to Jeremiah in Jer. 1:1, Septuagint (henceforth LXX). This cumulative evidence suggests implied readers who are not primarily from Palestine but from elsewhere in the Roman Empire, and who are either Gentile Christians or Jewish Christians concerned about the continuity between Judaism (with its scriptures) and contemporary Gentile Christianity.

The heavy use of biblical Greek and the frequent, sometimes subtle, allusions to the Greek Bible suggest that the implied readers have a more than superficial familiarity with the Greek scripture that enables them to recognize biblical allusions without direct quotations or explicit references, as are common in Matthew 1–2: "Then was fulfilled what had been said through Jeremiah the prophet . . . " (Matt. 1:17, RNAB). This subtle Lukan biblicism is strong evidence against Luke-Acts being addressed to non-Christian Romans, for such familiarity with the Greek Bible presupposes a Christian or Jewish readership.

That the audience was expected to be Christian and not primarily non-Christian Jews seems evident from the comparatively lesser concern than in Mark and Matthew about peculiarly Jewish issues; from the predominant focus on Jesus in the Gospel and on the apostles and spread of Christianity beyond Jews to Gentiles in Acts; and from the statement in the Gospel prologue that this book concerns "events accomplished among us" (Luke 1:1) and is to give assurance to Theophilus concerning the things "about which you have been instructed" (1:4). Especially the prologue evidence, when combined with the other indications, makes a Christian implied readership most likely.

Other important evidence that the implied readers of Luke-Acts are Christian are the prophecies that pertain especially to Christianity after the time of Paul. The clearest such prophecies occur in Paul's farewell to the Christian elders of Ephesus in Acts 20:29–30, where he foretells that after his death false teachers will beset the Christian church both from within and without. These prophecies from Paul's farewell confirm the interpretation that Jesus' parting provision of the Eucharist, his conferring the thrones of the twelve tribes of Israel on the twelve apostles and their primary leadership on Peter, and his prophecies of harsh times for them (Luke 22:19–20, 29–32, 35–37) also focus especially on Christian concerns and imply Christian readers.[23]

In context with these prophecies and provisions for apostolic and post-apostolic Christians, Jesus' prophecies in the eschatological speech in Luke 21 provide added confirmation of a Christian implied readership. In the midst of the kinds of apocalyptic predictions common to Jewish and Christian apocalypses (e.g., Luke 21:9–11), some prophecies seem especially significant for Christian implied readers: persecution of Christians (21:12–19); a time of punishment for Jerusalem when its inhabitants will be captured by Gentiles during protracted "times of the Gentiles" (21:22–24, which could be addressed to Jews but would function as special vindication for Christians); Jesus' return in glory as Son of Man to redeem his followers (21:27–28); and his warning to his followers to be ready to stand before him at his return (21:34–36). Added to this evidence, the prophecies at the end of Acts—where Paul cites Isa. 6:9–10 against the Jewish leaders and announces to them, "this salvation of God has been sent to the Gentiles; they will listen"—confirm the Christianity of the implied readers.

All this cumulative evidence argues persuasively that Luke-Acts handles predominantly Christian concerns, viewpoints, and interests, many of which would probably be of little interest to non-Christian pagans and aggravating for non-Christian Jews. Luke-Acts is intended primarily for Christian readers.

The fact that Luke and Acts are addressed to Christian readers puts even more restrictions on contemporary free play of interpretation than their traditional character alone would require.[24] All narratives have gaps in what is explicitly recounted, the filling of which is a major aspect of their interpretation. The gaps in Luke and Acts that are meant to be filled are gaps that would occur to Christian readers, and they are meant to be filled from a Christian perspective. The points of view of the text, both in its original setting and in its later context as part of the Christian Bible, are grounded in and express Christian faith. The most empathetic reading of the text would therefore ordinarily proceed from Christian faith and experience. Readers from many backgrounds and faiths can execute historical-critical methods to glean historical answers from the text or engage in literary analysis of the text, but reading Luke-Acts as biblical requires a biblical perspective and strong imaginative empathy for the Christian faith. Some obvious examples where faith facilitates filling biblical gaps in Luke concern Jesus' identity and accounts of providence or the miraculous, including Jesus' resurrection and relationship to God as his Father.

Christian catechesis and experience presumed for filling gaps

Many gaps in Lukan narration also presume that intended readers have Christian catechesis and experience. They therefore would be much easier to fill for those having such background. Readers with experience of prayer and of manifestations of the Holy Spirit or even of healings through prayer might spontaneously fill gaps that prove problematic for interpreters without such experiences. In this respect, lay Christian believers sometimes manifest clearer insight into the main issue behind a biblical narrative (*Sachkritik*) than academic biblical scholars. For example, many scholarly confusions about tongues in 1 Corinthians and Acts have found a consensus solution only after the charismatic experiences of the 1970s.[25]

Knowledge of Christian doctrine and catechesis also makes many Lukan gaps easier to fill. Before reading the elliptical narrative of Jesus' baptism in the Lukan Gospel, catechized readers already know that John baptized Jesus, that Jesus is Son of God anointed by the Spirit (therefore "Anointed" or "Christ," Luke 4:18, 41), who baptizes Christians in the

Holy Spirit, usually in conjunction with their baptism in water (Luke 3:15–16, Acts 2:33, 36, 41; 9:17–18). Christian catechesis and practice of baptizing Gentiles from all nations alerted Christian readers of Luke 4:24–29 to the irony of the resistance at Nazareth to this message and to how it foreshadowed Jesus' death and its effects for Gentiles.

Knowledge of the Greek Old Testament presumed for filling gaps

Many other Lukan gaps presuppose readers with a knowledge of the Greek Old Testament. Luke-Acts is permeated with indirect allusions to persons, events, and teachings of the Greek Old Testament. Unlike the many announced Old Testament quotations of the Greek in Matthew in the form, "This was done to fulfill . . . " (e.g., Matt. 1:22–23; 2:5–6, 15, 17–18; 4:14–16), Luke generally alludes to the Old Testament without announcing that he is doing so. This indirect approach presumes an ability on the part of intended readers to understand the allusions and to make the connections. For example, Lukan readers were expected to note the similarities between the angelic announcement to Zechariah in Luke 1:13 and those in the Old Testament (as in Dan. 10:12 and Gen. 17:19), and how John's abstention from wine (1:15) recalls the Nazirite vow in Num. 6:3 as practiced by Samson (Judg. 13:4–5) and Samuel (1 Sam. 1:1 LXX). They were expected to catch the echoes in Mary's canticle (1:46–55) of Hannah's song (1 Sam. 2:1–10). Jesus' identity is often described through implicit comparisons to Moses, Elijah, the Davidic anointed one, the prophets, the persecuted, just one in the psalms and wisdom writings, and so on. The pattern of the majority of the chosen people rejecting both the spirit-filled prophet and his successor (Jesus in the Gospel and the spirit-filled disciples in Acts) parallels the rejection of Elijah and Elisha as described in Sirach 48:1–16 LXX. Familiarity with the Greek Old Testament makes many Lukan gaps easy to fill.

Concepts of narrative criticism like implied authors and readers, as well as the sense of reading Luke and Acts as part of the Christian Bible for contemporary concerns, advance the treatment of Luke and Acts far beyond questions about the original author and community and life setting, and the scholarly impasses over many of those issues. These approaches help to reclaim for ordinary Christian believers some of the scriptural uses they most often make of Luke and Acts from a kind of historical-critical elitism, where academic "scribes" lock the scriptures into the distant past and intimidate even trained systematic theologians from using the scriptures without the key they alone can provide.

3 Plotting and Gaps

T he characteristic that distinguishes a narrative from a recorded series of undifferentiated incidents is its plot. A twenty-four-hour security video recording of a bank is not a narrative; an adventure movie or TV mystery is. From the continuum of experience a plot artificially isolates a series of actions having a beginning, middle, and end.[1]

Authors enjoy considerable freedom over where to begin their narratives. For example, conversion narratives could begin anywhere from immediately prior to the conversion to as far back as the person's birth, childhood, or youth. The choice of an end is similarly without constraint. Conversion narratives could end immediately after the conversion, or days, weeks, or years later. Authors also have comparable freedom regarding the middle of their narratives. They can select events to include or to leave out, or choose among alternate series of episodes that arrive at the same end, as when they follow one set of characters rather than another till the two sets meet later in the account. The temporal ordering of the middle of their narratives is also discretionary: they can flash back, flash forward, or use chronological order.[2]

The freedom of selection regarding beginning, middle, and end of a plot line is evident in a comparison of the parallel Gospel narratives of Mark and Luke. Of all the events known about the life and times of Jesus, the Markan narrator begins with the adult Baptist to preface Jesus' baptism and ends with the women fleeing from the empty tomb. The Lukan narrator begins much earlier in Jesus' life, with angelic proclamations of the conceptions of both the Baptist and Jesus, and ends later, after resurrection appearances. The Lukan narrator also adds many intermediate episodes to those in Mark but drops a series of Markan incidents. Although Luke usually follows the same order of events in the middle as

17

Mark, his order sometimes differs, as in Jesus' visit to Nazareth at his incipient rather than later ministry.

The process of selection necessary for creating a plot, while it may emphasize some events, deemphasizes and even omits numerous others, which are left to be filled in by the readers' imaginations. Writers' omissions, meant to require attention from readers, are often called gaps. (Omissions that are not consequential for the narrative, like hair color, are called blanks.)[3] The gaps that all narratives contain perform essential functions. No narrative can provide all conceivable descriptive details of characters or settings, nor can narratives mention all the steps in narrated actions. Excessive detail, moreover, is boring to read; imaginatively filling narrative gaps provides much interest for readers.[4]

Comparison of Luke with Mark alerts us to some of the more significant gaps Luke left in his account of Jesus' baptism by John. These include the failure to specify who baptized Jesus or where Jesus came from, to repeat mention of the Jordan River, or to indicate where Jesus was praying when the Holy Spirit descended on him (cf. Mark 1:9 and Luke 3:21). Especially since most readers would have known about John's baptism of Jesus before reading the Lukan Gospel, they would fill in these gaps by presuming that John baptized Jesus in the Jordan (despite the proleptic mention of John's [later] imprisonment in Luke 3:20 before narrating Jesus' baptism in 3:21). Readers would also tend to imagine Jesus' experience of the Holy Spirit and of the Father's voice as either in the Jordan or somewhere nearby. Where Jesus came from would be a blank. Only after recounting Jesus' baptism does the narrator mention Jesus' approximate age, his being reputed son of Joseph, and his genealogy through Joseph (Luke 3:23–38).[5]

This chapter will investigate how Luke plotted his narrative, beginning with what he says about this in his prologue, and testing what he says by observing the beginning and samples from the middle of the Gospel and the end of both Luke and Acts. It will also treat how gaps left in the plot are meant to be filled by readers as they respond to the text.

Plotting the Narrative

The Prologue, Luke 1:1–4

In his prologue, Luke explicitly mentions plot ordering when he compares to his own attempts what previous writers have done: "Many have tried to compile [order, ἀνατάξασθαι] a narrative about the things that have been accomplished among us" (Luke 1:1). Then he expresses his own decision to compose a similar narrative: "It seemed good to me also, having followed all things closely for some time past, to write an orderly account for you, most excellent Theophilus . . . " (1:3 RSV). The words ἀνατάξασθαι in v. 1 and καθεξῆς in v. 3 imply putting in order, which phenomenologically describes what the earliest Gospel writers had to do with the many independent stories and sayings of Jesus that they had collected.[6] In the absence of clear geographical and temporal clues, they were often unable to ascertain the original chronological order in which the episodes had occurred and had to find some other rationale for the order in which they narrated them in their respective Gospels. This partially accounts for some of the differences between the Lukan Gospel and one of his probable sources, Mark. But the most radical Lukan innovation is adding Acts as a sequel, with some plot overlapping between his Gospel and Acts.

PLOTTING TWO VOLUMES: LUKE AND ACTS

Luke's sequel raises the question whether it is envisaged as early as the preface to the Gospel, and therefore whether that preface (Luke 1:1–4) refers beyond the Gospel to both Luke and Acts. I will argue that it introduces both books, despite the presence of a second preface in Acts.[7] The preface is part of a larger prologue that includes at least the infancy narratives in Luke 1–2. One of the main plot functions of these two chapters, along with much of Luke 3–4, is to foreshadow later events in the Gospel. But Symeon's prophecies in Luke 2:29–35 go beyond the Gospel to foretell the main plot turn of Acts, when Jews become divided over the risen Jesus and the gospel goes out to the Gentiles. They find their clearest fulfillment in the Jews' excommunication from or continued membership in God's people in Acts, according to whether they reject or accept the risen Jesus proclaimed by the disciples (see Acts 3:23).

Luke 3–4, the events of which correspond to many in Mark's prologue (Mark 1:1–13 or 15),[8] also foreshadow later plot developments. The theme of the Baptist's preaching, a baptism of repentance for forgiveness of sins, points forward to the risen Jesus' promises in Luke 24 that repentance and forgiveness of sins would be preached in his name to all the nations. John's prophecy that a stronger one would come and "baptize you with the Holy Spirit and fire" (3:16) is echoed by the risen Jesus' promise in Acts 1:5 of baptism through the Holy Spirit. In Luke, the narrator's application to the Baptist of Isa. 40:5 according to the Greek Old Testament, "and all flesh shall see the salvation of God," goes beyond the shorter citations in both Mark and Matthew and is most clearly fulfilled when the Gentiles accept the risen Jesus and the Holy

Spirit in Acts.[9] The reference to children of Abraham in the Baptist's preaching (which occurs also in Matthew) becomes a major salvation motif only in Luke-Acts (the Magnificat in 1:55 and Benedictus in 1:73; the bent woman in 13:16; the saying about Jews excluded from God's kingdom in 13:28; the Lazarus parable in 16:22–30; Zacchaeus in 19:9; receiving the promises to Abraham in speeches of Peter and Paul in Acts 3:13, 25 and 13:26).

Further events in Luke 3–4 also foreshadow important plot elements of both the Gospel and Acts. After a description of the Holy Spirit's descent on Jesus and a record of Jesus' genealogy, there follows a description of Jesus' test by the devil in the wilderness. This temptation scene obviously foreshadows Jesus' later testing, especially when Satan enters into Judas (22:3), when Jesus gives an example of prayer against temptation (22:40–46), and when the Jewish officials arrest him on the Mount of Olives (22:53). Luke 4:13 underscores this foreboding: "When the devil had finished every temptation he departed from him until [another] time (ἄχρι καιροῦ)."[10]

Jesus' "inaugural address" at Nazareth has such a strong foreshadowing element that it is often described as programmatic for the Gospel as a whole.[11] In it Jesus announces that "today" Isa. 61:1–2 (with 58:6) has been fulfilled. The Spirit of the Lord is upon him (3:22); therefore he has "anointed" (ἔχρισέν) him. His mission is to preach good news to the poor (the beatitudes and passim in Jesus' ministry in Luke), to announce release (or forgiveness) to captives, to restore sight to the blind, to let the oppressed go free, and to proclaim the acceptable year of the Lord.

The mixed but ultimately negative reaction in which his own town rejects him strongly forebodes Jesus' rejection as a prophet by his own country. The Nazarenes cast him out of the city and take him up on a hill to kill him, which portends the Place of the Skull (23:33) and Stephen's expulsion from Jerusalem and martyrdom (Acts 7:58).

Finally, the Lukan version of the miraculous catch of fish has a strong foreshadowing component. Simon is the clear leader and almost sole focus. His efforts without Jesus have been fruitless, but in obedience to Jesus his catch is overwhelming. Simon stresses his sinfulness and fear, but Jesus commissions him to catch humans, and Simon, James, and John leave all to follow Jesus (Andrew is not mentioned). These three play major roles later in the Gospel and early in Acts, but except here and in lists of the Twelve, Andrew plays no other role in Matthew or Luke.[12] Luke's omission of Andrew makes this call scene a clearer foreshadowing of the episodes with Peter, James, and John at the raising of the girl (8:51) and at the transfiguration (9:28).[13]

TRANSITION BETWEEN LUKE AND ACTS, WITH OVERLAP

An important aspect of Lukan plotting is his overlapping transition between his first and second volumes. One of his main plot devices to achieve this transition is foreshadowing future events through prophecies.[14]

Luke 24:46–49: Prophecies Leading into Acts

The last words of the resurrected Jesus to his followers refer both backward into the plot of Luke and forward into Acts.[15] Jesus first refers to the words he spoke in his earthly ministry, that the things written in the Law of Moses and the Prophets and Psalms about himself had to be fulfilled (24:44). Then in vv. 45–47 he enables them to understand the words of scripture, that the Christ was to suffer and rise from the dead on the third day (Luke 23–24) and that repentance for the forgiveness of sins is to be preached in his name to all the Gentiles (Acts 10–20), beginning from Jerusalem (Acts 2–7). His emphasis in 24:48 that "you are witnesses of these things" provides one of the main themes in Acts. Finally, his promise in v. 49, "I will send the promise of the Father upon you: but you wait in the city until you are clothed with power from on high," obviously foreshadows and prepares for Acts 1–2.

The End of Luke's Gospel

With this preparation for Acts by words of the risen Lord, the Gospel ends in ways that overlap the beginning of Acts, with some incompatibilities of detail between the two. The impression in Luke 24:50–51, where Jesus gives his farewell blessing and is lifted up into heaven, is that the ascension occurred on Easter Sunday in Bethany. But Acts 1:1–11 says that the risen Jesus appeared to his disciples for forty days before his final ascension from the Mount of Olives. Luke 24:52–53 portrays the disciples returning to Jerusalem and spending their time praising God in the Temple, whereas Acts 1:12–14 prepares for the Pentecost account by showing them in the upper room awaiting the Spirit in prayer.[16]

It is clear that Luke had different purposes in these overlapping accounts. The first is to find a fitting end to his first book, the Gospel. It ends as it began, with worship of God in the Temple. Luke goes out of his way to emphasize the setting of the Jesus story within the promises to God's holy people. The Gospel begins in the Temple with this people's expectations for a messianic deliverer. It ends in the Temple praising God for the messianic deliverance that has taken place in the life, death, and resurrection of Jesus.[17]

Though I believe Luke planned his two books together, with the result that they have cross-referencing and modifications both from the Gospel to Acts and from Acts to the Gospel, it seems quite plausible that the actual writing and appearance of the two volumes may have been separated by some time, as is often the case with multi-volume works.[18] If this is so, then Luke ended his Gospel in a way appropriate to it, without having a beginning of Acts with which to compare it. Later, when he actually wrote the second volume that he had planned and implicitly promised in the preface of the first, his purposes of preparing for the Pentecost account and the story of Acts led to some retelling of details already written at the ending of his first volume, which was now public and not subject to further adjustments in light of the second.[19]

The Prologue of Acts

The plot of the second Lukan volume begins with a preface that both refers back to the first and imperceptibly merges into the narrative of the second. Luke reintroduces the first-person *histor* narrator from the preface of his Gospel ("it seemed good to me also"): "The first book [word, λόγος] I made about all which Jesus *began* (ἤρξατο) to do and teach until the day . . . he was taken up" (Acts 1:1–2). The use of *began* to describe Jesus' deeds and teaching in the first volume explicitly treats the Gospel as preliminary to the plot of Acts. But the *histor* disappears in favor of the usual third-person omniscient narrator as the introduction unfolds through vv. 3–8.[20]

Acts 1:3–8 doubles back over some events at the end of the Gospel but with an entirely new focus on the forthcoming events of Acts, especially Pentecost. The omniscient narrator recounts how Jesus presented himself to the apostles for forty days and ordered them not to leave Jerusalem but to await the promise of the Father: "You shall be baptized with the Holy Spirit after not many days" (v. 5). In response to the disciples' question, which betrays their misunderstanding about restoring the kingdom to Israel (v. 6), he corrected them (v. 7) and promised (v. 8): "You shall receive power of the Holy Spirit coming upon you [in Acts 2] and you shall be my witnesses in Jerusalem [in Acts 2–7], in Judea and Samaria [in Acts 8–9], and to the end of the earth [Acts 10–28 and beyond]." Thus, this prologue to Acts introduces the rest of the book by functioning as a summary of some key aspects of the upcoming plot line.[21]

The narration of Jesus' ascension sets the stage for both Pentecost and Jesus' return in judgment ("Jesus will return the same way you saw him going into heaven" [on a cloud]). Emphasis that the disciples watched as he was lifted up and taken by a cloud grounds the event in literary allusions to Elisha watching Elijah being taken up before receiving Elijah's spirit and continuing his mission (2 Kings 2:9–15). Thus, in Acts the disciples too were to receive Jesus' spirit and carry on his mission, beginning at Pentecost.[22] Returning to Jerusalem, they prepared for this by remaining in the upper room with the women and Mary the mother of Jesus and his brothers and devoting themselves to prayer (Acts 1:12–14).

COMPOSITE ARTISTRY IN PLOTTING LUKE-ACTS

One way in which the Bible and other traditional writings differ from works for which a single author is completely responsible is in the use of sources to create narratives. Sternberg points out that there has been a false dichotomy in some literary studies of the Old Testament between focus on sources and on the final product.[23] He remarks that it is foolish for literary critics to ignore completely the fact that some works are a montage of sources. Focus on the final product does not preclude also observing the composite artistry that has produced it.[24]

The abiding consensus is that Luke has used written sources, especially in his Gospel. I continue to subscribe to the most widespread hypothesis that Luke used both Mark and the hypothetical Q document of material common to Luke and Matthew alone, and that he added content from sources that only he had (= L), as well as history that resembles historical narratives in his Greek Bible.[25] For example, Luke 3:1–2 provides a historical introduction to his source material about John the Baptist that parallels Jer. 1:1–3 but is written in Greek sophisticated enough to be based on the genitive absolute.[26]

Luke 3 as an Example of Composite Artistry

Luke 3 provides a good sample of how the plot line combines several sources. Luke introduces his source materials about John the Baptist by inserting a historical setting styled after the beginning of the Greek book of Jeremiah.[27] To the LXX citation he found in his source, about the voice crying in the wilderness, he adds several lines climaxing in "and all flesh shall see the salvation of God" (v. 6), which foreshadows Acts. He drops all the traditional references to John's camel hair clothing and wild food and interweaves from Q and possibly another source John's preaching of repentance, which foreshadows both Jesus' preaching of repentance in the Gospel and Peter's in Acts 2 and 3. In 3:15 he adds to his source that the crowd was wondering if John the Baptist was the Christ, to provide a context for John's statement in the source about the stronger one coming who would baptize them with the Spirit and fire.

After this introductory Baptist material, Luke follows the Baptist plot line to his imprisonment (3:20) before focusing exclusively on Jesus at his baptism in 3:21–22. To report that Herod put John in prison, where he is at the next occurrences of his name (5:33–35; 7:18–23), Luke has to jump ahead chronologically. The question in 5:33, why Jesus' disciples do not fast as John's do, and its answer that they shall fast when Jesus is taken away from them, further foreshadow the similar fates of Jesus and John. In 7:18–23, Jesus' answer to the imprisoned John's disciples ends with the foreboding statement: "And blessed is the one who takes no offense at me" (7:23, RNAB).[28]

Following the proleptic mention in Luke 3:20 of John's imprisonment, with its auguring of John's and Jesus' deaths, Luke 3:21–22 now focuses exclusively on Jesus, and John is not mentioned by name. Except as the occasion for Jesus' baptism, John is passed over in the scene between Jesus and his Father, despite his probable presence there in Luke's source and his actual presence there in Mark and Matthew. The Lukan scene is greatly simplified, ignoring everything except Jesus' prayer and his Father's response, "You are my beloved son; with you I am well pleased."

At 3:23, Luke inserts a genealogy for Jesus in the same inverse LXX form as the genealogies of Tobit and Ezra: "being son, as was supposed, of Joseph of Eli of Matthat . . . of Adam of God" (3:23–38).[29] Luke's choice of where to insert Jesus' genealogy differs from Matthew, who began his Gospel with it (perhaps in imitation of 1 Chronicles, which begins with genealogies). Instead, Luke may have been imitating the placing of Moses' genealogy in Exodus 6 after the account of his call in Exodus 3.[30] Immediately after Jesus is called by God, with the statement, "You are my beloved son; with you I am well pleased," the narrator mentions Jesus' age and that he was "the son, as was supposed, of Joseph of Eli of Matthat . . . of Adam of God." This merging of two different sources, probably Mark and L, supplies a biblical genealogy for Jesus before resuming the narrative with his temptation (from Mark and Q) in Luke 4:1–13, as well as providing a kind of commentary on God's addressing Jesus as his son in 3:22.

PLOTTING "IN ORDER"

We have seen that Luke's narrative was composite and involved an interweaving of multiple sources into one continuous plot. Most scholars think that as a guide to order these independently transmitted traditions he used not only previous Gospels like Mark, but also plot skeletons like kerygmatic summaries and the prophecy of worldwide witness in Acts 1:8.[31] He probably used Mark's Gospel as the basis for the structuring of his Gospel, with adjustments like the following: he moved the Nazareth pericope forward to function as an "inaugural address"; he omitted the repetitious Markan second feeding and the material between

those two feedings; he supplemented his Markan source with Q and L
materials that he organized somewhat artificially as a longer journey-to-
Jerusalem section than that in Mark. This provided a stronger parallel
between Jesus journeying on mission, first to preach the kingdom and
then to suffer at Jerusalem, and Paul doing similarly in Acts.

Another important Lukan method of plotting traditions is his interweaving of separate plot lines that pertain to John the Baptist and Jesus,
somewhat like a two-plot novel.[32] The infancy prologue in Luke 1–2
intertwines plot lines about John and Jesus similarly to the way Luke 3
does in imitation of the Markan source, which began with the Baptist
preaching repentance and baptizing, turned to Jesus coming down from
Nazareth to be baptized by John, then followed Jesus' call and temptation
(Mark 1:1–13).

In his alternation between John and Jesus, Luke finishes one plot line
up to the point where that character is next needed, then alternates to the
other.[33] Thus, he follows John the Baptist's story to Elizabeth's song of
thanksgiving, then Jesus' plot line until Mary visits Elizabeth, then John's
birth and his father Zechariah's prophecy until the end of the chapter
(1:80), where he mentions that John grew and was in the desert until the
day of his manifestation to Israel (to be treated in Luke 3). He turns then
to Jesus' birth and visits to the Temple to the end of chapter 2, resuming
with John again in chapter 3, in the desert where he had left him in 1:80.

A similar alternation of plot lines is more briefly indicated when Satan
left Jesus, after his temptation, "until [another] time" (ἄχρι καιροῦ)—
namely, when he returns with special force at the onset of Jesus' passion
(Luke 22:3, 40–46, 53). Another occurs in Acts 8 when, after his incident
with the Ethiopian eunuch, Philip is transported to Caesarea, where he
will next be mentioned in Acts 21 when Paul visits that city. The "we"
account at Philippi in Acts 16 breaks off in a similar way, until it is
resumed again in Acts 20:5, when the "we" are again mentioned, still at
Philippi. Another example of following plot lines up to the place of the
character's next appearance or to his death is Acts 12, in which, after
Peter's escape from Herod, the plot follows Herod to Caesarea and his
eventual death in v. 23, then returns to the spread of the word after
Peter's escape in v. 24.

The following examples illustrate a related kind of intertwined ABA'
plot lines. In Luke 1:64 Zechariah opens his mouth and speaks, praising
God (= A). Before reporting what he said the narrator recounts in
1:65–66 the crowd's fear and question, "What will this child be?" (= B).
Finally, in 1:67–79, he reports what Zechariah says (= A'). A similar
ABA' plot line occurs in Luke 3:19–20: the narrator describes the

Baptist's preaching (= A), then his imprisonment (= B), then Jesus' baptism (= A'). A striking third example of this ABA' pattern appears in Luke 8:34–38, where the narrator first recounts how the Gentiles from the area saw the healed demoniac sitting clothed at Jesus' feet (= A), then how they asked Jesus to leave them so that Jesus departed in the boat (= B), and finally how the healed demoniac asked to be with Jesus (= A'). Here the violence to chronological order is particularly conspicuous, since the demoniac must have asked to go with Jesus (= A') before Jesus left (= B).

Similar patterns of intertwined plot reappear in Acts. For example, a first subplot describes Paul's conversion (Acts 9); a second concerns Peter and Cornelius (Acts 10–12); the narrative returns to Paul and Barnabas (Acts 13–14); and finally both subplots converge in the apostolic council at Jerusalem in Acts 15.

Techniques of Repetition and Redundancy in Plotting

Luke-Acts is well known for its important use of repetition of key incidents and themes, which resembles the redundancy for which many Old Testament narratives are distinguished.[34] All that needs to be added here is how this relates to plotting. Repetition involves analepses (flashbacks) or prolepses (foreshadowings) in the plot line, as in AB–C–DE–C––FG–C–HIJ, rather than a straightforward plot progression, ABCDEFGHIJ. From the frequently treated examples of the threefold repetitions of Paul's call in Acts 9, 22, and 26, of the Peter-Cornelius incident in Acts 10–11 and 15, and of the "apostolic decree" in Acts 15:20, 29, and 21:25, the re-use of Paul's call in Acts 9, 22, and 26 can provide a sufficient illustration of how Luke uses repetition in plotting Luke-Acts.

As Meir Sternberg and many others have pointed out, repetition in biblical narratives tends to be partly verbatim, partly with variations, and partly telescoped.[35] Thus the narrator's version of an incident tends to be repeated by a messenger with many of the same words, but some variations and abbreviation. The Lukan examples of Saul's call tend to confirm this judgment. On the one hand, they have a good deal of verbatim repetition, especially in the core of the call account in the dialogue between the risen Jesus and Saul. On the other, each repetition has minor variations, some within this core, but most in the surrounding narrative. As obvious examples, the latter two versions occur in the first person, Acts 9 in the third. The quoted discourse, "Saul, Saul, who do you persecute me?" and what follows tends to be verbatim, but Acts 26:14 adds a Greek proverb about kicking against the goads. Jesus tells Saul to go into the city (Acts 9) or Damascus (Acts 22) for instructions, whereas Acts 26 drops all mention of that and retrospectively telescopes with this initial encounter what Acts 22 treats as his later commission to the Gentiles.

Within the developing plot of Acts, the three versions of Saul's call provide three perspectives on what happened. The first occurs in its chronological setting, where the narrator recounts the event from an omniscient point of view, with access to the inner experience of both Saul and Ananias. The first narration of Saul's commission through one who initially objected to it (Ananias) provides an objective aura. Acts 22 offers Paul's retrospective personal point of view on what happened, stressing what his Jewish listeners would find important. Since Paul did not have access to Ananias' inner experience, he only mentions what he could observe, namely Ananias' good reputation among Jews and his behavior with Saul. Here Paul's narration of his receiving his commission through Ananias, combined with his own later vision sending him to the Gentiles, is provided with a personal and objective perspective. The point of view in Acts 26 looks back on Paul's call with more inclusion of its later consequences, dropping all mention of Ananias and telescoping this with Paul's later commissionings into one retrospective summary of the risen Jesus' mandate to him. The point of view is now entirely personal, but the setting in a formal trial defense before rulers increases the credibility of Paul's personal witness. This third account of his initial encounter with Christ now already adumbrates Paul's later career.

Thus the Acts 9 account plays its expected chronological and causal function within the plot line for what follows. Acts 22 and 26 are increasingly retrospective personal flashbacks by Paul to emphasize this centrally important event and to show its further implications in the account of Paul's work and the spread of the word in Acts. In view of the statement by Paul and Barnabas in Acts 13:47, "for thus has the Lord commanded us, 'I have set you as a light to the Gentiles,' " Paul's commission in Acts 26:16–18, "to serve and bear witness . . . to whom [the Gentiles] I send you to open their eyes that they turn from darkness to light . . . ," demonstrates his intimate association with the Christ's own role of announcing light to the people and to the Gentiles (26:23).[36]

JOURNEY MOTIFS AS PLOT DEVICE
FOR GATHERING INDEPENDENT TRADITIONS

As is well known, a major Lukan principle for organizing and ordering independent traditions and sources into a unified plot line is the journey motif.[37] After applying other principles of plot order, such as plot lines of previous Gospels and kerygmatic summaries, the Lukan compiler would have found many leftover episodes and sayings that gave no obvious indication of their original chronological or geographical setting. Apparently the exigencies of the plot of Acts influenced how Luke would order these extra materials in his Gospel. Whereas Matthew ordered similar materials into collections of miracles and of sayings organized as speeches, Lukan emphasis on the three journeys of Paul in Acts probably led him to expand in his Gospel a theme found in Mark—Jesus' journey to Jerusalem. Thus, most of Luke's material that was not found in Mark and that had no temporal identification appears within Jesus' journey to Jerusalem.

This plot device of the journey supports the dynamic view of the spread of God's word, first through Jesus in the Gospel and then through the disciples in Acts. It also underscores the journey toward and willing acceptance of suffering by Jesus and Paul. Thus the Lukan Gospel shows Jesus on mission journeys around Galilee to preach and to heal, then later on the journey to Jerusalem to suffer. Similarly, Acts shows Paul making two types of journeys: first, to call the Gentiles from darkness to light (Acts 13–14, 15:36–20:38); second, toward his own suffering witness at Jerusalem and on to Caesarea and Rome (Acts 21–28).

CLOSURE IN PLOTTING LUKE-ACTS

Applying the terms and approach of Marianna Torgovnick to the Gospel of Luke, Mikeal Parsons describes two ways of achieving narrative closure by having the end recall earlier portions of the text. In circularity, the end recalls the beginning. In parallelism, the end recalls from the narrative's middle the important plot devices of conflict, prophecy and fulfillment, and the journey motif.[38]

We can extend these useful insights to Acts as well. Many scholars have noted how the end of the Gospel of Luke recalls its beginning, especially the settings in the Temple and the expectations of salvation. Parsons tests how Luke 24:50–53 recalls 1:5–23, then compares the broader contexts 24:36–53 and Luke 1–2, and finally examines similarities in language, situation, and character groupings between resurrection and infancy narratives.[39] He finds that the Gospel's end recalls the beginning in the themes of priestly blessings (Zechariah is unable to bless; Jesus blesses at the end); returning to Jerusalem; pious people of God; the Temple and Jerusalem; and angels as actors only in the resurrection and infancy accounts (though they are frequent throughout Acts).[40]

The beginning and end of Acts are not as closely related as those in the Gospel, primarily because the beginning of Acts is so closely intertwined with the end of the Gospel, linking the two volumes together. But there are at least three important allusions at the end of Acts to its beginning that provide some closure along with an ongoing openness to the future. Acts 28:23 and 31 stress preaching the kingdom of God, as in Acts 1:3. Acts 28:23 features the term *witnessing* for Paul, which recalls "You shall be my witnesses" in Acts 1:8. Acts ends with Paul in Rome, promising that God's salvation has been sent out to the Gentiles (28:28), which recalls Acts 1:8's promise that the disciples will be Jesus' witnesses "to the end of the earth." These themes are not peripheral to Acts.

The end of Acts also has some important resonances to the beginning of the Gospel, thus providing some closure for Luke-Acts as a whole. Perhaps the most significant are the common ground covered by Paul's use of Isa. 6:9–10 in Acts 28:24–28 and Symeon's prophecy in Luke 2:29–35. Paul divides the Jewish people into those who believe and those who disbelieve (Acts 28:24–28), which recalls Symeon's prophecy that Jesus' presence would result in the falling and rising of many in Israel. Paul's statement in Acts 28 that God's salvation is now sent to the Gentiles has important resonances with Symeon's prophecy that Jesus would be a light to the Gentiles.

The closure of conflict, prophecy and fulfillment, and the journey motif from the middle of the narrative is correspondingly important, according to Parsons.[41] The prophecy theme, in particular, involves prolepsis and analepsis in plotting, sometimes within Luke, sometimes beyond Luke into Acts, and sometimes beyond both. The analepses from Luke 24 back into the Gospel resolve its prophecies. The prolepses generate suspense by anticipating coming events so that the question is not what will happen but how.[42']

The end of Acts likewise resolves many of its important plot devices, such as the conflict and mixed reactions of other Jews to Peter, Stephen, and Paul; the threefold repetition of the theme of Jewish rejection and consequent turn to the Gentiles; the theme of culpable blindness and deafness (Isa. 6:9–10 in Acts 28:26–27 recalling the warning in Acts 13:40–41 and Jesus' weeping over Jerusalem in Luke 19:42); the fulfillment of prophecies like that in Acts 1:8 and the scriptural prophecies about Jesus; and the resolution of the journey motif with Paul's arrival in Rome.

REMAINING OPENNESS IN PLOTTING LUKE-ACTS

Two types of openness that remain at the end of Luke, linkage and incompletion, prevent complete closure of the plot. Linkage ties the narrative to the next volume.[43] The most obvious linkage is the departure of Jesus (with disagreements) in Luke 24:50–53 and Acts 1:9–11. Other linkage between Luke 24 and Acts is provided by themes of repentance and forgiveness of sins, Jerusalem, witnessing, and the command to await empowerment.[44] Since there is no third volume, linkage does not apply to the end of Acts.

Incompletion, however, applies to the ends of Acts and Luke. Closure is not complete, and the end of a text is not the end of the work when the narrator leaves material for readers to complete from their imaginations, rather than from the text.[45] Such incompletion at the end of the Lukan Gospel includes confrontations, which continue in Acts and beyond, and which make of Luke-Acts a tragic story in which the expectations of the pious for Israel in Luke 1–2 remain at least partially unfulfilled;[46] promises unfulfilled until Acts (like the coming of the Spirit and Jesus as light to the Gentiles) or after Acts (like the destruction of Jerusalem and the eschatological cosmic signs); and the journey motif, which continues into Acts (and "to the ends of the world" probably extends beyond Acts). Incompletion is also found at the end of Acts, which fails to include Paul's history after his two years' Roman house imprisonment.

Thus, Luke-Acts has sufficient narrative closure to be satisfying as a story, but some remaining openness beyond the story time, which engages the readers in the spread of the word and the victory of God's promises that Luke-Acts relates.

PLOTTING THE END OF ACTS

Perhaps the most important decision in plotting a narrative is how and where to end it. The end sheds light on all that has gone before. According to whether the end is happy or sad, the entire plot is characterized as comic or tragic. If the end is incomplete—that is, open to continuing the narrative—it relativizes what has gone before and leads readers to expect another volume. In retrospect, therefore, the end appears as the goal to which the rest of the plot has been tending.[47]

The end of Acts has been highly problematic in the history of interpretation and scholarship. The last section seems a bit artificial. It shows Paul witnessing to the Jews of Rome, even though Christianity was already established there. When some of the Jews accept and some reject Paul's witness, Paul's response seems to exceed the provocation, as he cites the Isa. 6:9–10 topos about Israel's blindness and promises a turn to the more receptive Gentiles. Finally, and most disturbing to commentators since, Acts seems to stop "before the end" in a most peculiar place, before not only Paul's death but even before the end of the stated time of Paul's (two-year) house imprisonment in Rome.[48]

According to St. John Chrysostom, deliberate ending before foreshadowed outcomes was a common Greco-Roman narrative practice.[49] It also was the practice of Luke's apparent source, the Gospel of Mark, which ends unexpectedly and even more enigmatically than Acts. Apparently many later Christian readers and scribes were not as aware as Chrysostom of how common a practice this was, for several attempts were made to provide a more satisfactory end to Mark, one of which became the Gospel's canonical conclusion. I would argue that Luke was not one of these revisors, but Luke did notice the deliberate Markan gap. Although he chose to fill that gap at the end of his own Gospel, to lead into his second volume, he imitated Mark's gap at the end of Acts.

To have ended Acts with Paul's death would perhaps bring more closure to the story than desired, for it would stop the dynamic thrust of the spread of the word that had permeated the narrative. Rather, to end with Paul preaching the gospel boldly and unhindered propels the narrative toward the future and the time of the intended readers. The proclamation carried on by Paul continues at the time of writing and the intended times of reading, and the open ending of Acts draws attention to that.[50]

READERS AND GAPS

INTERRELATIONSHIP BETWEEN TEXT AND READER

We have seen that some gaps in the text have to be filled in by the readers for the narrative to make sense. To imagine the scenes narrated, readers also have to fill in some of the blanks by forming an imaginative image of Jesus and visualizing the actions (filling in unmentioned details). Thus, the Lukan narrator invites readers and listeners to imagine a scene in which a large crowd of people are being baptized (Luke 3:21a), then the baptism of Jesus (3:21b, all of this presumably by John), then Jesus praying (3:21b, in the Jordan or after he leaves it). After readers visualize what the narrator merely mentions, they can then follow the narrator's account to imagine Jesus' experience of heaven opening and of the Holy Spirit descending upon him (3:21b–22).[51]

Text "Dead" Until "Raised Up" by Reader

The reader's role is even more basic than filling gaps through imagination. In a real sense, the texts of Luke and Acts are "dead" until they are "raised up" by a reader. The narrative, although inscribed in an encoded text, needs readers' minds to be decoded and thus experienced or "heard." In this sense, the reader creates the narrative in the process of reading it, quite apart from the author, who might be long dead.[52]

Reader Guided by Text in Reading

But the reader does not create the narrative entirely from nothing (*ex nihilo*), as God created the world, according to traditional Christian belief. Reading is not ungoverned fantasizing: readers' imaginative pictures are guided by the codes already inscribed in the text by the writer. Although, admittedly, codes can have more than one possible interpretation, there are limits to which interpretations are possible for any configuration of words, especially in their contexts.[53]

Yet there are unavoidable cultural and other biases affecting not only the writer's choice of words, but also the meaning of those words in other cultural milieus. Readers in turn understand the text according to the meanings they have personally learned for words and signs and with their own emotional associations. Readers thus bring varying presuppositions and ways of decoding to the reading of a text. They can also refuse to read parts or all of the text, can let their minds wander away from attention to the text, or can hurry over or merely skim sections of the narrative. But to whatever extent the readers choose to read the text, their reading creates in their minds some version of the basic narrative that the writer inscribed in the text. When several readers compare what they understand from a single narrative, they recognize that it is the same narrative they are discussing. They fill in the gaps separately, but the writer supplies the coded signposts showing the way to do so.[54]

READER RESPONSE AS RELATED TO GAPS IN THE TEXT

Reader's imaginations are quite active in visualizing actions in a narrative, even when only a few skeletal steps of those actions are stated: "After all the people had been baptized [scene 1] and Jesus also had been baptized [scene 2] and was praying [scene 3], heaven was opened and the holy Spirit descended upon him in bodily form like a dove [scene 4]" (Luke 3:21–22a, RNAB; my bracketed insertions). Reader-response criticism generally presumes spontaneous and habitual imaginative reading activities and focuses on the conscious steps readers must take to fill in gaps in the information provided them in the narrative. Besides visualizing the four scenes mentioned in Luke 3:21–22a, alert readers notice that Jesus' baptizer is not named and that John's imprisonment has just been mentioned in the previous verse (3:20). Most spontaneously fill the information gap by presuming that John is nevertheless the one who baptizes Jesus. They recognize that verse 3:20 is a proleptic mention of a future event. Since v. 21 is connected to v. 20 by the purely transitional particle δέ[55] ("And it happened that . . . ," Ἐγένετο δὲ ἐν τῷ βαπτισθῆναι ἅπαντα τὸν λαὸν), mention of John's imprisonment in 3:20 puts the focus in 3:21 totally on Jesus, not on John.

The endings of Luke and Acts and beginning of Acts provide good illustrations of readers' filling gaps in the plots of narratives.

GAPS IN THE END OF LUKE

At first reading, the Gospel of Luke seems to close with no significant gaps remaining to be filled. By ending where it begins, in the Temple, the text provides unambiguous closure through circularity, as Parsons has argued.[56] But comparing the beginning and end of Mark (and of all the Gospels) also reveals the uniqueness of the Lukan Gospel's beginning and ending in the Temple. When readers ask why it should begin and end there, they perceive more clearly the thematic Lukan concern with symbolically linking "the events fulfilled among us" (Luke 1:1) to their Jewish roots. This theme of Jewish roots is further developed in the speeches of Acts.

A second plotting gap involves ending the Gospel with the disciples waiting for power from on high. Parsons fills this gap by interpreting it as openness of the Gospel to its sequel—a way of implying, "to be continued."[57]

Another sign of incompletion, despite the partial closure from ending in the Temple where the Gospel began, is the very grammar used in the final sentence. Instead of using a tense like the aorist or perfect, which would finish the narrative with a completed action, the writer concludes with an awkward periphrastic construction using a verb in the imperfect tense with a present participle: "and they were continually in the Temple praising God" (24:53, RNAB: καὶ ἦσαν διὰ παντὸς ἐν τῷ ἱερῷ εὐλογοῦντες τὸν θεόν). The grammatical forms emphasize by their very awkwardness the continuous state of the disciples' praising God in the Temple. The narration thus closes in the midst of an action that continues beyond the end of the story.

GAP IN THE CONFLICTING OVERLAP
BETWEEN THE BEGINNING OF ACTS AND END OF LUKE

The most conspicuous plotting gap at the end of Luke is its conflicting overlap with the beginning of Acts. Scholarly struggles to reconcile these conflicts justify their description by Parsons—historically intolerable.[58] The literary gaps are easier to deal with. For instance, Parsons points out that the close-up scenic conclusion of the Gospel (the day of resurrection) keeps its end temporally close to the body of the narrative, rather than providing an overview epilogue relating what later happened to characters in the story, or *Nachgeschichte* (Acts functions as the Lukan *Nachgeschichte*). But the beginning of Acts uses a basic biblical symbol, the forty days, as part of its legitimizing the disciples as they begin their mission.[59]

GAP OF THE END OF ACTS

Through the centuries, the most problematic gaps for interpreters of Acts have occurred at the end, Acts 28:23–31. One gap concerns the point of view toward the Jews. Why does Acts three different times portray Paul turning from the Jews toward the Gentiles (Acts 28:25–28, as well as 13:46; 18:6)? After the first two rejections of Jews, why is Paul again shown speaking to Jews in the next town (14:1) or converting a synagogue official (18:8)? Does this pattern imply that even after Acts 28:28 Paul continued to appeal to Jews, or does its climactic and final position in the narrative imply that the appeal to the Jews was in the past?[60]

A related gap concerns the mixed response of the Jews to Paul in Acts 28:24–25. Since some were persuaded by him, many interpreters wonder about the apparent harshness of Paul's final statement (ῥῆμα) to them all, Isa. 6:9–10 in Acts 28:26–27. One plausible attempt to fill this gap is Robert C. Tannehill's explanation that the lack of agreement among the Jewish leaders dashed Paul's hopes for their endorsement of his message and hence its acceptance by the entire Roman Jewish community. Although individual Jews may continue to accept the message, this failure of the leadership to agree and thus lead the Jewish community to acceptance occasioned Paul's turn to the Gentiles.[61]

The gap at the end of Acts that has aroused the most attention is the flat statement in Acts 28:30 (RNAB): "He remained for two full years in his lodgings" ('Ενέμεινεν δὲ διετίαν ὅλην). The verb *remained* is in the aorist, implying a simple (past) act that is over. The duration of Paul's house imprisonment is stated—"two full years." The narrator could not describe a past situation that lasted a specific amount of time without knowing that that situation changed at the end of the two years. This grammatical fact undermines the arguments of those who claim that Acts ends during Paul's imprisonment because it was written during Paul's imprisonment. If that were so, the narrator would not have referred to the imprisonment as past by using the aorist, nor could he have known how long the imprisonment would last.

If the two years of captivity are over by the time of writing, the major gap remains: What happened after that second year passed? Was Paul tried or just released? If tried, was he convicted and executed or acquitted and released (for further travel, such as his desired trip to Spain)? There are foreshadowings in the narrative that can be interpreted as intimating Paul's execution, such as his prediction to the Ephesian elders that they would never see him again (Acts 20:25, cf. v. 38). But although the majority of Lukan specialists hold that Acts implies that Paul was executed after the two years, evidence for complete agreement is no longer available.[62]

Although the narrator's remark that Paul's house imprisonment lasted "two whole years" implies knowledge about what happened at the end of those two years, by choosing to withhold this knowledge from the audience he leaves an obvious deliberate gap in the plot at the climactic position of its conclusion. Already, Chrysostom noted and explained this in his *Homilies on Acts* 55: "At this point the historian stops his account and leaves the reader thirsting so that thereafter he guesses for himself. This also non-Christian writers . . . do. For to know everything makes one sluggish and dull."[63] The gaps at the ends of Mark and Acts invite readers to fill them using their knowledge from outside the narrative. The intended readers of Mark knew about the resurrection appearances and could supply these. Similarly the original intended readers of Luke were probably expected to know what happened after Paul's two-year imprisonment, even if this gap is difficult to fill for later readers like ourselves.

But the failure to supply such information in the narratives of Mark and Acts raises other issues to their readers' attention. The point of Mark ending so enigmatically, "And they said nothing to anyone, for they were afraid" (Mark 16:8), seems less concerned with the story time of the women at the tomb than with stimulating the intended readers to reflect on their own faith and witness or deficiency therein.[64] The end of Acts also has another purpose more important than simply rounding out the story line. By not closing out Paul's life but ending Acts on a note of bold, unhindered preaching, the story ends with an open thrust toward future evangelization up to and beyond the time of the intended audience.

We have seen how the narratives of Luke and Acts were plotted by composite artistry that arranged (put in order, ἀνατάξασθαι, Luke 1:1) disparate source materials around previous plots (like Mark's), by kerygmatic summaries, and by motifs like the journey to Jerusalem. We have seen how the writer linked independent episodes in patterns of foreshadowing and fulfillment, in mnemonic ABA' patterns, and with deliberate redundancy for emphasis. The resultant plots of Luke and Acts have both closure of the main plot action and openness to the future.

Plotting necessarily leaves gaps in the recounting of incidents for readers to fill in. Gaps are necessary to maintain interest and audience participation in the experience of the narrative. The problematic beginning of Acts and end of Luke and Acts prove to be gaps that in some cases would have been much easier for the original intended audience to fill than for readers today. Even these gaps, problematic though they may be today, are important for linking Luke and Acts and, by avoiding excessive closure at Paul's death, for maintaining openness to a future of evangelization beyond Paul's work. Further, the kinds of gaps that are left and the information that is provided to the implied readers are indications of the kind of readers implied by the narrative, as the previous chapter showed.

Since the order of events in a plot is not fully predetermined, the narrator has a number of free choices in the narrative sequence, such as chronology, flashback, and foreshadowing. Thus the narrator is the key link among authors, plot, and readers. Part 2 shall present applications of these methodological considerations, with special focus on the central figure of the narrator—in the prologues (chapter 4), in the Gospel (chapter 5), in Acts as a whole (chapter 6), in the special "we" passages (chapter 7), and when a character (e.g., Paul) is the narrator (chapter 8). Part 2 will end with a study of the narrator's implicit commentary on the story (chapter 9).

2

Applications:
Narration

4 The Prologue to Luke's Gospel: Narrative Questions

PREFACES AND THEIR HISTORIOGRAPHICAL FUNCTIONS

It is practically a consensus in Lukan scholarship that the preface of the Gospel of Luke is a conventional ancient preface in its form, style, and content.[1] Its conventionality cautions against taking too literally all its claims, such as that "many" (πολλοί) have tried to compile Gospel narratives (Luke 1:1). But the presence of convention in a literary preface does not in itself imply that none of its claims can be taken seriously. Not only all writing but all use of language is necessarily conventional.[2] One simply cannot communicate without using customary linguistic and extralinguistic signs understood by others in the same culture and language group. Paul Ricoeur remarks:

> Language is itself the process by which private experience is made public. Language is the exteriorization thanks to which an impression is transcended and becomes an expression, or, in other words, the transformation of the psychic into the noetic. Exteriorization and communicability are one and the same thing for they are nothing other than this elevation of a part of our life into the *logos* of discourse. There the solitude of life is for a moment, anyway, illuminated by the common light of discourse.[3]

To be understood one must use conventional grammar and vocabulary and genres (with minimal neologisms or departures from the standard). Since the writer of Luke-Acts had to use some convention to begin his Gospel, his use of a preestablished preface genre does not automatically empty his preface of all meaning. His very choice among possible preface

39

conventions of this literary rather than a biblical kind provides some indication of his intent to produce a professional writing.[4]

Moreover, any study of art and writings must examine not only the genre but the individual adaptations of that genre and its functions within the entire work.[5] It is just as important to investigate how Luke modifies and applies the preface genre for his purposes as it is to be aware of the genre that he uses. One must also ask to what extent the conventional statements and claims made in Luke's preface are fulfilled in the body of the text. The preface and the main body are mutually interpretative. For example, even a casual reading of Lucian's *A True Story* demonstrates that the main body does not confirm its preface, but that its title is ironic in the ways that its preface had promised.[6]

Like other prefaces, Luke 1:1–4 refers to predecessors who had attempted similar histories, but unlike most, Luke's does not explicitly criticize or reject them. Like other prefaces, this one indicates both the content and ideological point of view of the narrative, but it does so in a way that more strongly identifies with the tradition being described than most self-conscious prefaces. Thus it refers to a narrative "of the events which have been accomplished *among us* [ἐν ἡμῖν] just as they were delivered *to us* [ἡμῖν]" (Luke 1:1–2). Like other prefaces, this one refers to its sources anonymously and to the labor of research and writing involved, but more briefly than most. Like many prefaces, this one is addressed to a named patron, Theophilus, but with no flattery other than the honorific "most excellent [κράτιστε]." Like other prefaces this one states its purpose, the common one of providing "assurance" or "certainty" (ἀσφάλειαν, 1:4) or truth about events already known to the narratee. Unlike most other prefaces, this one draws almost no attention to the person of the author: it does not give his name nor say anything about him other than that he has followed all things closely and intends to write an ordered account for Theophilus. Of course, Theophilus would know his name so he would not be expected to give it, just as Josephus does not give his name in his preface addressed to Epaphroditus in *Against Apion*, although he does in his preface addressed to subjects of the Roman Empire in *Jewish War*.[7]

Since Luke's preface individualizes the genre in several respects, there is no a priori reason to dismiss as merely conventional its stated purpose: "to *write* [a narrative] . . . that you may know the truth [*assurance*, ἀσφάλειαν] concerning the things of which you have been [orally] *informed* [κατηχήθης]." To understand the full meaning of this vaguely stated purpose one must interpret it in light of what the narrative actually does.

NARRATIVE'S PREFACE AND BODY: TRADITIONAL, NOT ORIGINAL, TALE

The Lukan preface promises a traditional narrative, and the body of the Gospel confirms this promise. It is in fact "a narrative of the events that have been fulfilled among us" (Luke 1:1, RNAB), not an account original to Luke in the way that contemporary novels are original to their authors (and fictional). Most of the events narrated are attested in other Gospels. Except for the infancy narrative in Luke 1–2, most of the other events narrated only in Luke are of the same (traditional) kind as those found in other Gospels. Like Mark and Matthew, Luke narrates primarily traditional material about Jesus. Also like the other Synoptic Gospels, the Lukan Gospel recounts this material primarily from the church's traditional point of view, not from some idiosyncratic perspective.

However, the Lukan preface does claim some originality in the Gospel's presentation of these events found in the Christian tradition. The Lukan author is not anonymously submerged in the tradition, like most of the authors of the narrative books of his Greek Bible, but calls attention to his personal contribution in this preface. The preface's claims to originality apply to the implied author's investigation and plotting of the events (Luke 1:1, 3), not to the creation of new (and therefore fictional) events. The inclusion of episodes in Luke that are not found in other Gospels but are quite similar to those in other Gospels confirms the preface's claim to original investigation of Christian events. The differences and additions between the Lukan and Markan plots confirms the preface's claim to original plotting.

DRAMATIS PERSONAE IN THE PROLOGUE

The prologue singles out at least four different individuals or groups: (1) "*Many* [πολλοὶ] have tried to compile a narrative"; (2) "events fulfilled among *us* [ἐν ἡμῖν]"; (3) "it seemed good to *me* also [κἀμοί]"; (4) "to write to *you* [σοι]." Among these four are a first-person narrator who presents himself as a *histor* (3),[8] a second-person narratee named Theophilus (4), an earlier group of writers of similar Christian narratives (1), and a group of Christians in whose midst the recounted events took place (2). The *histor* narrator distinguishes himself from other narrative writers (1), but includes himself in the Christian community among which the events took place (2).

Speaking in the first person (3) to a second-person narratee (4) removes the narrative from the "folk history" common in the Bible, in which an anonymous community member narrates to it the communal story. First person distances the narrator from both the community and other narrators by individualizing him and calling attention to his existence at the beginning of the narrative, even though he quickly gives way to an invisible, omniscient third-person narrator until he reappears for the opening of the second volume: "In the first book, O Theophilus, I have dealt with . . . " (Acts 1:1). It does the same for the narratee Theophilus, who probably belongs to the Christian community (which we have said seems to be the intended audience of Luke and Acts). Theophilus also quickly fades from reader awareness until reappearing briefly at the beginning of Acts.

Use of first- and second-person voices in the prologues makes a professional claim that the main body does little to sustain.[9] This special claim may be intended to differentiate Luke-Acts from the previous Christian narratives about "these events." In all probability (certainly if the previous writings included the Gospel of Mark) the earlier narratives were written after the manner of biblical narratives on which both writers and readers were nurtured.

Yet this distanciation of narrator and narratee is qualified by the inclusion of at least the narrator (and quite possibly Theophilus) among the persons in whose midst the events took place (Luke 1:1). These deeds, of which Theophilus was informed (1:4), were "fulfilled among us [πεπληροφορημένων ἐν ἡμῖν]" and their accounts were "handed down to us [παρέδοσαν ἡμῖν]" by original eyewitnesses and ministers of the word (1:1–2). Luke does not distance himself and Theophilus from the community whose narrative is being told the way Josephus distances himself from the Jewish community in telling Romans about the Jewish War. Whereas Josephus implies that the Jewish people, of which he was a member and former leader, were "kicking against the Roman goad" and the yoke willed by God for them, Luke approves of and is committed to the directions taken by Jesus and the disciples in Luke and Acts. Whereas the *Jewish War* accuses the Jews of bringing God's punishment on themselves through the instrumentality of the Romans, Luke-Acts defends Christians from charges of apostasy from their Jewish matrix and covenant community.[10]

NARRATORS IN THE IMPLIED AUTHOR'S PLACE IN LUKE-ACTS

As previously mentioned, Luke uses four different kinds of narrators to tell his tale: (1) a *histor*, "I," in the prologue; (2) an unobtrusive, omniscient narrator speaking in the third-person through most of Luke and Acts, with only occasional obtrusive asides to the implied readers; (3) a marginal observer and participant "we" narrator in sections of Acts after 16:10; (4) character narrators of stories within the story such as Paul of his call in Acts 22 and 26. This multiplicity causes some confusion about narrative perspective but had precedent in some late old or intertestamental writings like 2 Maccabees, Tobit, and parts of Ezra.[11]

Luke's principal narrator is obviously the third-person omniscient narrator who recounts most of Luke-Acts. This is the same kind of narrator commonly used in Old Testament biblical narratives. But the use of the two kinds of first-person narrators seems intended to modify the image of the implied author that exclusive use of an omniscient narrator would convey. Use of the individual *histor* suggests that the implied author is an educated writer who has made the same kind of historical investigation and narrative plotting expected of other historians. This claim is not followed up by the usual skeptical interjections employed by other *histor* narrators, as in Josephus, about the veracity of some miraculous accounts or variant conflicting accounts of the same incidents.[12]

Use of the "we" narrator, a marginal character in some episodes, makes a claim that the implied author was present at the events he narrates. Since these events only take place on some of Paul's later journeys, the claim is limited and does not apply to the Gospel nor to most of Luke's account of the origins of the church or early career of Paul in Acts. But "we" passages do provide a personal link with the main character of Acts toward the end of his career. Other historians of Luke's milieu likewise claim to have been present at the later events of longer narratives: Josephus claims eyewitness participation in the latest part only of the history of the Jewish people and limits his *Jewish War* to the time after those in earlier Jewish histories. "Of the subsequent history, I shall describe the incidents of the war through which I lived with all the detail and elaboration at my command; for the events preceding my lifetime [τὰ δὲ προγενέστερα τῆς ἐμῆς ἡλικίας]I shall be content with a brief summary [ἐπιδραμῶ συντόμως]."[13] Some scholars interpret Luke 1:3 in ways that support a similar claim in the later part of Acts, arguing that "having followed all things [παρηκολουθηκότι] closely" implies not only gathering information but actually participating in some events recounted.[14]

Luke's use of these three kinds of narrators in Luke-Acts indicates to his intended audience a narrative that is primarily biblical in form and function, but with some professional sophistication and first-hand knowledge in a few later sections. Including himself with those among whom the deeds described have been accomplished (1:1) affirms that this narrative is recounted by an insider who shares the beliefs of and identifies with its main characters, Jesus and his disciples.

Narrative approaches to the Lukan prologue have presented its combination of conventional and original intent and the seriousness of its stated purpose. The results have indicated that the Gospel narrative confirms the preface's claims to be a traditional rather than original narrative, in which the implied author's original contributions apply not to creation of new and consequently fictional stories but to the investigation and plotting of the traditional fund of accounts. They also drew attention to the four different groups or persons who make up the dramatis personae of the prologue. Finally, they illustrated some of the effects of using four different kinds of narrators in Luke-Acts: the discriminating *histor* who speaks in the first person in the prologues, the usually unobtrusive, omniscient narrator of most of Luke and Acts, the witness narrator who speaks as "we" in some later sections of Acts, and character narrators telling stories within the story. Let us now examine the narrator of most of the Gospel account.

5 Narrators in Luke

NARRATORS OF THE INTRODUCTION TO THE GOSPEL

After the brief study in the preceding chapter of narrators in the prologue and the passage immediately following it, we turn to Luke's diverse use of narrators for different parts of the plot of his Gospel, then of Acts. Luke's diversity of narrators is closely related to the Lukan plotting of the narrative, treated in chapter 3. From the prologue, one can probably assume that Luke began his plotting with many traditional stories and sayings about Jesus, some of them already in plotted form, as in the Gospel of Mark.[1] One can hypothesize that the most creative Lukan plotting of the Gospel, and consequently his most creative use of narrators in it, would come in the beginning, in the end, and in the devices used to organize and frame the middle section.[2] (Previously plotted material, as in the Gospel of Mark, already had its own narrators.) The non-Markan traditional episodes and sayings in the Lukan middle (which are usually referred to as belonging to the hypothetical Q source of materials common to Matthew and Luke or to L content peculiar to Luke or his sources) were also already narratives with their own narrators during their pre-Gospel circulation as independent Gospel pericopes. Therefore, the clearest Lukan contributions in traditional narratives were in the ways he framed and linked them: introducing them and placing them into a new narrative context; concluding them and preparing for his second volume; and ordering and framing disparate traditional pericopes and sayings in relationship to his already plotted (Markan) Gospel material.[3]

Let us look at the varying uses of narrators in the successive parts of the Lukan Gospel: Luke 1–2; Luke 3:1–4:30; Luke 4:31–9:50; the travel narrative, Luke 9:51–19:44; the Jerusalem account, Luke 19:45–21:38; the passion, Luke 22–23; and the resurrection accounts and transition to Acts, Luke 24.

45

THE NARRATORS IN THE PROLOGUE AND INFANCY NARRATIVE,
LUKE 1–2

The first striking diversity in Lukan narrators appears at the very beginning. We have seen that the narrator in the prologue is a *histor* who openly speaks to his patron, Theophilus, about how he gathered and organized the materials of his narrative, and what his purpose is in telling it.[4] He is at pains to emphasize his professional credentials and the credibility of his narrative. The narrator of the rest of Luke 1–2, however, is clearly a third-person folk narrator in the biblical tradition. In contrast to the literary periodic sentence of the prologue's narrator, this folk narrator writes a very unpolished biblical Greek: heavily Semitic in sentence structure and full of Septuagintal expressions.[5] Like most biblical narrators, he recedes behind his story, becoming virtually unnoticed, and exercises a quasi-omniscience from a bird's-eye perspective.

THE LUKAN NARRATOR AND INTENDED READERS

The relationship between the Lukan narrator and intended readers is especially important in Luke 1–4, the introductory material to the traditional episodes and sayings about Jesus' ministry.[6] In these chapters, the narrator shows the most independence from and modifications of his primary Markan source. In them he provides the intended readers with a good deal of orientation and background information through which to interpret the individual traditional episodes and sayings to follow. As would be expected both in Hellenistic biographies and biblical historiography, the Lukan narrator portrays the hero's parentage and circumstances of his birth (in this case for both John and Jesus) in a setting of national and cultural (biblical) expectations and promises.[7] These two chapters portray pious members of Israel, like Zechariah, Elizabeth, Symeon, and Anna, awaiting God's promises to save his people. The narrator pictures the parents of the Baptist as righteous Jews, despite what was often interpreted as the curse of sterility in his mother, who was not only childless like the mother of Samuel (1 Sam. 1), but old besides. He shows Jesus' parents fulfilling the law both of Caesar and of Moses (2:1–5, 22–24) and finding the boy Jesus in the Temple discoursing with the teachers (2:46), which foreshadows his later teaching in the Temple.[8]

The readers are shown that the births of John and Jesus are miraculous and portend respectively a great prophet "in the spirit and power of Elijah" (Luke 1:17), and the "Son of the Most High" whose Davidic reign will never end (1:32–33). Before the narration of the public life of either John or Jesus, the readers are reminded that John is a special prophet, filled with the Holy Spirit from his mother's womb (Luke 1:15, 41), whose role is to prepare the way of the Lord (Jesus). They also view Jesus, because he was conceived through a special act of the Holy Spirit in his virginal mother, as son of God rather than of Joseph (Luke 1:35, cf. 3:22–23, 4:22 ironically). The narrator has also informed Lukan readers that Jesus is destined for both acceptance and rejection in Israel and to be light to the Gentiles (Luke 2:32, 34–35). In other words, even before Jesus' baptism at the Jordan, the omniscient narrator has provided readers with all the information necessary for recognition of the ironic fulfillment of God's plan, especially through Jesus' death, that they will need to interpret the words and deeds of Jesus from the tradition.[9]

Most of the information in Luke 1–2, from traditions peculiar to Luke, provides a special Lukan perspective for interpreting Gospel traditions shared with Mark and Matthew. Luke 3–4 adds further orientation to Jesus' mission, death, and resurrection. These two chapters are structured according to the Markan prologue (Mark 1:1–15), with additions both from material shared with Matthew (Q) and peculiar to Luke (L).

NARRATORS IN LUKE 3:1–4:30

According to the practice of historians, the Lukan narrator places the Baptist pericope within a world historical context—the reign of Tiberius Caesar, when Pilate was procurator, when Herod, Philip, and Lysanias were tetrarchs, and Annas and Caiaphas were high priests (Luke 3:1–2).[10] (This corresponds to the statement by Paul to the Roman governor Festus and Herodian king Agrippa in Acts 26:26b about Christ's suffering and resurrection being preached to the people and to Gentiles: "this was not done in a corner" [RNAB].)[11]

The narrator also supplies a biblical backdrop for the call of John the Baptist, reporting it with an allusion to Jeremiah's call (Luke 3:2, Jer. 1:1 LXX) and interpreting John's mission with a citation of Isaiah 40 (expanded beyond the Markan citation and dropping the incorrect citation of Mal. 3:1 as Isaiah in Mark 1:2 [Luke 3:4–6]).

The narrator makes explicit what is only implied in Mark—that the people were wondering whether John might be the Messiah (Luke 3:15). This inside view exemplifies the narrator's omniscient point of view as well as one of his explanatory asides to readers. The non-chronological reference here to Herod's later imprisonment of John further illustrates the pattern of Lukan retrospective narration, which completes one plot line (John's) before turning to another (Jesus').[12]

In the baptism account that follows, the focus rests predominantly on Jesus; there is no mention of John and only passing reference to the others who were baptized. The narrator slightly modifies the traditional language of his source(s) to portray Jesus' baptism experience with apocalyptic resonances: the opening of heaven, the visible descent of the Holy Spirit as a dove on Jesus, and a voice from heaven, "You are my beloved Son; with you I am well pleased" (Luke 3:22, RNAB).[13]

After this privileged view of Jesus' prayer experience of being called God's son, the narrator reverts to a more external retrospective on Jesus' human age and origins and inserts a long explanatory digression—Jesus' age and genealogy (3:23–38): "When Jesus began his ministry he was about thirty years of age. He was the son, as was thought, of Joseph, the son of Heli . . . the son of Adam, the son of God" (Luke 3:23, 38, RNAB). He thus contextualizes Jesus' divine sonship with a genealogy of Jesus that goes back through all the biblical generations to Adam (son) of God (3:23–38). This in effect demythologizes the title son of God (in an apparent discrepancy to his earlier narration that Jesus would be conceived by the Holy Spirit in 1:35). In Luke 1:35 the narrator had supplied God's perspective on Jesus' identity as son of God (by quoting his angelic messenger to Mary). In providing Jesus' human genealogy the narrator acts more from a historian's perspective (though the link to Adam and thus to God is also biblical). This view "from below" seems intended to complement, not contradict, his earlier more theological explanation of Jesus' divine sonship, a view "from above."[14]

In repeating traditional material about Jesus' temptation by the devil, the narrator keeps the omniscient point of view found in his sources. He reserves the climax of the temptations for Jerusalem, which corresponds to the climactic place Jerusalem holds in Luke's Gospel as destination for Jesus' journey. He also links the temptation account more closely to its immediate context by specifying that Jesus returned from the Jordan full of the Holy Spirit (4:1). After the temptations, the narrator foreshadows the devil's return in Jesus' passion by his conclusion: the devil "departed from him until an opportune time" (ἄχρι καιροῦ, 4:13, RSV).

The narrator also frames the temptation between two references to "returning" with the Spirit: "Filled with the holy Spirit, Jesus returned from the Jordan" (4:1, RNAB) and "Jesus returned to Galilee in the power of the Spirit" (4:14, RNAB).[15] He provides an overview (unique to Luke) of Jesus' spreading reputation and the praise he received for his teaching in the synagogues (4:14–15). Neither Mark nor Matthew mention any of these details, but rather focus on Jesus proclaiming the good news of repentance prior to the approaching kingdom of God. In stressing Jesus' reputation and reception and especially his teaching in synagogues, the narrator heightens the parallels with his reports about Paul in Acts.[16] This kind of foreshadowing through parallelism only becomes noticeable to readers when they read about Paul in Acts and notice the echoes of narratives about Jesus in the Gospel.

The narrator moves the Nazareth account forward to provide additional introduction to Jesus' public ministry and death. He uses this incident as a programmatic foreshadowing of all of Jesus' mission as anointed ("Christ"-ed) healer and preacher and of his rejection and death by his own land (πατρίς).[17] He portrays Jesus' actions as a direct parallel to Paul's in the synagogue in Acts 17:2–3. He uses Isaiah 61 to provide intertextual depth to his portrait of Jesus as Spirit-anointed and prophet, and he alludes ironically to the Nazarenes' mistaken view of Jesus as only Joseph's son (4:22). Luke foreshadows Christian outreach to the Gentiles, as well as Jesus' rejection by his people and death at their hands "outside the city" (4:29, cf. Calvary and Acts 7:58). The narrator thus has set the context for his account within God's biblically revealed plan for his anointed Messiah and has foreshadowed Jesus' climactic death in the Gospel and the mission to the Gentiles in Acts.

NARRATORS FOR MOST OF THE TRADITIONAL EPISODES AND SAYINGS

NARRATORS IN LUKE 4:31–9:50

Although the narrator of Luke moves some events forward, he postpones the call of the first disciples (Luke 5:1–11 vs. Mark 1:16–20) until after some exorcisms and healings, including that of Peter's mother-in-law (Luke 4:31–44, Mark 1:21–39). This move plus the miraculous catch of fish (Luke 5:4–7, cf. John 21:1–11) add motivation for the disciples' otherwise abrupt following of Jesus when he first calls them. The narration of the miraculous catch maintains the same external point of view as in the previous episodes. The use of "Simon" for Peter focalizes the account from an earlier perspective, though v. 8 shifts to a later perspective by calling him Simon Peter.[18] The narrator also displays his inside knowledge of the astonishment of Simon, James, and John and explains in an aside that the latter were the sons of Zebedee and Simon's partners.

The narrator then follows the Markan order in recounting about seven episodes from the same kind of biblical omniscient point of view as in Luke 5:1–11. These culminate in the synoptic traditional story of the choice of the Twelve, the importance of which he had emphasized by mentioning Jesus' preparation through the previous night of prayer on the mountain. After this choice, the Lukan narrator uses the "showing point of view" simply to "show" Jesus preaching a sermon to the people (of God, λαός, 6:17, 7:1), with special attention to his disciples (6:17, 20), at the foot of the mountain. The narrator does not intrude between his introduction of the sermon in Luke 6:20 and his transition in 7:1 to the healing of the centurion's son.[19] Most of this sermon is a series of Jesus' traditional sayings simply linked together to give the impression of a longer sermon.

After the sermon, the narrator adds episodes missing in Mark but common to Matthew, except for the raising of the widow's son at Nain (7:11–17). In recounting this incident, the narrator makes many intertextual allusions to the raisings of a widow's son by the prophet Elijah in 1 Kings 17:17–24 and of a married woman's son by Elisha in 2 Kings 4:32–37.[20] His final quotation of the people's acclamation of Jesus as a great prophet, and reference to his spreading fame, function as plot bridges, leading directly into the Q story of the Baptist's question "to the Lord" from prison (where he was last mentioned as being in Luke 3:20): "Are you the one who is to come, or should we look for another?" (7:19, RNAB). By calling Jesus "the Lord," the narrator slides into post-resurrection retrospection. He also refers to the cures and exorcisms performed by Jesus before quoting from the Q tradition Jesus' answer to the Baptist's disciples, which in turn is studded with expressions from Isaiah. He then provides the traditional (Q) assessment of John the Baptist as the greatest of prophets but least in the kingdom (7:24–28), and Jesus' condemnation of this generation for rejecting both the Baptist and himself (7:29–35). Narrating disparate episodes from the Jesus traditions gives an overall impression of Jesus' spreading fame, recalling other prophets like Elijah, Elisha, and the Baptist.[21]

The Lukan narrator then recounts the episode of the penitent woman, who anoints with oil the feet of Jesus. This tale could be modified from the pre-passion traditions of Mark and Matthew, where it functions as a remote anointing of Jesus' body for burial.[22] In Luke 7:36–50, however, it focuses on her love and Jesus' forgiveness of her sins. Jesus' final words to the penitent, "Your faith has saved you; go in peace," will become a refrain, returning like a contrapuntal melody line to the travel notices spanning both the so-called Galilean ministry section (4:14–9:50) and in the famous travel section that follows.[23]

Thus, the refrain returns in Luke 8:48 where Jesus, on his way to Jairus's daughter (see 8:41–42 and 51), is interrupted by the woman with the flux of blood. His final word to her is, "Daughter, your faith has saved you; go in peace" (8:48, RNAB). In the so-called travel narrative after Luke 9:51, the refrain recurs in 17:19 as the end of a pericope begun with a specific travel notice in 17:11: "As he continued his journey to Jerusalem . . . " (RNAB). At the finale, Jesus says to the Samaritan leper who alone came back to thank him, "Stand up and go; your faith has saved you" (17:19, RNAB). A slight variant on the refrain occurs one final time when Jesus heals the blind beggar near Jericho: "Have sight; your faith has saved you" (18:42, RNAB). This contrapuntal refrain seems to be a Lukan four-part expansion (primarily in Lukan passages or modifications on traditions) of a refrain that occurs only twice in Mark.

Jesus' final saying to the woman, "Go in peace," leads into a narrator's aside about his travels with the Twelve and with women who ministered to him (8:1–3). This summary notice serves not only as a bridge between disparate segments of plot but also prepares for the women's reappearance at Jesus' passion and resurrection (23:49, 53, 56–24:11).[24]

The narrator then recounts the sower parables and other Markan episodes leading up to Jesus' feeding of the five thousand, after which he omits a good deal of Markan material. (He does, however, return to the Markan plot line with Peter's confession and Jesus' first prophecy of his passion.) This "great omission" eliminates the most enigmatic section of Mark, which deals with a second almost identical feeding, riddles about the numbers of leftovers (Mark 8:19–21), and provocative sayings about the disciples' blindness and hard hearts (Mark 6:52, 7:18, 8:17–18).[25]

Immediately following the feeding of the five thousand, the narrator relates Peter's pivotal confession of Jesus as the Christ, as well as Jesus' prediction of his suffering, his statements on the necessity of his disciples to suffer, and Jesus' transfiguration (9:18–36). Although composed of disparate episodes, the narration of this section builds to a climax from questions about Jesus' identity to the revelation of Jesus' glory as God's son. The section is rounded out with traditional incidents that are apparently unrelated (9:37–50), except for a second passion prediction (9:43b–45).

NARRATORS IN THE TRAVEL NARRATIVE, LUKE 9:51–19:44

Many scholars have tried to find a coherent plot structure behind the Lukan travel narrative, basing this section on parallels to Deuteronomy, sections of the Deuteronomistic History, or the like.[26] No consensus has been reached, however, regarding the nature of the structure or its Old Testament roots. Some recent literary critics have simply renounced any claim that the Gospels (including Luke) are unified narratives. Rather, they claim, we should admit that Luke's Gospel is primarily episodic, not a developed narrative plot.[27]

However, it is clear that the Lukan Gospel at least intends to plot a narrative about Jesus (Luke 1:1–4) and that the narrator subsumes the Markan plot line and provides some other unambiguous plot developments (see Luke 1–4 and other examples above). It seems equally evident that the many traditional non-Markan episodes, inserted into the Markan plot line in the long travel narrative, resist formation into any obvious plot development. The Lukan narrator has succeeded in little more than superimposing a loose journey motif over a collection of many traditional episodes and sayings of Jesus, simply by means of a narrator's frame and periodic reminders of the journey theme.[28] Thus the section begins with a solemn notice of time fulfilled and Jesus's departure for Jerusalem: "When the days for his being taken up were fulfilled [ἐν τῷ συμπληροῦσθαι τὰς ἡμέρας τῆς ἀναλήμψεως αὐτοῦ], he resolutely determined to journey to Jerusalem" (Luke 9:51, RNAB). This solemn introduction is echoed later, in Acts 2:1, at the introduction to the Pentecostal inauguration of the church's spread: ἐν τῷ συμπληροῦσθαι τὴν ἡμέραν τῆς πεντηκοστῆς.[29]

Despite such a solemn introduction to Jesus' final and predestined journey to Jerusalem, the narrator keeps this journey in sight only briefly, before the many apparently unrelated episodes crowd it from most readers' minds. The narrator begins with explicit reference to a travel motif. He reports that Jesus sent two messengers ahead to a Samaritan village to prepare his way (9:52), and he ends this episode with their journeying by way of another village (9:56). In 9:57, the narrator notes their traveling "on the way." In Luke 10:1, he recounts how Jesus sent off seventy-two in pairs to each town and place he intended to visit.[30] But now his references to journeying come separated by longer narrative stretches. In 10:17 he reports their return to Jesus, but with little suggestion of his continued journey toward Jerusalem. After several more episodes the narrator remarks in 10:38 that on their journey they came to a certain village, where Martha hosted him. The next episode on prayer begins with a vague mention that Jesus "was praying in a certain place" (11:1), but with no reference to movement toward Jerusalem. After several sayings on prayer, the narrator reports an exorcism of a mute demon with no indication of locale or journey in progress (11:14). A series of interchanges with various groups follows, with still no reference to a journey (11:14–52). Finally the narrator mentions almost in passing (through a genitive absolute participial construction rather than a main clause) that when Jesus left, the scribes and Pharisees plotted to catch him (11:53). Even though this expresses movement by Jesus, it makes no explicit mention of progress toward Jerusalem.

Luke 12:1–13:9 add further incidents and sayings of Jesus, none obviously related to any movement toward Jerusalem. Luke 13:10 mentions merely that he was teaching in a synagogue on the sabbath, with no indication of its location or of any journey context. The narrator adds further deeds and sayings with no apparent journey motif until 13:21.

In Luke 13:22, the narrator once more summarizes Jesus' travels through and teachings in towns and villages on his way to Jerusalem. But the following episodes in 13:23–14:24 again seem unrelated to a journey theme. His subsequent journey allusion in 14:25 to crowds traveling with Jesus leads to sayings on discipleship and forgiveness and miscellaneous sayings and parables in 14:26–17:10, before his next summary reference to Jesus' journey: "As he continued his journey to Jerusalem, he traveled through Samaria and Galilee" (17:11, RNAB). This summary narrative reverses the order in which Jesus would have gone (from Galilee through Samaria to Jerusalem in Judea).[31] The curing of the ten lepers is set on Jesus' journey: "As he was entering a village, ten lepers met [him]" (Luke 17:12, RNAB).* But the narrator adds other sayings in 17:20–18:14 with no mention of travel. The incident about people bringing children to Jesus in Luke 18:15–17, which after Luke 9:50 is the first Lukan rejoining of the Markan plot line, has no locale. Nor do the next story of the rich official and the sayings about possessions that develop from it (18:18–30). There is perhaps a figurative allusion to a journey in references to following Jesus: "Then come, follow me" and Peter's "We have given up our possessions and followed you" (18:22 and 28, RNAB).[32]

The narrator reemphasizes the journey motif in Jesus' third passion prediction, but by now he has reincorporated the Markan journey theme, and Jesus rather than the narrator mentions it: "Behold, we are going up to Jerusalem and everything written by the prophets about the Son of Man will be fulfilled" (18:31b, RNAB). Compared to the Markan and Matthaean parallels, the Lukan narrator has taken from tradition the reference about going up to Jerusalem but added the reference to the fulfillment of everything written by the prophets. This further explicates the intertextual grounding of the Lukan journey motif in Old Testament prophecies and God's plan.

The journey motif continues as an explicit frame for the story of the healed blind man. The Lukan narrator begins the episode by noting Jesus' approach to Jericho and resolves it with the penultimate comment, "He immediately received his sight and followed him, giving glory to God" (18:43, RNAB). The narrator introduces the next episode, about Zacchaeus (only in Luke), by portraying continual movement: "He came to Jericho and intended to pass through the town" (Luke 19:1, RNAB). He notes how

---

*Unless otherwise noted in the text, bracketed material found in quotations from the New American Bible With Revised New Testament appears in the original. Brackets do not indicate alterations to the RNAB text by the present author except where the original Greek has been added.

Zacchaeus ran ahead to where Jesus was to pass (19:4). Within this setting of movement toward Jerusalem he narrates the story of Zacchaeus and the composite parable of the nobleman going to receive the kingship (from L) and giving his servants ten gold coins to invest in his absence (from Q, 19:1–27).

The narrator culminates his journey motif with Jesus' entry into Jerusalem. "After he had said this, he proceeded on his journey up to Jerusalem" (Luke 19:28, RNAB). The sense of movement toward Jerusalem remains primary as the narrator recounts how Jesus draws near to Bethphage and Bethany, sends two disciples ahead to get a colt (19:29–35), and rides the colt toward the Mount of Olives while the crowds acclaim him (19:36–40). The motif continues to intensify as Jesus nears Jerusalem and weeps over it (19:41), prophesying doom for the city "because you did not recognize the time (καιρός) of your visitation" (19:44, RNAB). By quoting Jesus' prophecy of destruction just before his entry into Jerusalem, the narrator provides a foreboding backdrop for all of Jesus' conflicts with the Jerusalem leaders and for his death at their instigation. The readers are aware, as the Jerusalem leaders were not, of the dire consequences for Jerusalem from their rejection of Jesus, their Davidic and prophetic messiah.[33]

The ultimate destination of the journey motif is the Temple (19:45–47).[34] The summary about the Messiah Jesus teaching daily in the Temple closes this section with a frame recalling the boy Jesus with the teachers in the Temple in Luke 2 and sets into motion the next phase in the plot line, the leaders' plotting to put Jesus to death (19:47–48). Jesus' journey to Jerusalem begins now to mutate into his exodus through suffering to glory (see Luke 9:31; 24:26).

NARRATORS OF THE LUKAN CONFLICT AND PASSION AT JERUSALEM

NARRATORS IN LUKE 19:45–21:38

Luke 19:45–48 is a transition passage from Jesus' journey to Jerusalem to the beginning of his conflicts with authorities there. On the one hand, these verses about the Temple cleansing furnish the end point and goal of all the preceding travel narrative section. On the other, Jesus' commandeering the Temple sets the stage for all the Temple conflicts and Jesus' passion, which follow in the next section of the Lukan plot (which here follows the Markan plot line closely, with some significant adjustments).[35]

Following the Markan lead, the Lukan narrator builds tension by noting how the authorities were seeking Jesus' death but were prevented by the people's attraction to his teaching. He thus sets the stage for Judas's betrayal, which he had already foretold by labelling him a traitor when first introducing him among the Twelve in Luke 6:16 (as had Mark 3:19). He explains beforehand why Judas's betrayal of Jesus was necessary, to enable the leaders to arrest Jesus when he was away from the crowds (as Mark 11:18).

In the ensuing traditional accounts of Jesus' conflicts with various Jewish leaders, the Lukan narrator heightens the suspense before Jesus' passion. He centers the tension around who shall teach "the people" (τὸν λαὸν, his technical term for the people of God, Israel, the recipients of God's promises) in the Temple.[36] The struggle between the same Sanhedrin and Jesus' apostles over leadership of the people will carry over into Acts.[37] As the setting for the leaders' first challenge to Jesus' authority, the narrator specifies (beyond Mark 11:27) that the Temple was where Jesus was teaching (Luke 20:1, where the apostles also teach in Acts 3–5). He specifies that the subsequent parable of the wicked tenant farmers was also spoken "to the people" (Luke 20:9; "to them" in Mark 12:1) but against the scribes and chief priests (Luke 20:19 as in Mark 12:12). Though the parable was already against the leaders, the Lukan narrator underlines the seriousness of Jesus' challenge to those leaders by mentioning that he challenged them in the presence of "the people." As in Mark, he repeats that the leaders sought to lay hands on him then but feared "the people" (of God), although Mark 12:12 says merely, "they feared the crowd (τὸν ὄχλον)."

The Lukan narrator does not allow the natural endings between originally independent episodes to break the steadily mounting tension toward Jesus' passion. Instead, he links these episodes to form a single chain of events leading to the cross. Thus, he omits Mark's "And leaving him they went away" at the end of the clash over the tenant parable, which in Mark signals a temporary break in the confrontation. Rather, he moves directly from reporting that the leaders knew that Jesus had told the parable against them (Luke 20:19) to mentioning that they watched him closely and sent agents to trap him in his speech so they could hand him over to the governor (20:20).

He thus closely relates the tenant parable and the question about tribute to Caesar, which were two independent conflicts in Mark 12. And in Luke 20:20 he alone specifically mentions the leaders' intent to hand Jesus over to Pilate, which explains their plot against Jesus and foreshadows what will happen in Luke 23 and what the Acts speeches will refer back to.[38] Only after some Sadducees challenge resurrection (as in Mark) does the narrator show the retreat of Jesus' questioners by mentioning some scribes' positive response and the fear of others to question him further (Luke 20:39–40).

Tension is maintained, however, as Jesus moves from defense to attack. After his enemies retreat, the narrator shows Jesus challenging them, linking his challenge to their retreat by the grammatical signal "and" or "then" (δέ). "And they no longer dared to ask him anything. Then [δέ] he said to them [εἶπεν δὲ πρὸς αὐτούς] . . . " (20:40–41). Jesus goes on to challenge a common expectation about the Messiah in the light of a biblical quotation that apparently contradicts it. "How do they claim that the Messiah is the Son of David?" (20:41, RNAB). Since he quotes David in the Psalms calling the Messiah "lord," how can the Messiah be David's "son"?

The narrator moves immediately into a further attack by Jesus, this time directed against the scribes. The attack is public, "within the hearing of all the people" (20:45, RNAB). In this group setting, he tells his disciples, "Be on guard against the scribes . . . " (20:46, RNAB), and he makes some severe charges against them, culminating in the accusation, "They devour the houses of widows . . . " (20:47, RNAB).

From the reference to widows the narrator moves directly to the next incident, in which Jesus uses the example of a poor widow's Temple contribution to make a point about not judging by appearances. While the denunciation of the scribes (Mark 12:38–40) and the observation of the widow (Mark 12:41–44) are separate in source material, the Lukan narrator links the two incidents in Luke 21:1 with the same linkword (δέ) used to tie occurrences in 20:39, 41, and 45. "When he looked up [ἀναβλέψας δὲ] he saw some wealthy people putting their offerings into the treasury and he noticed a poor widow putting in two small coins" (21:1–2, RNAB). In other words, though the narrator used traditional episodes that were already in this order, his narration smoothed and quickened the transition between them with the linkword δέ to depict a more unified occasion of conflict and tension than was in the tradition.

The narrator retains the same setting, Jesus teaching the people in the Temple, as he proceeds to show him prophesying about the destruction of the Temple: "While some people were speaking about how the Temple was adorned . . . he said, 'All that you see here—the days will come when there will not be left a stone upon another stone . . . ' " (Luke 21:5–6, RNAB). This initiates Jesus' long eschatological discourse, which was in the Markan tradition but which the Lukan narrator modified regarding its recipients and locale.[39] In Mark 13:3, Jesus addresses it to

Peter, James, John, and Andrew "privately" [κατ' ἰδίαν] on the Mount of Olives facing the Temple. In Luke 21:7, however, the narrator signals no change of place, with the resulting implication that Jesus is still teaching "the people" in the Temple.

The narrator uses this speech of Jesus to foreshadow the whole Lukan plan of God for "the final days" (cf. Acts 2:17), from the time of Jesus beyond the narrator's own time until the cosmic cataclysms and return of the Son of Man (Luke 21:25–28). Jesus' speech thus provides a temporal setting for the rest of Luke and Acts, up to and beyond the time of all future readers. To a far greater extent than in Mark 13, the speech in Luke 21 emphasizes eschatological periodization, a technique in apocalyptic writing of dividing the future into distinct periods leading up to the final end.[40]

Jesus' prophecy of the Temple's destruction introduces the apocalyptic scenario of Luke 21. To his listeners' question, "When will this happen?" Jesus warns them not to focus on the question *when,* nor to believe those who say that now is the time of the end. Wars and insurrections and natural disasters will precede the end. But these in turn will be preceded by persecution of believers and the fall of Jerusalem. It is clear from this summary that the predictions in the speech do not follow chronological order but jump forward and backward in time. One effect of such narration is to give readers an impression of being caught up in the vortex of the final days. They find themselves experiencing persecution, the destruction of Jerusalem, the times of the Gentiles, wars, natural disasters in their past and present, and looking forward to cosmic catastrophes and the ultimate parousia of the Son of Man.

The narrator ends Jesus' eschatological discourse with the summary notice that Jesus taught in the Temple area during the days and spent nights at the Mount of Olives (Luke 21:37). He thus prepares remotely for Jesus' arrest there (22:39, 47–53).

NARRATORS IN THE LUKAN PASSION, LUKE 22–23

The narrator sets the time by remarking that "the feast of Unleavened Bread, called the Passover, was drawing near" (22:1, RNAB). He thus explains as synonymous what in Mark had been simply juxtaposed: "The Passover and the Feast of Unleavened Bread were to take place in two days' time" (Mark 14:1, RNAB).

He begins the passion account repeating that the leaders "were seeking a way to put him to death, for they were afraid of the people" (Luke 22:2, RNAB). This is a close variation on his earlier explanation, after the parable of the tenant farmers, that the leaders "sought to lay their hands on him at that very hour, but they feared the people . . . " (20:19, RNAB).

This theme, the leaders' inability to seize or kill Jesus or his followers because of their fear of "the people," becomes a significant link between Luke's Gospel and Acts. In Luke 19:47–48, the narrator reports that after Jesus drove out the sellers in the Temple and began teaching there daily, the leaders "were seeking to put him to death, but they could find no way to accomplish their purpose because all the people were hanging on his words" (RNAB). In their following challenge to Jesus' authority, the omniscient narrator explains that they were afraid to deny the Baptist's baptism because "all the people will stone us, for they are convinced that John was a prophet" (20:6, RNAB). After the next confrontation between Jesus and the leaders, the narrator repeats the statement in 20:19 about them trying to kill Jesus. Now as he begins his passion account, the narrator's repetition of this theme increases the foreboding and tension, implicitly underlines the importance of the traitor Judas's role, and recalls readers' attention from the foreshadowing predictions in Luke 21 of the end times to the abiding current threat that the leaders present to Jesus.

Repetition of a similar theme in Acts, wherein occurs the clash between the Sanhedrin and the apostles, links the two sets of confrontations closely and interprets them mutually.[41] As the leaders had been unable to move publicly against Jesus because of the people, so the Sanhedrin released Peter and John, "finding no way to punish them, on account of the people who were all praising God for what had happened" (Acts 4:21, RNAB). After a second arrest of the apostles and their miraculous escape from prison, someone reported to the Sanhedrin, " 'The men whom you put in prison are in the temple area and are teaching the people.' Then the captain and the court officers went and brought them in, but without force, because they were afraid of being stoned by the people" (Acts 5:25–26, RNAB). Both Jesus and the apostles taught in the Temple, and the leaders were unable to stop either because of their fear of the people.

This repetition underscores a struggle between the old authorities (the Sanhedrin) and the new (Jesus and his apostles) about who shall teach the people of God in the Temple.[42] For the Lukan narrator, the old leaders' helplessness symbolizes the transfer of authority over God's people from the Sanhedrin to Jesus the Anointed One (Messiah) and his spirit-anointed apostles. The large numbers of "the people" in Acts 2–5 who repent and accept Jesus as the Messiah continue to be recipients of God's promises to "the people," but under new spirit-anointed leaders. Meanwhile the former leaders are cut off from the people by their continued rejection of the messianic prophet like Moses (see Acts 3:19–23).

The Lukan narrator uses his omniscient viewpoint to add to his tradition a fuller explanation of Judas's treachery: "Then Satan entered into Judas

. . . " (Luke 22:3, RNAB). This also places the action within a larger cosmic setting of spiritual warfare between the kingdom of God and the kingdom of Satan.[43] It recalls the foreboding narrator's aside after Jesus had initially overcome Satan's temptations: "When the devil had finished every temptation, he departed from him for a time (ἄχρι καιροῦ)" (Luke 4:13, RNAB). This is now that time (καιρός).

Besides cosmic setting, the narrator also adds historical explanations to his traditional material, as when he appends "in the absence of a crowd" (22:6, RNAB) to Judas's search for a favorable opportunity to hand over Jesus. The narrator immediately goes on to highlight Jesus' initiative in instructing Peter and John to prepare the Passover at the place to which a man carrying a jar of water will go (22:8–13). He thus implies, by hiding from Judas the location of their Passover meal, that Jesus is aware of Judas's treachery. In this way, the narrator hints, Jesus guards against being arrested until after his final Passover meal with his disciples, a fact that becomes clear to readers only in retrospect.[44]

After the farewell supper, the narrator adds to traditional material a second reference to Jesus' custom to go to the Mount of Olives (22:39, ἐπορεύθη κατὰ τὸ ἔθος). He had been the only Gospel narrator to have also previously referred to the pattern Jesus had of teaching in the Temple by day and withdrawing to stay at the Mount of Olives by night (21:37). This information clarifies how Judas would know where to lead the arresting party to find Jesus.

By beginning Jesus' farewell supper with the notice, "When the hour came" (Luke 22:14, RNAB) instead of the Markan "When it was evening" (Mark 14:17, RNAB), the narrator may be maintaining the cosmic overtones of the time or "hour" (almost as in John's Gospel) of Satan's return (Luke 4:13) and of the beginning of Jesus' exodus in Jerusalem (9:31). These hints are later confirmed when readers encounter Jesus' answer to those coming with Judas to arrest him: "Day after day I was with you in the temple area, and you did not seize me; but this is your hour, the time for the power of darkness" (22:53, RNAB). The addition of "your hour" is only in Luke among the Synoptic Gospels but is reminiscent of John's passion account. By this added motif—the hour of powers of darkness—the narrator places Jesus' passion in the context of spiritual warfare, as the Johannine Gospel does.[45]

The Narration of Jesus' Farewell Address, Luke 22:14–38

In other works I have treated Luke 22:14–38 as a special Lukan redaction of traditional Last Supper materials into the form of Jesus' farewell address to his apostles.[46] Those works showed how source materials were re-ordered, edited, and redacted into the loose form of a farewell address, a shape that they did not have in Mark or other traditions. Those works also ground the present narrative critical study of how the narrator functions in showing his audience Jesus' farewell address.

The narrator begins Jesus' farewell address with the solemn notice, "When the hour came, he took his place at table with the apostles" (Luke 22:14, RNAB). Thereafter, he simply introduces Jesus speaking and shows him making his farewell address, including the apostles' reactions. Jesus begins by foreshadowing his imminent suffering, stating that he would not eat the Passover again until it is fulfilled in the kingdom of God, nor drink wine until God's kingdom comes (22:15–18). Next Jesus gives to his apostles a memorial of him, the Eucharist, which is to be a new covenant for them: "Then he took the bread, said the blessing, broke it, and gave it to them, saying, 'This is my body, which will be given for you; do this in memory of me.' And likewise the cup after they had eaten, saying, 'This cup is the new covenant in my blood, which will be shed for you' " (22:19–20, RNAB).[47] The reference to Jesus' body to be given for them and his blood to be shed for them reinforces the prediction of his death from the previous verses. But now it places that death in the context of a new covenant, grounded in God's previous covenantal promises to his people. It also places Jesus' death in a Christian eucharistic setting.

When the narrator relates Jesus' eucharistic sayings, he does so according to the wording of the liturgy of his intended audience. If, as the later parts of Acts suggest, Luke-Acts has close links with Pauline churches, it is not surprising that the wording of the eucharistic formula in Luke is closer to the version of Paul (1 Cor. 11:23–26) than to that of Mark and Matthew. By using the eucharistic wording of his intended readers, the Lukan narrator correlates the farewell words of Jesus with the eucharistic celebrations, grounding the latter in the former. Doing this stimulates them to recall their eucharistic worship as they hear the words of Jesus at the Last Supper. Similarly, when they later participate in the Eucharist, they would be likely to recollect Jesus' words at his farewell supper.[48]

After giving the apostles the eucharistic memorial to him, Jesus delivers to them a prophetic warning about the one who would betray him. Premonition of future troubles and prediction of the circumstances of one's death are important aspects of many farewell addresses, especially in scripture.[49] Mark reported this prediction of Judas's betrayal at the beginning of the Last Supper. But since such a prediction would not be a natural way to begin a farewell address, in Luke 22:21–23 it is postponed until after the eucharistic sayings. These words of Jesus deepen the foreboding of his death, repeat the theme of his betrayal, and make explicit what was already implicit—that Jesus knew beforehand of Judas's treachery. After Jesus' warning, the narrator adds the comment that they began to debate who would do such a thing (22:23), which leads into a squabble among them over who should be regarded as the greatest. Jesus' rebuke and teaching about how Christian authority is service takes on added ironic pathos in the context of his impending death. This setting within Jesus' farewell discourse emphasizes his teaching about authority far more than the traditional context of this incident as part of Jesus' public life (as in Mark 10:41–45).

After this rebuke and lesson, Jesus reassures the apostles that they have remained faithful to him in his trials, "and I confer a kingdom on you, just as my Father has conferred one on me, that you may eat and drink at my table in my kingdom; and you will sit on thrones judging the twelve tribes of Israel" (22:29–30, RNAB). This promise establishes their authority over the people of Israel, which will be activated via conflict with the old authorities in Acts 4–5. As is common in farewell addresses, Jesus is providing leaders to guide the people after he is gone.

He specifies the new leadership structure further with a special role for Simon Peter. Jesus announces this role in the context of a prediction that Simon and the others would be tested by Satan, but that Jesus' intercession for him would keep his faith alive and enable him to strengthen his brethren after his repentance. Jesus thus makes clear that Simon's leadership over the others is to be grounded on grace and repentance, not on his special merits. When Peter goes on to protest that he would go to prison and death with Jesus, Jesus prophesies he will deny him three times this very day (22:31–34). By simply showing this dialogue between Jesus and the apostles, the narrator not only exhibits Jesus providing a successor to lead his people, but deepens the narrative foreboding about the traumatic events about to take place that very day.

The narrator shows Jesus ending his farewell on an enigmatic note, as Socrates had ended his farewell to his disciples in Plato's *Phaedo*.[50] Jesus refers back to his earlier directives to his missionaries not to carry provisions (esp. Luke 10:4) and warns them that in the future they will be persecuted rather than provided for. He is ending his farewell by trying to strengthen his followers for the trials they will face. But they misunderstand him and refer to two swords they have, and Jesus abruptly ends the dialogue (Luke 22:35–38).

Jesus' Testing on the Mount of Olives, Arrest, and Sanhedrin Trial

The narrator reports how Jesus followed his custom in going to the Mount of Olives, thus specifying how Judas could find him. His reference to the disciples "following" Jesus provides mild irony in view of what would soon take place. He then shows Jesus teaching his disciples a final urgent lesson on the need to pray for strength in the impending trials, with echoes from the Lord's Prayer: "Pray that you not enter into temptation" (22:40, my translation). He then models this lesson for them, by withdrawing out of earshot but within their view, kneeling and praying.[51]

Of the Synoptic Gospels, only the Lukan narrator omitted reference to angels helping Jesus after his temptations in the desert, and now only he speaks of an angel in this trial (compare Luke 4:13 with Mark 1:13 and Matt. 4:11, plus Luke 22:43 with Mark 14:32–42 and Matt. 26:36–46). The case of the missing angel at the end of Jesus' temptations in the desert appears solved by the angel's appearance to fortify him here, in his prayer struggle at the time of his greatest test.[52]

The narrator contrasts Jesus' teaching and example of prayer against the disciples' failure to stay awake. Their failure to "pray that you may not undergo the test" (22:46, RNAB) leaves them unprepared for the arresting party's arrival (22:47).

The narrator's use of "behold, a crowd" (ἰδοὺ ὄχλος) to signal the abrupt arrival of the crowd with Judas to arrest Jesus is a Semitic biblicism, based on the common Hebrew expression, "and behold" (ve'hinneh), used to introduce many sentences in biblical narratives (e.g., Judg. 19:1). As Sternberg has pointed out, even though this expression is used by the narrator, it can focalize the action from the perspective of the characters seeing the action, rather than from the narrator's usually more distanced viewpoint.[53] In Mark the expression does not occur on the narrator's lips, but only in characters' quoted speech. In NT narratives this expression by the narrator occurs most frequently in Luke-Acts, Matthew, and Revelation. Often, especially in Revelation, the expression "and behold" introduces the content of a vision or an apparition of a heavenly being (so also in Luke 24:4, Acts 1:10, 10:30, 12:7). It draws the readers into the vision, or into the narrated scene, like a zoom-in, close-up shot by a movie camera.

Compared to Mark, the Lukan narrator initially does not mention the mob with weapons, but instead focuses primarily on Judas and Jesus (22:47). He quotes Jesus explicitly stating the irony of Judas betraying him with a kiss (22:48). He alone mentions the disciples asking if they should strike with the sword, which recalls their previous misunderstanding about swords at the end of the farewell supper in 22:38. When one of them then cuts off the right ear of the high priest's slave, only the Lukan narrator shows Jesus rebuke them and heal the ear (22:50–51).

After the initial focus on Judas and the sword-wielding disciples (22:52), the narrator refers to the priests, guards, and elders. He shows Jesus accusing them of coming after him as if a revolutionary or robber, with weapons, even though he taught daily among them in the Temple. Only he adds Jesus' comment that places his arrest in a cosmic context of spiritual warfare: "But this is your hour, and the power of darkness" (22:53, RSV). The Lukan narrator ends the scene on this dramatic note, not showing the arrest itself nor the flight of his disciples included in the other Gospels.

Rather, he shows the group taking Jesus after his arrest to the high priest's house, with Peter following at a distance (22:54). The Markan and Matthaean narrators cut away from Peter in the courtyard to Jesus' trial and the false witness against him, then back to Peter's denial after Jesus is condemned, thus framing Jesus' witness with Peter's denial (Mark 14:53–65, Matt. 26:57–68).[54] The Lukan narrator, however, shows without interruption Peter's threefold denial around the fire that evening; "the Lord" looking at Peter; and Peter's recollection of the prophecy and weeping. (The narrator's abrupt reversion to "the Lord" changes his temporal perspective to retrospection from Jesus' post-Easter lordship.) In what may be a more accurate historical reconstruction than Mark and Matthew, the Lukan narrator shows no night trial but only the soldiers mocking and tormenting Jesus overnight until taking him before the Sanhedrin in the morning.[55] The narrator also focuses immediately on the climactic challenge of the Sanhedrin to Jesus, disregarding the false witnesses (which are alluded to retrospectively in Stephen's trial in Acts):

> They said, "If you are the Messiah, tell us," but he replied to them, "If I tell you, you will not believe, and if I question, you will not respond. But from this time on the Son of Man will be seated at the right hand of the power of God." They all asked, "Are you then the Son of God?" He replied to them, "You say that I am." (22:67–70, RNAB)

Jesus' refusal to answer their direct question resonates intertextually with the prophet Jeremiah's response to King Zedekiah in Jer. 45:15 LXX (38:15 Hebrew): "If I tell you, will you not certainly put me to death? And if I counsel you, you will not heed me" (my LXX translation). The narrator makes it clear that Jesus has not directly claimed to be Messiah, which would lay him open to political charges. Therefore, when the leaders later accuse him before Pilate of claiming he is Messiah and king in 23:2, the narrator has ensured that readers will perceive this as a false charge. Nevertheless, he ends this scene with the Sanhedrin's verdict: "What further need have we for testimony? We have heard it from his own mouth" (22:71, RNAB).

Jesus' Trial before Pilate and Beginning of His Passion:
Luke 23

The Lukan narrator continues the rapid narrative pace by showing
without comment the Sanhedrin rising from their verdict and leading
Jesus directly to Pilate (Luke 23:1). He is the only narrator to show that
they immediately begin to make three political charges against Jesus:
(1) misleading the nation; (2) forbidding tribute to be given to Caesar; and
(3) claiming that he is Messiah (Christ) king (or "anointed king," χριστὸν
βασιλέα). The second charge, of forbidding tribute, is in direct contradiction to Jesus' own words in Luke 20:25, "Give to Caesar what belongs to
Caesar." The third accusation, that Jesus claims to be Messiah king, contradicts the testimony Jesus has just given in Luke 22:67–69, where he
refuses to answer whether he is the Messiah. The narrator does not have
to explicitly state that these charges are false. His way of structuring or
"ordering" his account (Luke 1:1, 3)[56] demonstrates their falsehood. For
he has juxtaposed the charge about Jesus claiming to be Messiah in the
very next scene, only a few verses after Jesus refuses to answer their
question about his Messiahship.

The narrator then turns directly to Pilate's question to Jesus, "Are you
the king of the Jews?" (23:3, RNAB), which is in all the passion traditions.
Jesus maintains his guarded responses: "You say so" (23:3, RNAB). The
narrator continues to simply show the main questions and answers without explanation. He is the only one to show Pilate reacting to Jesus' reply
by his verdict to the chief priests and crowds: "I find this man not guilty"
(23:4, RNAB). He is also the only one who mentions that Jesus' accusors
continue to insist that he is inciting the people by teaching throughout all
Judea, beginning in Galilee (23:5).

The narrator at once shows that the reference to Galilee spurs Pilate to
send Jesus to Herod. The narrator had previously disclosed Herod's curiosity about Jesus (Luke 9:7–9) so that readers are not surprised at Herod's
current eagerness to see some sign from Jesus (23:8). He had also indicated Jesus' apparent contempt for Herod as "that fox" in Luke 13:31–
33. Now he shows Jesus' refusal to answer Herod during extensive questioning, despite harsh accusations by chief priests and scribes (23:9–10).
Without clarification the narrator next shows Herod and his soldiers
treating Jesus contemptuously and sending him back to Pilate (23:11),
which he follows with a cryptic explanation, "Herod and Pilate became
friends that very day, even though they had been enemies formerly"
(23:12, RNAB).

At this point in the double narrative of Luke and Acts, this obscure statement and the rationale behind it leave a gap for readers. This whole incident is peculiar to Luke, and lays the narrative groundwork for the fulfillment of Ps. 2:1–2 in Acts 4:25–28. The prayer of the community in Acts 4 claims that the union of King Herod and "ruler" Pontius Pilate against Jesus, "whom you anointed [ὅν ἔχρισας]," fulfills the psalm's reference to kings and rulers uniting against the Lord (God) and against his Messiah. Governor Pilate sending Jesus to Herod will also find a parallel in Governor Festus bringing Paul to trial before (the Herodian) King Agrippa in Acts 26.[57]

Only the Lukan narrator shows Pilate addressing the chief priests, rulers, and "the people" a second time, repeating that he has not found Jesus guilty of their charges, nor has Herod. Pilate restates that Jesus has done nothing worthy of death. Therefore he proposes to release him after flogging him (Luke 23:13–16). Repetition of verdicts of innocence (the second of three by Pilate, plus Herod's implied verdict) underscores Jesus' innocence, a major motif of the Lukan passion account. It culminates in the centurion's witness at the death of Jesus, "This man was innocent [δίκαιος] without doubt" (23:47, RNAB).[58] The repetition also will be paralleled by the refusal of Roman and Herodian authorities to find Paul deserving of death (Acts 23:9, 29; 25:25; 26:31–32; cf. 28:18).

The rapid pace of narration continues, with each new scene linked to the previous one by the conjunction δέ (Luke 23:2, 6, 8, 13, 18). The response to Pilate's proposal to release Jesus after flogging is immediate: "But all together they shouted out, 'Away with this man! Release Barabbas to us'" (23:18, RNAB). Up to this point, Barabbas has not been introduced; by postponing his introduction (which Mark had logically presented before referring to the people's request for him), the narrator speeds up the pace of narration and emphasizes the irony of the people asking for a murderer instead of for the innocent Jesus. The narrator shows Pilate responding immediately, and only he adds the explanation that Pilate wanted to release Jesus (23:20). This procurator's desire to release Jesus will find resonance with Agrippa's statement in Acts 26:32 to the procurator Festus that Paul could be released if he had not appealed to Caesar.

To Pilate's proposal the people continue to shout, "Crucify him! Crucify him!" (23:21, RNAB). The narrator points out that Pilate "addressed them a third time, 'What evil has this man done? I found him guilty of no capital crime. Therefore I shall have him flogged and then release him'" (23:22, RNAB). Despite his rapid narrative pace, the Lukan narrator numbers the times Pilate declares Jesus not guilty. Finally he shows the people's shouts for crucifixion prevailing (Luke 23:23, an obvious miscarriage of justice). He shows Pilate giving the verdict to grant their request. With heavy irony, he concludes his report of the trial, "So he released the man who had been imprisoned for rebellion and murder, for whom they asked, and he handed Jesus over to them to deal with as they wished" (23:25, RNAB).

The Lukan narrator does not report the crowning with thorns but moves rapidly toward Calvary, with Simon of Cyrene's conscription to help Jesus carry his cross (Luke 23:26). At this point, only the Lukan narrator mentions the lamenting women, for whom Jesus prophesies a fate worse than his (23:27–31).[59] After this the narrator mentions something he had passed over earlier, that two criminals were led away with Jesus to be executed (23:32).

Jesus' Crucifixion and Death, Luke 23:33–56

The crucifixion and death of Jesus are the heart of every Gospel passion account and of the Christian proclamation itself. The Lukan narrator varies from other versions mostly in his pacing and selection of details. As soon as he recounts Jesus' arrival at the place called the Skull, he narrates that they crucified him and the criminals, one on each side of him, omitting mention of an offer of drugged wine (Mark 15:23). According to the canonical text of Luke, Jesus' first statement on the cross is his plea, "Father, forgive them, they know not what they do" (Luke 23:34a, RNAB).[60] The narrator then uses expressions from Ps. 22:19 to describe the division of Jesus' garments by casting lots, providing intertextual resonance back to an Old Testament prayer of a suffering just man.

Whereas Mark and Matthew blame everyone present for the blaspheming that follows, the Lukan narrator spares the people, blaming three groups for reviling Jesus: the rulers, the soldiers, and one of the criminals crucified with Jesus. After Jesus' death, only the Lukan narrator will mention how the crowds (ὄχλοι) who saw (Θεωρήσαντες) what happened left beating their breasts (Luke 23:48). Thus, in Luke the people are differentiated from the leaders. Although the people are guilty of demanding Jesus' crucifixion (Acts 3:13–15, cf. 2:23, 36), they do not stoop to blasphemy and are remorseful afterward (Luke 23:48).[61]

The Lukan narrator carefully distinguishes the kind of mockery given to Jesus by the three groups. The rulers challenge him to save himself if he is the Messiah (Christ) of God, the elect one (23:35). The soldiers mock him as king of the Jews. The narrator then pauses to explain in an aside why the soldiers use this title for Jesus: "Above him there was an inscription that read, 'This is the King of the Jews' " (23:38, RNAB). Finally one crucified criminal taunts him, if he is the Messiah, to save himself and them (23:39). And again unique to Luke, the criminal is rebuked by his crucified companion, who attests to Jesus' innocence, and asks Jesus to remember him when he enters his kingdom (23:39–42). He alone shows Jesus' promise to him that "today you will be with me in Paradise" (23:43, RNAB). Through this interchange and without comment of his own, the narrator attests his own belief that Jesus truly was both innocent and king, as even one of those crucified with him could see, and that he would be vindicated by God after his death.

This interchange with the crucified man slows the pace of narration and adds to the impression of time passing with Jesus on the cross. With Mark and Matthew, Luke 23:44 states the time as the sixth hour or noon, and recounts how darkness came over the land until the ninth hour, 3 P.M. (which the Lukan narrator explains as an eclipse of the sun). From his omniscient point of view he relates how the Temple veil was torn at this point, something that would not be visible to someone at the scene of the cross, but which symbolizes a divine break with the Temple. Matthew and Mark do not mention the tearing of the veil until Jesus' death. The Lukan narrator omits their account of Jesus' cry of abandonment by God, as well as of the confusion over Elijah and offering of sour wine (Mark 15:34–36, Matt. 27:46–50). Instead of reporting merely a loud cry as he expired (Mark 15:37, Matt. 27:50), he shows Jesus quoting Ps. 31:6, "Father, into your hands I commend my spirit," as he dies (Luke 23:46, RNAB). Thus he portrays a deeper sense of calm and control in Jesus than appears in their versions.[62]

Unlike Mark and Matthew, the Lukan narrator relates that the centurion at the cross proclaims Jesus' innocence rather than his divine sonship (Luke 23:47, Mark 15:39, Matt. 27:54). Not only does he thus strive to increase historiographical plausibility, but by reasserting Jesus' innocence, he confirms his central theme of the innocence of Jesus in Luke and of his disciples in Acts.

Finally, only the Lukan narrator ends his account of Jesus' death by noting that the crowd who witnessed all this went away beating their breasts (Luke 23:48), by which he foreshadows and prepares for their repentance in Acts 2–3.

All the Gospels mention the women who witnessed Jesus' death, but the Lukan narrator also shows all Jesus' acquaintances (πάντες οἱ γνω-στοὶ) standing at a distance, implying the presence of men as well as of the women from Galilee to whom he explicitly refers (Luke 23:49). He thus also deepens the intertextual connotations both of pathos and of fulfillment of God's biblical plan for Jesus by alluding to Ps. 38:12 about the sufferer's acquaintances standing afar.[63]

The narrator draws his readers into the next episode as eyewitnesses: "And behold (καὶ ἰδοὺ) a man by the name of Joseph. . . . "[64] He is the only narrator to use this Hebraic form of expression here, and the only one to specify that Joseph as a member of the council had not consented to their plan, and that Arimathea is a Jewish town (Luke 23:50–51). He also adds that Joseph was expecting the kingdom of God (23:51b, also in Mark 15:43). He shows Joseph simply going to Pilate and asking for Jesus' body, and after taking it down, wrapping it and laying it "in a rock-hewn tomb in which no one had yet been buried" (23:53, RNAB). Only after showing the action completed does the narrator give a time indication: "It was the day of preparation, and the sabbath was about to begin" (23:54, RNAB). The time explains both why Jesus was not anointed when he was wrapped for burial, as well as what the narrator next shows, that the women follow, observe the tomb, prepare spices and oils (to complete his burial when the sabbath is over), and obey the commandment to rest on the sabbath (23:55–56).[65] The narrator has fully set the stage for the narration of Jesus' empty tomb and resurrection in Luke 24.

NARRATORS OF LUKE 24: RESURRECTION EPILOGUE, TRANSITION TO ACTS

Immediately after displaying the women resting on the sabbath, the Lukan narrator shows them at dawn the following day going to the tomb with the burial spices they had prepared (Luke 24:1). Omitting any questioning about who would roll back the stone (as in Mark 16:3), or even the women's names (Mark 16:1), he straightaway shows them finding the stone rolled back (Luke 24:2), entering the tomb, and not finding the body of "the Lord Jesus" (24:3). They were puzzling over this, "and behold [καὶ ἰδού] two men stood before them in shining clothing" (24:4, my literal translation). The narrator again zooms in on the scene, having the audience share the women's apparition. He shows them terrified and bowing their faces to the ground, the common reactions to biblical theophany or angelophany. At this point only the Lukan narrator has the angelic figures provide the first post-Easter analepsis or retrospection, as they tell the women to remember what Jesus told them while yet in Galilee and repeat to them Jesus' predictions about the Son of Man being crucified and rising on the third day (24:6–7). "And they remembered his words" (24:8, RNAB).

The Lukan focus is much sharper than the Markan version. Mark's dealt with a call to meet Jesus again back in Galilee, which would distract from the Lukan preferred emphasis on Jerusalem, and perhaps from historical memories of the first apparitions being in Jerusalem (as attested by Luke and John against Mark).[66] With at least historical plausibility, the

Lukan narrator flashes back to Jesus' Galilean prophecies and repeats them in the new light of the empty tomb. He emphasizes memory of what Jesus had foretold, thus tying Jesus' prophecy more closely to its fulfillment. In describing the women remembering what Jesus had said, he implicitly invites his audience to remember along with them.

The Lukan narrator maintains his rapid pace and focus on the present action of the women. Right after noting that they remembered Jesus' words, he shows the women returning from the tomb and announcing everything to "the eleven" and the others. Only after they had fulfilled their mission does the narrator pause to give their names. After naming them, he shows them reporting to the apostles, who disbelieve the women's story (Luke 24:10–11). All of this is a plausible alternative to the vexing ending of Mark, where the women said nothing out of fear (Mark 16:8).[67] Despite the apostles' disbelief, the narrator shows Peter running to the tomb, seeing only the burial cloths, and leaving in amazement (Luke 24:12).

Though the Lukan narrator uses less mystery than Mark in narrating this scene, he too narrates not Jesus' actual resurrection from the tomb, but only its aftereffects: the empty tomb, reaction of witnesses, angelic apparitions, and appearances of the risen Jesus to disciples. Nor does the narrator impose hindsight on his narrating; he shows the consternation of the women at finding the empty tomb, the disciples' disbelief of their story, and Peter's amazement. The narrator does not even recount the scene of Jesus' first appearance, that to Peter, but merely leaves Peter in his amazement in 24:12 and turns to Jesus' appearance to two disciples on the road to Emmaus (24:13–32). After the Emmaus narrative, in 24:33–34 he shows the Eleven informing Cleopas and his unnamed companion, "The Lord has truly been raised and has appeared to Simon!" (24:34, RNAB). Thus the reader is informed that Jesus first appeared to Simon, without the narrator actually including that event.

The narrator jumps to the new Emmaus scene, using the special focalizing introduction, "and behold [καὶ ἰδοὺ] two of them on this day were going to a village . . . named Emmaus" (Luke 24:13, my literal translation).[68] After thus bringing his audience into the scene, he narrates the disciples' consternation and conversation and how Jesus joined them, "but their eyes were prevented from recognizing him" (24:16, RNAB). Though this indicates the audience's advantage in knowledge over the two disciples, it leaves a gap, not indicating how or why Jesus avoided recognition (except for a "theological passive" that hints that God may have prevented it).[69] The whole conversation is full of pathos and irony, as the narrator skillfully simulates the confusion the disciples felt between the first discovery of Jesus' empty tomb and his first reported appearance. He recreates for Christian readers (who know the end of the story of Jesus' resurrection) that period before his disciples understood the full implications of the empty tomb.

By quoting opinions about Jesus, the narrator presents the impression the earthly career of Jesus made on his contemporaries, before the deeper christological awareness of Christians after Jesus' resurrection. They saw him as "a prophet mighty in deed and word" (24:19, RNAB). He also recreates the disciples' disillusionment before the good news of Jesus' resurrection: "But we were hoping that he would be the one to redeem Israel" (24:21, RNAB). Thus he underscores that the mere news of the empty tomb did not solve their disillusionment and confusion. The report of the women brought no consolation to them (24:21–24).

The empty tomb was a necessary condition of Jesus' resurrected life for Luke. Acts 2:29–32 refers to David's full tomb as absolute refutation of any claims that David rose from the dead. But the empty tomb alone was not sufficient to ground the good news of Jesus' resurrection. It took the appearances of the risen Jesus to do that. The priority of Jesus' appearances beyond just a discovery of his empty tomb recalls a similar juxtaposition in the foundational good news in 1 Cor. 15:1–11 of entombment, "the third day," and appearances (with "the third day" presumably referring to the datable discovery of an empty tomb, not to an undated string of appearances).[70]

The narrator shows Jesus providing a second analepsis back to the biblical prophecies of the Christ's death and glorification (24:25–27). Jesus' interpretation of the scriptures concerning himself also parallels the first Christians' search in the scriptures for an understanding of Jesus' death and resurrection. The key to the next scene at Emmaus is the disciples' recognition of Jesus. The Lukan narrator had hidden the identity of the protagonist, a device common both to Greek literature and drama (e.g., Odysseus' disguised return in the *Odyssey*, the ironic hidden identity of the one causing the plague in *Oedipus the King*) and to some biblical narratives (e.g., the culprit in Nathan's parable of the slaughtered pet lamb, 2 Sam. 12:1–6; the hidden identity of the angel Raphael in Tobit). He makes similar expert use of the corresponding recognition scene, so important for drama and narrative. The recognitions of Odysseus by his wife and her evil suitors, of Oedipus as slayer of his father and husband of his mother, of David by Nathan in 2 Samuel, and of Raphael by Tobias in Tobit were all climactic within their respective plots. In a similar way, the disciples' recognition of Jesus is climactic for the Emmaus narrative.[71]

The Lukan narrator presents recognition on at least a two-fold level by narrating their recognition of Jesus in words evocative of the Eucharist, in which his intended Christian audience recognizes the continued presence of the risen Jesus among them. Thus he narrates, "while he was with them at table, he took bread, said the blessing, broke it, and gave it to them. With that their eyes were opened and they recognized him, but he vanished from their sight" (Luke 24:30–31, RNAB). Lest anyone miss the eucharistic allusion, the narrator ends the episode by showing the two disciples telling (ἐξηγοῦντο) "how he was made known to them in the breaking of the bread" (24:35, RNAB).

By also quoting the disciples' remark after Jesus' disappearance— "Were not our hearts burning [within us] while he spoke to us on the way and opened the scriptures to us?" (24:32, RNAB)—the narrator alludes to the Christian search in scriptures for knowledge of Jesus. He implies that his audience will deepen their understanding of his narrative to the extent that they too allow the risen Jesus to open the meaning of the scriptures to them.[72]

The narrator links the Emmaus incident closely to the following one with, "While they were still speaking about this, he stood in their midst . . . " (Luke 24:36, RNAB). After announcing such a startling appearance, he shows Jesus greeting them with peace. From his omniscient point of view, he recreates their past situation realistically when he explains how terrified they were, thinking they were seeing a ghost (even after discussing his previous appearances). He shows the risen Jesus reading minds and hearts and quieting their doubts by touch and eating, proving that he was not a mere spirit (24:36–43).

Then he shows Jesus providing a final analeptic reprise of his Jerusalem exodus event (cf. Luke 9:31): "These are my words that I spoke to you while I was still with you, that everything written about me in the law of Moses and in the prophets and psalms must be fulfilled" (24:44, RNAB). In principle, he thus grounds the entire passion of Jesus in the scriptural will of God. "Then he opened their minds to understand the scriptures. And he said to them, 'Thus it is written that the Messiah would suffer and rise from the dead on the third day and that repentance, for the forgiveness of sins, would be preached in his name to all the nations, beginning from Jerusalem' " (24:45–47, RNAB). This refers not only back to his passion and resurrection (thus summarizing the Gospel), but also forward to the events of Acts and the spread of the gospel. This statement by Jesus functions as a hinge between the two Lukan volumes, the Gospel and Acts, grounding both in scripture.[73]

The narrator shows Jesus continue by calling them his witnesses and promising the Holy Spirit, which he terms the promise of his Father, for whose power they are to wait in Jerusalem (24:48–49). With this proleptic word by Jesus, the stage is set for the events of Acts.

After allowing his audience to listen to Jesus' parting words in the upper room, the narrator pulls back from the close-up scene, as it were fading to a distance.[74] The narrator ends his first volume by showing without comment Jesus' final blessing at Bethany and his departure and the disciples' continual praise of God in the Temple.

We have followed the Lukan uses of narrators throughout the various parts of his Gospel and seen how he provides an interpretive point of view for understanding Jesus' ministry and death in the first four chapters, using Jesus' "inaugural address" at Nazareth in Luke 4:31 to foreshadow and enter the story of Jesus' ministry and rejection. We have observed how the narrator weaves together many episodes from varying sources, adding transitions and placing them in a somewhat artificial context of a journey that will parallel the Pauline journeys in Acts.

In Jesus' conflicts and death in Jerusalem, the narrator highlights the contest over who shall lead "the people [of God]," the current Jewish leadership or Jesus, as the beginning of Acts will highlight a similar contention between the Sanhedrin and the apostles. The narrator avoids what might distract from the building tension of Jesus' approaching passion. Through Jesus' eschatological forecast in the Temple area, the narrator lays the framework of periodization of future times, from those of Acts to that of the Lukan writing (such as the "times of the Gentiles"). He portrays the passion as "the hour" of Satan, emphasizing its cosmic overtones. He re-orders several traditions to portray the Last Supper as Jesus' farewell address, somewhat like Paul's in Acts 20. He thus interprets Jesus' death from a eucharistic perspective and with an eye to his own lifetime. After emphasizing Jesus' testing in the garden, the narrator focuses in the rest of Jesus' suffering on his calm acceptance of the Father's plan. In the appearance accounts he underlines how it was God's will that the Messiah should so suffer and thus enter his glory.

In the next chapter, we shall follow the moves the narrator makes in recounting the growth and spread of the word about the Lord Jesus through apostolic witness, persecution, and journeys, culminating in those of Paul.

6 Narrators in Acts

NARRATORS OF THE INTRODUCTION TO ACTS

As we have done for the Gospel, let us similarly follow the various narrators through the story line and main sections of Acts: the prologue (Acts 1:1–11) and introduction, Acts 1; the growth of the Jerusalem church, Acts 2–3; conflict with Jewish authorities, Acts 4–5; the Seven and Stephen, Acts 6:1–8:3; the initial outreach of Philip, Saul, and Peter, Acts 8:4–12:24; Barnabas and Saul, Acts 12:25–14:28; the Pauline missions, Acts 15:1–20:38; the Pauline defense, Acts 21:1–28:16; the end, Acts 28:17–31.

Acts has the same first-person singular narrator in its prologue as the Gospel and similar third-person omniscient narrators for the bulk of the narrative. But Acts also introduces a special first-person plural narrator ("we") in selected sections after Acts 16:10, who was not present in the Gospel. Acts also has some characters narrating stories within the story, such as Paul in Acts 22 and 26 about his call. We will devote separate chapters to detailed analysis of those "we" sections and character narrators, but this chapter is to provide a sense of the use of narrators throughout the entire Acts plot line.

The Lukan narrator's situation in Acts is different from in the Gospel. The basic Gospel story was already familiar to his audience, as were earlier written versions of it. The Lukan narrator manifests dependence on the Gospel of Mark both in its content and in its ordering of episodes, as well as on many traditional stories and sayings found also in Matthew and called Q by scholars. In Acts, however, he has far more freedom. He seems to be the first to provide a written narrative of these apostolic events and therefore was not reliant on the order of a previous narrative as he had been in his Gospel.[1]

Because of their familiarity to his audience, the Lukan narrator had

73

limited freedom to modify the Gospel deeds and sayings of Jesus. In Acts he has no comparable store of remembered sayings of the apostles. To show Jesus speaking in the Gospel, his usual method is simply to insert traditional sayings or collections of sayings of Jesus or to order originally independent sayings into a quasi-sermon, as in Jesus' farewell address at the Last Supper in Luke 22.[2] When he shows Peter or Paul speaking in Acts, he has no similar store of their remembered or written sayings and therefore creates speeches to approximate what he knew or estimated they would have said on that occasion.[3] He also has far fewer independent episodes passed down to him, which in the Gospel he had to combine by somewhat artificial schemata like the journey to Jerusalem travel narrative. In Acts, more of the incidents build on those that preceded, so that the story line becomes more manifest than in the Gospel.[4]

NARRATORS IN THE PROLOGUE, ACTS 1:1–11

At the beginning of Acts, the narrator immediately identifies himself as the narrator who began the Gospel account. He uses the same first-person singular "I," refers to the Gospel as "the first word [or 'book,' λόγος]," and addresses the same patron Theophilus (Acts 1:1).

The sustained switch from the "showing" mode of narration to the "telling" mode of direct address has been, up to this point, peculiar to the prologues of Luke and Acts.[5] We have seen that the narrator introduces himself, so to speak, in the manner of a professional writer. After this direct comment to his audience about his goals and methods, the narrator reverts entirely into an unobtrusive, third-person voice showing the action, with only occasional asides to his audience in the telling mode of narration.

In the Gospel the shift in modes is dramatic and quite overt, even in the sharp contrast in styles. In Acts the transition from telling to showing evolves without warning, and it becomes fully evident when the narrator switches in mid-sentence from citing Jesus in indirect address to letting Jesus speak the rest of the sentence in direct address:[6] Jesus "enjoined them not to depart from Jerusalem, but to wait for 'the promise of the Father about which you have heard me speak; . . . in a few days you will be baptized with the holy Spirit'" (Acts 1:4–5, RNAB).[7]

Besides beginning Acts with the same obtrusive first-person "I" narrator that began the Third Gospel, the writer provides additional links between his second volume and his Gospel, one of which is the apostles' question whether Jesus would now restore the kingdom to Israel (Acts 1:6). This question is surprising to the audience, for the passion narrative in the first volume has already revealed to them the nature of Jesus and the kingdom of which he preached. But the apostles in Acts 1 do not yet share the readers' clarity about Jesus' kingship and kingdom. The narrator has disclosed to the readers many details of the passion and how they fulfilled scripture, which the disciples as a group would not have witnessed. The privileged knowledge that the narrator has provided to the audience becomes available to the apostles in Acts only after the Pentecostal outpouring of the Spirit upon them.[8]

The narrator also uses their question as an opportunity to show Jesus referring to the times and seasons established by the Father, which Jesus' speech about the final days in Luke 21 had at least partially delineated. The apostles are not to know when the final end will come; instead they are promised that they will receive the power of the Holy Spirit upon them and will witness to Jesus "in Jerusalem, throughout Judea and Samaria, and to the ends of the earth" (Acts 1:8, RNAB). Thus, through Jesus' prophetic response, the narrator foreshadows in outline the main movements and mission of Acts.[9]

Immediately following this promise, the narrator shows Jesus being taken up in a cloud while the apostles watch, as the prophet Elijah had been lifted up with his disciple Elisha watching (2 Kings 2:9–14). By this intertextual reference, the narrator provides an important biblical clue to his intended audience. As Elisha's witnessing Elijah's assumption was the sign that he would receive Elijah's spirit as his successor, so the apostles' watching Jesus being taken into heaven foreshadows their reception of his spirit at Pentecost.

With the disciples continuing to stare up into the heavens, the narrator draws in the audience with his focalizing expression, "and behold" (καὶ ἰδού): "And behold two men stood beside them in white clothes." The introduction of these angelic figures echoes a similar apparition to the women at the empty tomb in Luke 24:4: "And it happened as they were perplexed about this and behold two men stood by them in dazzling clothing" (my literal translations).

Similar language in the descriptions of these two apparitions invites readers to relate the two appearances to each other. Both occur as special revelations to disciples: first to women, then to (primarily) men according to the narrator's pattern of frequently balancing similar incidents between male and female participants.[10] Both occur when disciples are disturbed by Jesus' unexpected absence, first from the empty tomb, now as he has been taken up from them into heaven. Both apparitions impart aspects of the good news of Jesus' departure to his Father: his resurrection from the tomb and his being lifted up into heaven from which he would return at the end of time. Both challenge the disciples about looking for

Jesus in the wrong place: "Why do you ["the women who had come from Galilee with him," Luke 23:55] seek the living one among the dead?" (Luke 24:5, RNAB); "Men of Galilee, why are you standing there looking at the sky?" (Acts 1:11, RNAB). The response of both groups of Galileans was to return to Jerusalem: "And they remembered his words. Then they returned from the tomb and announced all these things to the eleven and to all the others" (Luke 24:8–9, RNAB); "Then they returned to Jerusalem from the mount called Olivet . . . " (Acts 1:12, RNAB).

In both cases the narrator chooses a nonchronological plot order: he waits until after narrating the apparition before naming the women (in Luke 24:10) and the men (the Eleven in Acts 1:13). But Acts rounds out the female-male doublet by noting that the eleven men just named were united in prayer "with women and Mary the mother of Jesus and his brothers" (1:14, my literal translation).

NARRATORS IN ACTS 1:12–26: PREPARATIONS FOR PENTECOST

Verses 12–14 act as transition verses and can thus be treated with both the introduction in vv. 1–11 and as part of this immediate preparation for Pentecost.[11] Through this first of his summary passages, the narrator shows the Eleven preparing for Pentecost by retiring to the upper room.[12] He names the Eleven and shows them devoting themselves to prayer with the women, Mary the mother of Jesus, and Jesus' brothers. He thus provides a transition from Jesus' ascension and the disciples' replacement of Judas. As in the Gospel, this transition emphasizes the protagonists at prayer.

After this summary about their prayer in the upper room, the narrator recounts an episode in Acts 1:15–26 in which the followers of Jesus directly prepare for the promise they are to receive at Pentecost. He shows Peter addressing the community of "about [ὡσεὶ] 120," apparently an approximation symbolic of the restored Israel.[13]

The narrator shows Peter taking the leadership role in restoring the Twelve, from which Judas had fallen away. He thus demonstrates that Jesus' promise to him at the farewell supper in Luke 22:31–32, that he would pray for Peter so that after his fall he would strengthen his brethren, is fulfilled.[14] He shows Peter explaining that Judas's betrayal was necessary to fulfill the scripture (Ps. 41:10). Peter's mention that Judas bought a field from the wages of his injustice (1:18) and fell to a hideous death on it illustrates God's plan being confirmed by Judas's punishment. This foreshadows a comparable sale of a field and downfall for Ananias and Sapphira in Acts 5, although the similarity is noticed by readers only in retrospect.

In the resurrection appearances, the Lukan narrator simply states that the risen Jesus revealed to his followers the meaning of the scriptures about himself, without actually letting the readers see what those interpretations were. Only now in Acts does he show Peter and Jesus' other followers proclaiming these specific biblical interpretations and applications. The result is that the audience in Luke 24 is kept in the dark about them until Jesus' disciples reveal them in Acts. In other words, the readers first learn these interpretations in Acts through the apostolic witnesses to whom alone Jesus had revealed them in the Gospel.[15]

Through Peter, the narrator also explicitly recalls his criteria for being one of the "twelve apostles": they were men who had traveled with Jesus and his band from the time of John's baptism to Jesus' ascension. Their function was to witness Jesus' resurrection. The narrator shows the community praying that God would reveal his choice of two candidates, Joseph Barsabbas or Justus, and Matthias. They then cast lots and enroll Matthias with the Eleven (1:20–26). The narrator simply assumes that after prayer the casting of lots reveals God's choice. Now that the Twelve has been reconstituted and is again able to sit on twelve thrones over Israel (Luke 22:30), the stage is set for Pentecost.

NARRATORS OF THE JERUSALEM CHURCH GROWTH

NARRATORS IN ACTS 2–3

The narrator signals a major new plot section and development with his solemn introduction, "And in the fulfilling of the day of Pentecost [Καὶ ἐν τῷ συμπληροῦσθαι τὴν ἡμέραν τῆς πεντηκοστῆς]" (2:1), which parallels his solemn introduction to his travel narrative in Luke 9:51: "And it happened in the fulfilling of the day of his being taken up ['Εγένετο δὲ ἐν τῷ συμπληροῦσθαι τὰς ἡμέρας τῆς ἀναλήμψεως αὐτοῦ] . . . "(my literal translations). By echoing his earlier solemn signal of the time when a new stage of God's preordained plan is to be fulfilled, the narrator also draws his intended audience's attention to the prophecy of Jeremiah that had seared itself into the national consciousness as evidenced in his Greek Bible (Jer. 25:11–12 LXX). Later writings of the Greek scriptures repeatedly referred to this prophecy of Jeremiah: After prophesying the Babylonian exile, Jeremiah foretold that the land would be in desolation, "and they shall serve among the Gentiles seventy years. And in the fulfilling of the seventy years [καὶ ἐν τῷ πληρωθῆναι (the important Alexandrian manuscript reads συμπληρωθῆναι) τὰ ἑβδομήκοντα ἔτη]. . . . " The Greek versions of 2 Chron. 36:21,

1 Esdr.1:58, and Theodotion Dan. 9:2 all refer explicitly to this prophecy of Jeremiah and the fulfillment [εἰς συμπλήρωσιν] of its seventy years of desolation.

The recurrence of this theme, the fulfillment of a set time in exile, in so many later writings of the Greek Old Testament (which are the only places to use these particular variants of *fulfilled* [συμπληρωθῆναι, συμπλήρωσιν]), increase the probability that the Lukan narrator expected his intended audience to catch the allusion to the prophecy of Jeremiah in his double use of συμπληροῦσθαι. That prophecy provides an intertextual backdrop of the fulfillment of prophesied epochs in God's saving plan, into which Luke-Acts is structured at Luke 9:51 and Acts 2:1. Thus the narrator inaugurates his account of Pentecost as the fulfillment of a new epoch of God's salvation.[16]

He begins from an omniscient, bird's-eye view, setting the context in God's plan and showing the group gathered together. Unobtrusively in the third person, he narrates the sudden noise and the appearance of "tongues as of fire" and how they were all filled with the Holy Spirit and spoke in various tongues as the Spirit gave them to proclaim (Acts 2:1–4). He does not bring the audience into the scene with "and behold," as at the angelic apparitions at the tomb and ascension, but keeps a more distant focal point.

At v. 5, the narrator shifts focus to a second group, explaining that Jews from every nation were staying in Jerusalem. He shows them attracted by the noise and gathering into a confused crowd, because each member of the crowd hears his or her own language. He shows some questioning the phenomena and others scoffing at them as signs of drunkenness (2:5–13).

With the scene thus set, he shows Peter speaking for the other eleven and addressing the crowd formally. He lets Peter's speech explain the meaning of the Pentecostal phenomena. He thus uses the historiographical pattern, common in both Greco-Roman and biblical narratives, of inserting speeches to explain the meaning of the events they accompany.[17]

Peter first answers the scornful interpretation of drunkenness by quoting Joel's prophecy and arguing that these phenomena fulfill it. For a second time in Acts, the audience hears not the narrator but one of the twelve apostles interpreting and applying scriptural prophecies. The narrator thus remains consistent with his procedure in Luke 24, where he shows that the risen Jesus taught the disciples to interpret and apply the Bible to himself, though the particular scriptures to which Jesus referred are not specified. Readers have had to wait until these speeches in Acts to hear the witnesses apply "from their own mouths" particular scriptures to Jesus.[18]

Redactional studies have shown how the Joel quotation is modified to fit the Pentecostal phenomena and Lukan theology: "the last days" in 2:17 places all of Acts in the end times of fulfillment; "and they shall prophesy" in 2:18 underscores the Lukan prophetic interpretation of Pentecost; additions in 2:19 balance out the biblical pair of signs and wonders, above and below.[19] As the Isaiah prophecy had functioned as programmatic for Jesus' ministry in Luke 4, so this Joel prophecy foreshadows the main events of the apostles' ministry in Acts: the Holy Spirit's outpouring on all nations, male and female prophetic figures, signs and wonders, salvation of people from any nation who "call upon the name of the Lord [Jesus]." Many of the consequences of the Spirit's outpouring on Jesus' followers in Acts are similar to those from the Spirit's descent on Jesus in the Gospel.[20]

At the conclusion of Peter's speech follows a second generalizing summary, Acts 2:42–47, which portrays the believers' communal life under the apostles and mentions their daily growth in numbers. After this transition, the narrator recounts in Acts 3 the healing by Peter of the lame beggar at the Temple gate, accompanied by its explanatory speech.

In this episode the narrator speaks of Peter and John repeatedly, yet Peter does all the talking and acting. (The insistence on continuing to mention John may stem from a desire to show the two working as a pair, as both Jesus had recommended [Luke 10:1] and as Barnabas and Paul, and Paul and Silas were later to do.)[21] The healing illustrates the power newly available to Peter and the apostles from the Spirit in the name of Jesus. It also functions in the Lukan narrative as a sign, but not as a proof. For like the Pentecostal phenomena that were interpreted as drunkenness, the healing retains an ambiguity that requires explanation to be fully persuasive.[22] In this case, the misunderstanding Peter warns against is believing that his or John's power or piety caused the healing. In Acts 14, Barnabas and Paul, after healing a lame man, will have to correct barbarians from a corresponding misunderstanding. In both cases, the healing is emphatically attributed to Jesus and his name (for Jews) or to the one true God (for pagans). Finally, the narrator underscores the healed person's joy and praise of God, as he often does in the Gospel and Acts.

As at Pentecost, the narrator shows a crowd rushing together, but this time he refers to the group as "the whole people (πᾶς ὁ λαός)." This reference to "the whole people" connotes that Peter is addressing God's chosen people as Moses and Jesus had done, with the current crowd representing the whole covenant people. Peter's explanations, call to repentance, and promises are all addressed to them as God's people. He threatens with excommunication those who fail to respond: "Everyone who does not listen to that prophet [like Moses] will be cut off from the people" (Acts 3:23, RNAB). Because a contest has arisen between the apostles and authorities over who shall teach God's people, Peter and John are interrupted by authorities (4:1–2).[23]

Peter's speech attributes the lame man's healing to the power of the name of Jesus, "whom you handed over and denied. . . . You denied the Holy and Righteous One and asked that a murderer be released to you" (3:13–14, RNAB). It thus recalls the key theme of Jesus' innocence in the Lukan passion narrative but concedes that neither the people nor their leaders were aware of the seriousness of their deed. Thus it allows an opening toward forgiveness (3:17), which corresponds to and is grounded in Jesus' words on the cross: "Father, forgive them, they know not what they do" (Luke 23:34, RNAB).[24]

Peter's subsequent explanation for how Jesus' death and resurrection fit into God's biblical plan of salvation provides the theological matrix, along with his use of Joel and other scriptures in Acts 2, for the rest of the Acts narrative. In this sense, Acts 2–3 function as integral to the introduction to Acts, as Luke 1–4 function as introduction to Luke. They provide the implied readers with the biblical context of God's saving plan within which to understand the rest of the events in the narrative.[25]

NARRATORS IN ACTS 4–5: CONFLICT WITH JEWISH AUTHORITIES

Chapter divisions in Luke and Acts are not original but were added to later manuscripts. In few places are these divisions more misleading than the division in Acts between chapters 3 and 4. The action of chapter 3 flows without interruption into chapter 4, as the narrator shows priests, captain of the Temple guard, and Sadducees interrupting Peter and John "[w]hile they were still speaking to the people" (Acts 4:1, RNAB). With his omniscience, the narrator explains their inner feelings and reasons for confronting Peter and John: they were "disturbed that they were teaching the people and proclaiming in Jesus the resurrection of the dead" (4:2, RNAB). He juxtaposes the scene of their throwing Peter and John into prison with the conversion of many who heard Peter's speech and the growth of the believing community to five thousand (4:3–4).

He thus sets the stage of confrontation and competition between Jewish authorities and the apostles over who shall teach "the people [of God]," which will continue through most of Acts 4–5. He shows a series of arrests and confrontations in their assembly between them and the apostles. In sharp contrast to the apostles' failure to support Jesus effectively during his passion, and especially to Peter's denial of Jesus before even a servant, Peter and the apostles always overcome the Sanhedrin's challenges and threats, even escaping from prison and resuming their teaching of "the people" in the Temple in defiance of the helpless authorities.

In effect, the narrator is showing that the apostles will judge the twelve tribes of Israel, as Jesus prophesied at his farewell supper (Luke 22:30). Though the primary meaning of this prophecy probably refers to the final advent of God's kingdom, the verb *judge* in scripture can also refer to contemporary authority over Israel, as in the biblical book of Judges. As the apostles teach the people of God in the Temple and the authorities prove helpless to stop them, the narrator is depicting the transition of authority over God's people from the Sanhedrin to the Twelve.[26]

The narrator explains Peter's advantage over the Sanhedrin with the aside that he was "filled with the Holy Spirit" (Acts 4:8), whose assistance Jesus had promised would be theirs when they came to court (Luke 12:11–12). He addresses the Sanhedrin as "[l]eaders of the people and elders," which is appropriate for the occasion but also overlaid with irony for the readers, who are witnessing a transition of leadership over "the people" from the Sanhedrin to the Twelve.

Peter and John's return to the community provides an epilogue in which the narrator uses the church's prayers of thanksgiving as a biblical interpretation of the healing and consequent confrontation with the Sanhedrin. First the prayer cites Ps. 2:1–2:

> Why did the Gentiles rage
> and the peoples entertain folly?
> The Kings of the earth took their stand
> and the princes [or rulers, ἄρχοντες] gathered together
> against the Lord and against his anointed [χριστοῦ].
> (Acts 4:25–26, RNAB)

Then it applies the psalm midrashically to the alliance of Herod (the king) and Pilate (the ruler, cf. Luke 23:12), the [Roman] Gentiles and "peoples" of Israel (plural only because in the psalm it is plural) against the anointed Jesus.[27] It thus situates the passion and its aftermath within God's foreordained plan. The helplessness of the Sanhedrin against the apostles simply illustrates the folly of the peoples rebelling against God and his anointed Messiah in Psalm 2.

The prayer concludes by asking that they be empowered for bold proclamation in the face of these threats and to continue healing, signs, and wonders. The narrator shows God responding to it immediately by shaking the place and filling them with the Holy Spirit and bold speech, which echoes, as it were, the original Pentecostal infilling in Acts 2.

Between this and the next scene, the narrator interposes a third summary in Acts 4:32–35. He uses Greek friendship language and Deuteronomic expressions to picture the believers as united in heart and sharing their possessions under the apostles' leadership.[28] As a transition to the scene with Ananias and Sapphira, he describes the community's pattern of selling property and laying the proceeds at the apostles' feet. He then incarnates this pattern in the positive example or *exemplum* of Barnabas, to be contrasted to the negative *exemplum* of Ananias and Sapphira.[29] His use of positive and negative *exempla* can best be understood within the tradition of Greek rhetoric, with which the implied author of Luke-Acts has demonstrated his familiarity.[30]

The narrator signals the close relationship between the accounts of Ananias and Barnabas with the conjunction δέ in Acts 5:1. Ananias imitates Barnabas's actions exactly, except that he held back some of the proceeds and laid only part at the apostles' feet. The narrator shows Peter immediately confronting him (with unexplained supernatural knowledge): "Ananias, why has Satan filled your heart so that you lied to the holy Spirit and retained part of the price of the land? . . . You have lied not to human beings, but to God" (5:3–4, RNAB).

The *exemplum* equates lying to the apostles with lying to God, which implies that the apostles are filled with God's Holy Spirit and have God's authority and knowledge. Ananias's sudden death, and that of his wife later, provides a horrifying lesson: it is dangerous to lie to the Holy Spirit by lying to spirit-filled authorities. The fear of the community is meant to typify fear of the readers to commit similar sins against their spirit-filled authorities. The horrible fate of Ananias and Sapphira is used as a lesson for the implied readers.[31]

The narrator frames this *exemplum* with summaries involving the apostles. He had preceded it with the summary of sharing possessions by laying proceeds at the apostles' feet. He now follows it by a summary of the apostles' signs and wonders (5:12–16).

This in turn leads to another scene in which authorities arrest the apostles, but this time the unobtrusive third-person narrator shows an angel freeing them during the night. Thus the Sanhedrin looks foolish the next day when it sends to the prison for the apostles but learns that they have escaped and re-occupied the Temple, where they are teaching the people (5:17–25). The narrator repeats his comment (5:26, cf. Luke 20:6, 19; 22:2) that they treated the apostles gingerly because they were afraid of being stoned by the people, who side with the apostles against the Sanhedrin (as they had sided with Jesus when he occupied the Temple and taught them in Luke 20–22).

In the ensuing confrontation with the Sanhedrin, the narrator remains in the background, simply showing without comment that the apostles reject the command not to teach in Jesus' name: "We must obey God rather than men" (5:29, RNAB). He shows Peter and the apostles accusing them of killing Jesus and witnessing that God has raised him from the dead and exalted him as savior of Israel from their sins. When they become furious, the narrator lets one of the Sanhedrin, the respected Gamaliel, express the theological truth behind their impasse, rather than himself telling his audience that in resisting the apostles they may find themselves fighting against God.[32]

Letting an opponent express what the narrator holds as the truth provides a strong ironic twist and is a powerful way to identify the Christian movement with God's action. Even when the Sanhedrin flog the apostles before freeing them, the narrator shows that the apostles are not only undaunted but actually rejoice, and they continue unabated to teach and proclaim that Jesus is the Messiah (5:40–42). As this set of confrontations comes to an end, the narrator's picture of the Sanhedrin's impotence vis-à-vis the apostles is complete.

NARRATORS IN ACTS 6:1–8:3: THE SEVEN AND STEPHEN

In Acts 6 the narrator begins a major new plot line. After concluding the apostles' confrontation with the Sanhedrin, he switches to a new scene at a new time and in a new situation within the community: "At that time, as the number of disciples continued to grow, the Hellenists complained against the Hebrews because their widows were being neglected in the daily distribution" (6:1, RNAB). He retains a distant, unobtrusive viewpoint, showing the Twelve responding to these complaints and the community's choice of Stephen, Philip, and the rest of the Seven. He shows the apostles commissioning them by laying hands on them and ends with another brief summary about the disciples' increase in numbers (6:2–7).

Then he focuses on Stephen, describing his wonders, signs, and debates with Hellenistic Jews. His comment that these opponents "could not withstand the wisdom and the spirit with which he spoke" (6:10, RNAB) recalls Jesus' promise in Luke 21:15. Then he refers to false witnesses who charge Stephen with blasphemy against Moses, the Temple, and the law, and with claiming that Jesus would destroy the Temple and change Moses' customs. Although the intended audience might not notice it, this apparently displaces false charges from Jesus' trial to Stephen's. The Lukan passion account had not mentioned these false charges, which are present in the other Synoptics and presumably in Luke's Gospel source. Now those charges are mentioned, but in retrospect at the later trial of Stephen.[33]

The narrator pauses dramatically before recounting Stephen's reply, showing the whole Sanhedrin staring at Stephen's angelic appearance (Acts 6:15). Then he shows the high priest asking about the charges and eventually cedes the stage to Stephen's response, a long, midrashic application of biblical salvation history. The history that Stephen cites usually complements the biblical history set forth earlier in Peter's speeches, with few repetitions. Such complementarity with minimal repetition seems directed to the level of the audience more than to the level of the speeches being portrayed and is meant to provide readers with a richer intertextual matrix for understanding church origins in Acts.

As Stephen ends his speech with an accusation of his listeners (Acts 7:51–53), the narrator shows their anger at him, then his vision of Jesus at God's right hand; he is then thrown out of the city (as happened to Jesus at Nazareth and Calvary) and stoned—during which the narrator goes out of his way to mention a witness "named Saul." He quotes Stephen's last words, which mirror the content if not the wording of the final words of Jesus, forgiving his murderers and handing over his spirit (7:54–60). After mentioning Stephen's death, the narrator mentions Paul a second time: "Now Saul was consenting to his execution" (8:1, RNAB).

By juxtaposing Stephen's prayer of forgiveness with Saul's part in Stephen's death, the narrator lays the groundwork for Saul's forgiveness in Acts 9. Similarly the narrator had prepared for the forgiveness of the Jerusalem Jews in Acts 2–3 by Jesus' prayer for their forgiveness in Luke 23:34.[34]

The narrator ends this episode and provides transition for the following scenes with Philip and Paul by narrating a persecution that scattered all but the apostles, especially Philip and the other Hellenist believers, focusing particularly on Saul's attempts to destroy the church (Acts 8:1–3).

NARRATORS OF THE INITIAL OUTREACH IN ACTS

The narrator presents the persecution ignited by Stephen's death as actually an occasion for the continued triumphal spread of the word. He prefaces several episodes concerning Philip by the general statement, "Now those who had been scattered went about preaching the word" (Acts 8:4, RNAB). Saul's attempt to destroy the church (8:3) merely resulted in furthering its dissemination (8:4).[35]

NARRATORS IN ACTS 8:4–40: SAMARIA AND PHILIP

The narrator illustrates the spread of God's word through several vignettes centered around Philip. In the first set, he introduces a magician named Simon as a foil for Philip. The narrative illuminates the power of the Spirit manifested in Philip's signs and wonders and contrasts it to pagan magic as practiced by Simon. When the apostles confirm Philip's ministry by imposing hands on Philip's converts, the phenomena caused by their reception of the Holy Spirit impress Simon even more than Philip's miracles. The narrator leaves a gap by not saying what particular signs of the Spirit's coming so impressed Simon, but most readers would presume that they included speaking in tongues as at Pentecost or speaking with boldness as in Acts 4:31.[36]

The narrator does not directly comment on Simon's request to buy this apostolic power of conferring the Spirit, but lets Peter's vehement denunciation and threat comment for him (Acts 8:20–23). In effect, he is using the Simon account as another negative *exemplum*, which illustrates the power of the Holy Spirit, its differences from magic, its origination from God according to God's plan, and its nature as something that humans cannot control, manipulate, buy, or sell.[37] Once he has clarified this point, he does not even bother to show his audience what happens to Simon after his request to be spared Peter's threat (8:24). He rounds off this incident with a brief summary notice of the apostles' return to Jerusalem, preaching to Samaritans on the way (8:25).

The narrator next features the omnipresent aspects of his omniscient point of view in his account of Philip and the Ethiopian.[38] His account of Philip overhearing the eunuch reading and of their conversation illustrates two points that would probably have been obvious to the originally intended readers but which are quite instructive for contemporary readers. It reveals that reading was normally done aloud, even when reading alone.[39] It also indicates a Lukan expectation often not shared by contemporary Christians, especially those having a *sola scriptura* emphasis on private interpretation of scripture. Both this anecdote, and those in Luke 24 about the risen Jesus needing to explain the scriptures to the disciples, indicate an expectation that Christians needed help to interpret the scriptures (which at the beginning of Christianity included only what Christians would later call the Old Testament), especially for its messianic content.[40] Luke-Acts does not treat the Christian interpretation of the Old Testament as self-evident but presupposes church instruction in scripture's meaning.

At this point the narrator lets his audience know which scripture the eunuch had been reading—Isa. 53:7–8, about someone being led like a sheep to the slaughter. The eunuch's question to whom the passage refers gets to the heart of Lukan exegesis of the Old Testament, which has affinities to the ways the Qumran community found applications in the

Hebrew scriptures to their situation.[41] A primary question for Lukan messianic exegesis is to whom prophetic passages refer—to the prophet, or to some future figure (8:32–34). After Philip's removal by the Spirit, the narrator first remains with the rejoicing eunuch, then switches to show Philip's progress until he reaches Caesarea, where he next is mentioned in Acts 21.

NARRATORS IN ACTS 9:1–30: SAUL

At the end of Acts 8, the omnipresent narrator has just left Philip in Caesarea. In Acts 9:1, he returns his attention to Saul in Jerusalem, whom he had last mentioned in 8:3 as trying to destroy the church. By the linking word δέ (9:1), he joins his current narrative about Saul to the previous stories about Philip. Since Acts 9:1–2 continues the theme of Saul's persecutions that had preceded the Philip accounts in Acts 8:1–3, the two notices of Saul's persecutions frame the stories about Philip. Thus the narrator interprets the stories of Philip's evangelization and the framing summaries of Saul's persecutions in light of each other. With irony he shows his most prominent missionary already responsible by his harassment of Christians for Christianity's spread even before his conversion. Saul's persecution caused Philip to leave Jerusalem and bring God's word to Samaria and beyond to Caesarea. The unstoppable spread of God's word that is illustrated in the reports about Philip continues without interruption, as the risen Jesus now changes the persecutor Saul into one of the foremost messengers of the very word he has been trying to suppress.

The narrator begins by showing an extension of Saul's persecutions beyond Jerusalem to Damascus. His terminology reflects his Christian ideological point of view, for he speaks of Saul "breathing murderous threats against the disciples of the Lord" (Acts 9:1, RNAB).[42] Such dramatic vocabulary extends into his picture of Saul's intent to bring men and women of the Way "back to Jerusalem in chains" (9:2, RNAB). But he shows Saul's "irresistible force" meeting Christ's "immovable object" and being defeated by it.

From an omniscient viewpoint the narrator recounts Saul's conversion and baptism, then provides another summary in 9:19b–22 showing people's astonishment at Saul's conversion and Saul's proofs to Damascus Jews that Jesus is the Messiah.

Thus the narrator sets the stage for the Jewish plots to kill Saul. He shows the understandable fear that Jerusalem believers had of Saul and how Barnabas took charge of introducing Saul to the apostles, reporting to them Saul's vision of the Lord and his preaching in Damascus.[43] Finally he shows Saul debating with the Hellenistic Jews as he had in Damascus, the Jews attempting to kill him, and the believers sending him on to Tarsus via Caesarea (9:26–30).

After this quick overview of Saul's initial activity, the narrator concludes this plot line with another general summary in 9:31 about how the church was at peace and growing throughout Judea, Galilee, and Samaria.

NARRATORS IN ACTS 9:31–12:24: PETER TRADITIONS

This summary in Acts 9:31 acts as a transition, rounding off the stories of Saul and leading into the episodes about Peter in Lydda and Joppa.[44] In 9:32 the narrator uses one of his general introductions to a new episode or plot line: "Now it happened [ἐγένετο δὲ] that as Peter was traveling through every region he came also to the saints living in Lydda" (my literal translation). Retaining this objective overview, he shows Peter healing the paralyzed Aeneas with a simple command. His report of the resulting widespread conversions because of this healing illustrates his summary about the church's growth in Judea in 9:31 (Acts 9:32–35).

The account of Peter raising Tabitha to life shows why Peter moves from Lydda to Joppa. It also fits his pattern throughout Luke-Acts of balancing examples of men with those of women. Peter's actions are described with allusions to how Jesus turned out all but the parents and three disciples at the funeral of Jairus's daughter, as well as to how Elijah and Elisha raised a dead person with no one else in the room (Luke 8:51, 1 Kings 17:19–23, 2 Kings 4:32–37). As Jesus had simply commanded the dead girl to rise, Peter commands Tabitha to rise. Without comment, the narrator shows Tabitha being raised and presented to the community.

Only then does he comment on how word of this spread and led to many more conversions. His final sentence provides the transition to the Cornelius incident that is a major turning point in Acts: "And he stayed a long time in Joppa with Simon, a tanner" (9:43, RNAB). In the following scene, the angel will tell Cornelius to find Peter there.

The narrator introduces the centurion Cornelius in terms reminiscent of the Jewish elders' recommendation of the centurion in the Gospel: "he loves our nation and he built the synagogue for us" (Luke 7:5, RNAB). Here the narrator describes Cornelius as "devout and God-fearing along with his whole household, who used to give alms generously to the Jewish people and pray to God constantly" (Acts 10:2, RNAB). With reference to prayer the narrator then introduces Cornelius's vision. The angel's reassuring words to him—"Your prayers and almsgiving have ascended as a memorial offering before God" (Acts 10:4, RNAB)—are reminiscent of Gabriel's reassurance of Zechariah in Luke 1:13: "Do not be afraid, Zechariah, because your prayer has been heard" (RNAB). With redundancy geared to audience recognition of the link with 9:43, he shows the angel commanding Cornelius to send for Simon Peter who is staying with Simon the tanner at Joppa.[45]

After showing Cornelius obeying the angel and sending three men for Peter (10:7–8), the narrator moves his viewpoint to Joppa the next day (10:9). From a bird's-eye perspective, he simultaneously shows the men nearing the city of Joppa and Peter praying at lunchtime on the roof. The narrator displays some psychological sophistication in juxtaposing mention of Peter's hunger with the report of his vision of food, implicitly allowing readers to find a natural link between the two. This is a subtle variant of the practice of Hellenistic historiographers of allowing readers to interpret wondrous events on either a natural or supernatural level.[46]

After recounting Peter's vision and his meeting with Cornelius in Acts 10:10–29, the narrator of Acts shows Cornelius narrating in 10:30–32 the same vision that he himself had reported in 10:3–6. Not only does this repetition emphasize the importance of the incident, but it provides a different point of view on the event, as does Paul's own narration of his call (from Acts 9) in Acts 22 and 26. This time the event is focalized through Cornelius, so that what the narrator called "angel," Cornelius calls "a man in dazzling robes." Cornelius skips the angel's initial salute and his fear and simply reports his basic message, that his prayer and almsgiving had been "remembered before God" (10:31, RNAB), instead of the narrator's "ascended as a memorial offering before God" (10:4, RNAB). The rest of the angel's message repeats the narrator's account with only minor variations. Cornelius's response is now reported from his own point of view: "So I sent for you immediately, and you were kind enough to come" (10:33, RNAB). He then invites Peter to speak.

Peter's speech opens with the principle that God shows no partiality, which alludes to Deut. 10:17 and is also a key Pauline theme (e.g. Rom. 2:11).[47] The narrator uses this speech to summarize the Gospel's main points about Jesus' ministry, death, and resurrection. Because of its Gentile audience, the speech emphasizes that Jesus will be judge of all (10:36–43).[48] The narrator repeats his artificial pattern of showing interruption of speeches only after the main points have been made.[49] Here Peter is interrupted by God sending the Holy Spirit upon his listeners, who then speak in tongues to the amazement of the Jewish believers who had accompanied Peter (10:44–46). After showing Peter having them baptized, the narrator ends with the comment, "Then they invited him to stay for a few days," which allows enough time for the Gentiles' baptism to be known and reacted to (10:49, RNAB).

Through Peter's retelling of the incident, the narrator exposes his audience for the third time to what happened, this time focalized through Peter's perspective.[50] The third repetition using much the same vocabulary, but from Peter's point of view rather than the narrator's or Cornelius's, both confirms for the audience the incident's importance and adds new insights into it.[51] One such insight is Peter's direct comparison to Pentecost: "As I began to speak, the holy Spirit fell upon them as it had upon us at the beginning" (11:15, RNAB).

The narrator then ties Acts directly to Luke when Peter remembers "the word of the Lord, how he had said, 'John baptized with water but you will be baptized with the holy Spirit' " (Acts 11:16, RNAB; Luke 3:16; and Acts 1:5). Peter's narrative concludes with an argument in the form of a rhetorical question: "If then God gave them the same gift he gave to us when we came to believe in the Lord Jesus Christ, who was I to be able to hinder God?" (11:17, RNAB).

The narrator shows how this combination of narrative and argument ends the objections and transposes them to praise that "God has then granted life-giving repentance to the Gentiles too" (11:18, RNAB). As he shows this story within a story changing objections to praise, so the narrator predisposes his intended audience to let his larger story of Luke and Acts supersede objections with praise for how God has reached out beyond the chosen people to save all flesh (Luke 1:3–4).

Having brought the Peter-Cornelius story to its conclusion, the narrator returns to other missionaries who had been scattered in the persecution of Stephen (8:4). Acts 8:4 and 11:19 thus provide a more inclusive frame for all the stories of Philip, Paul, and Peter. This frame associates all the major new directions of outreach to Samaria, Judea to the coast, and especially to the Gentiles, as well as the conversion of Paul, who would play the largest role in the later outreaches to the Gentiles in Acts. All these new initiatives, as well as the conversion of the one who would initiate many more, are associated with the persecution of Stephen and his prayer for his killers' forgiveness.[52] The point is reinforced still again: nothing can stop the spread of God's word, not even persecution.

The allusion to Stephen's persecution leads into the next major initiative in Acts, when missionaries who had been preaching to Jews in Phoenicia, Cyprus, and Antioch begin to preach at Antioch to Greeks as well (11:19–20). The narrator indicates that the Jerusalem church reacts to news of this by sending Barnabas to Antioch, who confirms their work and goes to Tarsus to bring Saul to help there (11:22–26). The narrator ends with a summary about Barnabas and Saul teaching at Antioch and with an aside in which he tells his audience that "it was in Antioch that the disciples were first called Christians" (11:26, RNAB).[53]

The narrator concludes this series of events by incorporating an independent incident from tradition about prophets coming from Jerusalem to Antioch. He reports retrospectively Agabus's prophecy of a severe famine as well as its later fulfillment under Emperor Claudius. He shows the Antioch disciples responding by sending relief to believers in Judea through Barnabas and Saul (11:27–30).

Between the note at the end of Acts 11 about Saul's and Barnabas's relief mission and their return in 12:25, the narrator inserts a final incident between Peter and Herod that ended in Peter's going underground (12:17) as well as in Herod's ultimate death (12:20–23). Thus the going and returning of Barnabas and Saul between Antioch and Jerusalem frames Peter's escape from Herod's prison, Herod's death, and the unhindered spread of God's word.

This framing device seems to make clear that the narrative is speaking of Barnabas's and Saul's return from Jerusalem to Antioch in 12:25, even though the manuscripts are quite confused and many of the earliest have them returning "to Jerusalem" instead of "from Jerusalem" (εἰς instead of ἐξ or ἀπὸ, or "to Antioch").[54] In this section of Acts, the narrator is going out of his way to intertwine the plot lines of Barnabas and Saul with those of Peter, all three of whom will meet again at Jerusalem in Acts 15. The inability of Herod's prison to contain Peter as well as Herod's ultimate death from blasphemy (11:23) illustrate how unstoppable is the growth of God's word (11:24). By framing these incidents with the travels of Barnabas and Saul between Antioch and Jerusalem and back, the narrator mutually interprets this uncheckable growth of God's word (Acts 12) in light first of the work of Barnabas and Saul at Antioch (Acts 11) and then of their mission from Antioch in 13:3–14:27.[55] Barnabas, Saul, and Peter then meet (with other church leaders) back at Jerusalem for the pivotal council in Acts 15.

NARRATORS IN ACTS 12:25–14:28: BARNABAS AND SAUL

In Jerusalem the narrator introduces five prophets and teachers in a list framed by Barnabas at the beginning and Saul at the end. With his omniscience he quotes the Holy Spirit commanding that Barnabas and Saul be set apart for mission, without indicating to his audience how the Spirit revealed to them this directive other than that it was during fasting and prayer. "Then, completing their fasting and prayer, they laid hands on them and sent them off" (13:3, RNAB). The narrator then equates this commission by the leaders with being sent by the Holy Spirit: "So they, sent forth by the holy Spirit . . . " (13:4, RNAB).[56]

The narrator has already shown Saul and Barnabas preaching in synagogues in Cyprus before mentioning that they had John (Mark) along as their assistant, which is necessary background for his upcoming report on John Mark's desertion in 13:13. In the middle of his account of their confrontation with the magician Bar-Jesus, he pauses with asides to explain that Bar-Jesus was a Jewish false prophet (13:6), that his name is translated as Elymas the magician (13:8), and that Saul has another name, "Saul, also known as Paul" (13:9, RNAB). From this point on he will generally use the name Paul, except in some flashbacks like those to Saul's call in Acts 22 and 26. He also begins naming Paul before Barnabas and other companions, whereas up till now Barnabas was usually the leader and mentioned first.

In rapid succession the narrator shows Paul bringing a temporary blindness on the magician, John Mark leaving them and returning to Jerusalem, and the synagogue officials in Antioch of Pisidia inviting them to speak. Only then does the pace slow dramatically to show Paul's speech in scenic detail. In the narrative this speech functions as Paul's inaugural address, similar to those of Jesus in Luke 4, Peter in Acts 2, and Stephen in Acts 7. Like those of Peter and Stephen, Paul's speech reviews salvation history, but it generally complements their foci rather than repeating the examples already stressed in their speeches.[57]

The main thrust of Paul's speech describes how the inhabitants of Jerusalem and their leaders fail to recognize Jesus and thereby fulfill the prophecies about him (13:27). This dramatic irony, lack of recognition leading to fulfillment of oracles, is familiar from both Hellenistic drama and historiography.[58] The speech stresses Jesus' innocence and fulfillment of scripture (13:28–29) as the narrator's account had done in the Third Gospel. It reports God's raising Jesus from the dead and his appearances for many days "to those who had come up with him from Galilee to Jerusalem" (13:31, RNAB), who are his witnesses before the people. Paul's speech maintains the distinction between the original resurrection witness of the Galileans and his own current proclamation of this good news to those in Pisidia (13:31–32).[59]

The narrator shows Paul being invited back to speak the following sabbath and "almost the whole city" gathering to hear God's word. He shows the Jews contradicting Paul out of jealousy and Paul and Barnabas retorting, "It was necessary that the word of God be spoken to you first, but since you reject it and condemn yourselves as unworthy of eternal life, we now turn to the Gentiles" (13:46, RNAB).[60] They end by applying to themselves the quotation of Isa. 49:6 about being the light to the Gentiles (13:47), which had been applied to Jesus in Luke 2:32.

After showing the Gentiles rejoicing, the narrator gives a summary view of the word of the Lord being spread throughout the region (13:48–49). He shows the Jews stirring up persecution and expelling Paul and Barnabas, who shake the dust from their feet as Jesus had instructed in Luke 9:5 and 10:11, and proceed to the next town, Iconium (13:50–51). The narrator maintains his practice of ending most episodes with a positive summary: "The disciples were filled with joy and the holy Spirit" (13:52, RNAB). Not even persecution impedes Christian joy and the spread of God's word.

The narrator presents the same pattern at Iconium as at Pisidia, only he merely gives a summary report that Paul had spoken, without elaborating his message. The overview goes on to report how the city was divided, some supporting the Jews, others the apostles. It also reports an attempt on their lives and their flight to Lystra and Derbe and the surrounding countryside, "where they continued to proclaim the good news" (14:7, RNAB).

The alternation of scenic and summary passages continues with a vivid scene of the healing of a lame man at Lystra. The narrator uses mocking humor here in showing Paul and Barnabas trying to quell a spreading belief that they are Hermes and Zeus in disguise. He even shows the priest of Zeus bringing oxen for sacrifice. The narrator consistently shows respect for Jewish religion, but mockery of pagan superstition (e.g., Acts 19).[61]

After a brief speech about the living God who will no longer allow Gentiles to go their own ways and who gives evidence of his existence in nature, Paul and Barnabas barely restrain the crowd. But in an amazing about-face that underscores the crowd's fickleness, the narrator reports Jews from Antioch and Iconium getting the crowds to stone Paul, drag him out of the city (which ironically recalls what happened to Stephen in Acts 7), and leave him for dead. He leaves gaps for the readers about Paul's real state, simply showing the believers gathering around him, Paul "rising" (with a pun on resurrection/getting up, ἀναστάς), and going back into the city.[62]

After this scene at Lystra, the narrator covers the rest of this first missionary journey by means of a summary overview of their many conversions in Derbe, their return to Lystra, Iconium, and Antioch in Pisidia to strengthen their converts, their appointment of elders in each church, and further stops until their return to their home port of Antioch in Syria. He prepares for the Jerusalem conference by his summary report that Paul and Barnabas reported at Antioch the faith of the Gentiles. He thus frames the whole journey: it begins by the Antioch church's commissioning of Paul and Barnabas and ends by their reporting back to that church the results of their commission. Implicitly, he also underlines the principle of accountability in the Christian mission. Paul was no unattached traveling evangelist but was commissioned by and accountable to the missionary church at Antioch. Finally, he allows for passage of time with this summary: "Then they spent no little time with the disciples" (14:28, RNAB).

NARRATORS OF THE PAULINE MISSIONS IN ACTS

NARRATORS IN ACTS 15:1–18:22: THE JERUSALEM COUNCIL AND PAUL'S MISSION JOURNEY

In Acts 15, the narrator depicts the confluence of the plot line about Peter with that about Paul and Barnabas, about the church of Jerusalem with that about Antioch. The conflict leading to the Jerusalem Council is fomented by Judean Jewish Christians pushing Judaizing practices at Antioch, which causes tension between Jerusalem and Antioch.

After showing the input of Peter, Paul, and Barnabas at the Council, the narrator portrays the mediating and deciding position as provided by James, the current head of the church in Jerusalem.[63] His solution is depicted as a spirit-given compromise (15:28) that respects the Gentiles' legitimate call without requiring them first to become Jews, yet enables table fellowship, intermarriage, and consequently full community between Jewish and Gentile Christians through Gentile respect for restrictions on Christian Jews. Whatever the historical impact of these compromises may have been, from the narrator's point of view they provide a mediating God-given solution to the controversy between Antioch and Jerusalem, and between Pauline and Petrine Christian practice.[64]

By showing the whole church choosing the leaders Judas Barsabbas and Silas to accompany Paul and Barnabas and to provide oral authentication of the letter they send to Gentile Christians in Antioch, Syria, and Cilicia, the narrator exposes his audience to a repetition of the apostolic decrees only ten verses after their first citation.[65] The letter clearly expresses also the narrator's point of view, in stating that the Judaizers were without mandate from Jerusalem (15:24) and that the decrees were a "decision of the holy Spirit and of us" (15:28, RNAB). The letter follows the ancient letter form with fewer changes than the canonical NT letters, which seem to have followed Christian innovations inspired by Paul. It limits itself to stating merely senders and recipients, "Greetings [χαίρειν]," the body, notice about the letter carriers, and "Farewell ["Ερρωσθε]" (15:23b–29).[66]

The narrator then provides a summary that shows the delegation delivering the letter and fortifying the community, and after some time, Judas and Silas returning to Jerusalem while Paul and Barnabas remain in Antioch (15:30–35). Some manuscripts indicate copyists' awareness of a gap: if Silas returned to Jerusalem, how can Paul take him to Syria and Cilicia?[67] But there is a similar gap about how Barnabas could take John Mark with him, since the narrator has not mentioned his leaving Jerusalem. The narrator leaves readers to fill this gap, perhaps by supposing that both Paul and Barnabas had to send to Jerusalem for their companions before embarking.

The separation between Paul and Barnabas provides the narrator with a clean finish to the intertwined plot lines about the Jerusalem and Antioch churches of the first half of Acts. He dedicates the second half to Paul's mission and trials. He uses a straightforward, almost naive approach to this narrative of a potentially scandalous rift between Paul and the Jerusalem leader, Barnabas, who had legitimated Paul with Christians in the first part of Acts. He avoids more serious charges of a dispute over Judaizing, as in Gal. 2:13, and focuses exclusively on a dispute over taking John Mark again after he had abandoned their first mission. The dispute is focalized from Paul's perspective: "but Paul insisted that they should not take with them someone who had deserted (ἀποστάντα) them at Pamphylia . . . " (15:38, RNAB). That their disagreement over this could become so sharp as to lead to their separation is rendered more probable by the awareness of Christians in Pauline churches that Barnabas was John Mark's cousin (Col. 4:10).

The narrator casts no blame on either side and mentions no evil consequences of their separation.[68] In fact, he seems to imply that it doubled their missionary force. Barnabas took Mark to Cyprus, and Paul took Silas to Syria and Cilicia (15:39–41). Moreover, he clearly implies that Paul's links to the Jerusalem church as well as to Antioch were not severed. He has just emphasized that Paul's new partner Silas is also a respected representative of the Jerusalem church (15:22, 27, 33) and noted that the Antiochene Christians commended their mission to the Lord (15:40).[69]

The narrator now focuses exclusively on Paul's mission, even to the extent of referring to Paul and Silas with singular forms (15:40–16:1).[70] He explains Timothy's background, from a Jewish Christian mother and Greek father, as a rationale for Paul's circumcizing Timothy to make him a more acceptable evangelist to Jews in the region. Apparently, he expected this explanation to be adequate for his intended audience, though twentieth-century readers have to fill in some historical gaps. Most scholars explain that because of his Jewish mother, Timothy would be legally considered a Jew; yet because his mother was married to a Greek his lack of circumcision was widely known. A Jew by race who was not circumcized would be offensive to Jewish congregations that Paul hoped to address.[71]

With Timothy added to Paul's group at Lystra, the narrator in summary mode shows them (presumably also Silas, though he does not mention him) traveling through several cities and promulgating the Jerusalem apostolic decrees. He ends the summary with his usual refrain about the growth of the churches in faith and numbers (16:4–5).

The narrator mentions unexplained resistance by the Holy Spirit toward their moving first toward Asia or later toward Bithynia, so that they went instead to the port of Troas. His use of shorthand notices for extensive travel, as well as his silence on what means the Holy Spirit used to steer them in these directions, leave large gaps in the account of the journey. His rapid narrative pace first begins to slow down with the scene of Paul's night vision of a Macedonian urging him to come to Macedonia, which he presents from his usual omniscient third-person point of view (16:6–9).

Then, without warning, a new narrator steps forward in Acts 16:10. He is a character within the story who speaks in the first person plural as "we." Since a separate chapter will be dedicated to the "we" narrator, this overview of narrators shall simply describe the alternation of all narrators of Acts. From 16:10 onward that alternation will be between the usual omniscient third-person narrator who shows and the participating first-person "we" narrator who tells.[72]

The "we" narrator tells the audience briefly of the Pauline group's journey to Philippi and their converting Lydia and her household before introducing the incident of the slave girl (16:11–17). Imperceptibly, the "we" narrator steps back and lets the omniscient narrator finish showing the incident, focusing in scenic detail on Paul's exorcism of the oracular slave girl and the consequent beating and imprisonment of him and Silas; their deliverance and the conversion of the jailor and his household; and their final departure from the city requested by magistrates embarrassed over beating Roman citizens (16:18–40). The "we" narrator will not return until Paul's next appearance in Philippi, in Acts 20:5–15.

The regular narrator follows Paul's party through Thessalonica and Beroea to Athens, alternating between summary journey notices and scenes of mission in those cities. At Thessalonica, the narrator provides some asides to his audience about the presence of a Jewish synagogue and Paul's custom of preaching there. Otherwise he simply shows Paul arguing with Jews that Jesus is the Messiah, consequent mob disturbance, and the Christians sending Paul secretly on ahead to Beroea during the night (17:1–10). He again interrupts his account to tell his audience that the Jews in Beroea are more fair-minded than those in Thessalonica (17:11). He shows many Jews becoming believers there, until Jews from Thessalonica stirred up trouble for them so that the community sent Paul to Athens, with Silas and Timothy remaining behind.

The narrator shows Paul waiting for Silas and Timothy in Athens, becoming exasperated at all the idols there, and debating in the synagogue with Jews and in the public square with passersby. He shows him even engaging some Epicurean and Stoic philosophers, and in an aside he perpetuates the stereotype of Athenian idle curiosity (17:16–21).

The core of this episode features in scenic detail Paul's speech at the Areopagus. The speech captures audience attention through the Greco-Roman rhetorical device *captatio benevolentiae*, a currying of the audience's favor, even though the narrator had earlier displayed Paul's annoyance over the very religiosity for which he now praises them (17:22, cf. 17:16)! The speech cites authoritative books and arguments from these texts, as did the speeches of Peter, Stephen, and Paul to Jews in Acts 2, 7, and 13. However, Paul uses Greek texts instead of scriptures and arguments sounding like "rational theology" from nature instead of christological arguments.[73] Nevertheless, when the speech finally points to Jesus as judge of the world appointed through his resurrection, the narrator presents still another artificial interruption even though he has presented all the points important to him. This time the listeners interrupt Paul when he mentions resurrection, the very notion of which, the narrator suggests, the Greeks despise.

In the Corinth account that follows, the narrator introduces Aquila and Priscilla and explains that they had moved there because of the emperor Claudius's expulsion of Jews from Rome. He also tells his audience that Paul stayed with them because they shared the tentmaker trade, but every sabbath Paul argued in the synagogue (18:1–4). In summary rather than scenic mode, he narrates how Paul preached full-time after Silas and Timothy came from Macedonia, but he leaves a gap about how their arrival enabled Paul's full-time ministry. Most readers would surmise that Silas and Timothy either helped support Paul or brought money from Macedonia for his upkeep (2 Cor. 11:8–9 refers to Macedonian provision for Paul in Corinth).[74]

At Corinth the narrator shows Paul responding to Jewish resistance with his second declaration that he would turn from them to the Gentiles (18:6; cf. 13:46, 28:28). Yet the narrative following this announcement leaves another gap for readers to fill in. Although Paul declared this turn to the Gentiles and moved his preaching from the synagogue to a private house next door, the next person whom the narrative mentions Paul converting is a synagogue official, Crispus (18:7–8).[75]

With his omniscience, the narrator reveals the Lord assuring Paul and then mentions a year and a half spent teaching at Corinth. Thus he leaves a large time gap before the next episode, the hearing before the proconsul Gallio. After that scene, he adds that "Paul remained for quite some time," before he finally sailed with Priscilla and Aquila for Syria (presumably for his home base in Antioch). In passing he mentions Paul's cutting his hair because of a vow (18:18), which his intended audience may have been expected to understand as a Nazirite vow, but which leaves a historical gap for later readers.[76] The narrative pace remains rapid, with quick references to stops on Paul's journey: Ephesus, Caesarea, and finally home to Antioch. But without warning, the narrator portrays Paul continuing his movements beyond Antioch, "[a]fter staying there some time" (18:23, RNAB), back to the churches he had previously founded in order to confirm them. Thus the narration of Paul's second missionary journey blends into his third one with little noticeable separation.[77]

NARRATORS IN ACTS 18:23–20:38: PAUL'S THIRD MISSIONARY JOURNEY

The narrator begins recounting Paul's new trip from an overview perspective. With omnipresence, he rapidly shows Paul visiting "in order" (καθεξῆς, Acts 18:23, cf. Luke 1:3) his converts throughout Galatia and Phrygia. He immediately turns to a new scene at distant Ephesus, where he introduces Apollos, shows Priscilla and Aquila explaining the Christian way to him more accurately (ἀκριβέστερον, cf. Luke 1:3), and shows the community sending a letter of recommendation with Apollos to Corinth, where he leads an apologetic effort against the Jews (Acts 18:24–28).

Using a kind of split-screen approach, the omnipresent narrator follows both Apollos and Paul: "While Apollos was in Corinth, Paul traveled . . . to Ephesus" (Acts 19:1, RNAB). He uses a mixture of short episodes, summaries, and longer vivid scenic passages to relay to his audience what seem to be unrelated traditional anecdotes. In the first he shows a dialogue between Paul and some inadequately catechized disciples. After Paul contrasts John's baptism with Christian baptism in Jesus' name, his hearers receive the Holy Spirit, as evidenced by their speaking in tongues and prophesying. The narrator ends his account with information one would expect at the beginning: "Altogether there were about twelve men" (19:7, RNAB). Postponement of this information to the ending, and the use of "about (ὡσεί) twelve," are both gaps that signal for readers some symbolic emphasis and allude back to the Pentecost filling of the Twelve among "about 120" disciples in Acts 2.[78]

The narrator then turns from scenic to summary narration, indicating that Paul debated in the synagogue for three months and was forced by resistance to withdraw with his disciples to the lecture hall of Tyrannus for two more years, "with the result that all the inhabitants of the province of Asia heard the word of the Lord, Jews and Greeks alike" (19:10, RNAB). Acts 19:11–12 continues to generalize, describing a pattern of such miraculous power from Paul that cloths that touched him healed the sick and cast out demons. This generalization recalls the mighty deeds through Peter's shadow mentioned in the summary in Acts 5:15–16.[79]

Using the general claims of this summary as a starting point, the narrator mockingly recounts a vivid episode in which seven Jewish exorcists try to cast out demons "by the Jesus whom Paul preaches," only to be ignominiously rebuked, stripped, and beaten by the spirits (19:13–17). He shows the reaction to this event—fear and the burning of a huge number of magic books by believers (19:18–19)—and ends with his generalizing refrain, "Thus did the word of the Lord continue to spread with influence and power" (19:20, RNAB).[80] His report of the reaction and his conclusion reveal his intent sharply to contrast magic with healing faith and to ridicule the former. This corresponds to the narrator's mocking of magic and other pagan beliefs and practices elsewhere in Acts (e.g., 8:9–24, 13:6–11, 14:11–18, 28:3–6).

Next the omniscient narrator briefly foreshadows Paul's upcoming trials at Jerusalem and Rome by showing him deciding "in the Spirit" (ἐν τῷ πνεύματι) to pass through Macedonia and Achaia back to Jerusalem, after which "I must visit Rome also" (19:21, RNAB). In preparation he sends two assistants on ahead to Macedonia (as Jesus had sent two disciples ahead of him to Samaria in Luke 9:51–52), while remaining "for a while" (χρόνον) in Asia (19:22).

The narrator depicts the disruption of Paul's plans through an unexpected riot led by the silversmith Demetrius, who was disgruntled because Paul's mission successes were threatening the sale of idols (19:23–27). The narrator omnisciently reports meetings of workers in idol-related crafts at which no Christians would likely have been present. He attributes an economic motive to pagan resistance to Paul, which corresponds to his treatment of the anger of the slave girl's owners in Acts 16:19, when Paul took away their livelihood through the oracular spirit within her.[81]

The speech that he shows Demetrius making uses Hellenistic rhetorical practices of assuming some persona and creating speeches appropriate for that speaker and occasion, or *prosopopoeia*.[82] The speech's ideological point of view is appropriately anti-Paul and anti-Christian, assuming the pagan view of the reality of gods denied by Paul. But when the narrator shows the crowds responding with mindless two-hour chanting, "Great is Artemis of the Ephesians," his own mocking point of view again becomes manifest. He ends the account by showing a reasoned intervention by the town clerk, who declares Christians innocent of temple robbing or insulting "our goddess" and insists that the group disband. He dismisses the mob, saying that if they have a case, they should bring it to the proper court (19:35–40). Emphasis on this kind of "neutral" intervention by Greco-Roman authorities also corresponds to the narrator's usual point of view (e.g., Acts 18:14–17).[83]

In a summary, the narrator then shows Paul resuming his interrupted plans, encouraging the disciples throughout Macedonia, spending three months in Greece, and returning through Macedonia when Jews plotted against him as he was about to sail for Syria (Acts 20:1–3).

Without warning, the "we" narrator again breaks in and notes which followers accompanied Paul: Sopater, Aristarchus, Secundus, Gaius, Timothy, Tychicus, and Trophimus. He tells how they "went on ahead and waited for us at Troas. We sailed from Philippi . . . and rejoined them . . . in Troas, where we spent a week" (20:4–6, RNAB).[84] This "we" narrator acts as a marginal participant in the account he narrates, indicating his presence at the Sunday Eucharist in which Paul raises up a young man who falls, apparently to his death, during Paul's long midnight sermon. The point of view is that of a participant and is therefore not omniscient and provides no more certainty than a spectator would have about whether the boy was actually dead (20:7–12).[85]

The character narrator tells how "we" preceded Paul to Assos, where "we" took him aboard. He reports further stops and finally Paul's decision to bypass Ephesus in his hurry to get back to Jerusalem in time for Pentecost (20:13–16). But he does not seem to accompany Paul off the ship at Miletus, where it is the usual omniscient third-person narrator who shows Paul's farewell address to the Ephesian elders (20:17–38). The "we" narrator does not reappear until Paul has returned to the ship and they set sail (20:38–21:1).

In the farewell account, the regular narrator resumes narrating and simply shows Paul's summons of the Ephesian elders to Miletus, his farewell address, and their reaction. Paul's farewell includes usual elements of farewell discourses—exhortation, predictions, blessing, and summation of his own example (20:17–35).[86] After the speech, the narrator uses pathos in showing them praying together and the weeping and farewell gestures and distress at Paul's words that they would never see him again (20:36–38).

The farewell address provides a fitting conclusion to Paul's missionary activity in Acts. His journey to Jerusalem after this speech will result in his arrest and trials, as had Jesus' journey to Jerusalem in the Gospel of Luke. As a farewell, the speech looks both backward to Paul's example and forward to future situations of the church. By showing Paul giving his last advice to elders who succeed him as authorities over the church, the narrator summarizes highlights of Paul's care of his churches. In the process, he also addresses indirectly the time after Paul, which is closer to the time and situation of the intended audience of Luke-Acts.[87] Through this farewell address, he allows Paul to address the situation of his readers.

NARRATORS OF THE PAULINE DEFENSE IN ACTS

NARRATORS IN ACTS 21:1–24:27: JERUSALEM ARREST, TRIALS BEFORE FELIX

As soon as Paul rejoins his party on board ship, the "we" narrator takes over again and briefly tells how "we" set sail, stopped at Cos, Rhodes, and Patara, changed to a ship heading for Phoenicia, passed to the left of Cyprus and put in at Tyre (Acts 21:1–3). While the ship was being unloaded, "we sought out the disciples and stayed for a week" (21:4, RNAB).

Except in 21:6, the narrator keeps the "we" group distinct from the local Christians and reports how the latter kept telling Paul "through the Spirit" διὰ τοῦ πνεύματος) not to set sail for Jerusalem (21:4). The "we" narrator here presumes an audience of Christians, or at least of people quite familiar with the Bible of the Jews, for he does not explain what he means by "through the Spirit." This remains a gap for contemporary readers, who have to speculate on the phrase's meaning. ("Through the Spirit" most likely refers either to prayer or prophecy, suggesting that the local Christians gave this advice to Paul during or as a result of their prayer [probably in common], or through prophecy, as the narrator shows Agabus doing later at Caesarea in Acts 21:10–11).[88]

The "we" narrator tells his audience how all the local believers escorted "us" to the beach, where after praying, "we bade farewell to one another [the "we" here includes the local Christians]. Then we boarded the ship, and they returned home" (21:6, RNAB). The "we" narrator shares with his readers how "we" continued the voyage, stayed a day with Christians at Ptolemais, then finally arrived at Caesarea, where "we" stayed with "Philip the evangelist, who was one of the Seven" (21:8, RNAB).

This identification of Philip refers back to Philip's introduction among the Seven in Acts 6:5 and to the narrator's reference in 8:40 to Philip's arrival at Caesarea. The term "evangelist" for Philip refers back to Acts 8:4–40: to Philip's evangelizing Samaria, the Ethiopian eunuch, and lastly the towns between Azotus and Caesarea (Acts 8:40 uses the very term "evangelized [εὐηγγελίζετο]"). The "we" narrator is thus making an express link back to the regular narrator's last mention of Philip in Acts 8:40, which underlines his solidarity and close teamwork with the overall narrator to produce one unified narrative. Despite the alternation between narrators from Acts 16–28, a single narrative to one audience is the goal throughout.[89] A contemporary comparison might be the alternation in one television news story between an anchorperson and a reporter on the scene expressing his or her own experiences of the reported event.

The "we" narrator's mention of Philip's four prophesying daughters seems a gratuitous afterthought, except as a literalistic fulfillment of prophecy from the overall narrator's Pentecost scene, in which Peter quotes Joel to say that "your sons and your daughters shall prophesy" (Acts 2:17, RNAB).[90] The confirmation by the "we" narrator of a foreshadowing from the main narrator of Acts further illustrates the close teamwork and unity of purpose between the two narrators. Yet the next episode strikingly illuminates how different the two narrators' points of view can be.

In Acts 21:10–12, the "we" narrator and Paul's other co-travelers join the local residents in urging Paul to avoid his capture, which Agabus prophesies. Whereas the overall narrator's ideological point of view and standard of judgment are virtually always identical with God's, in this unusual case, the "we" narrator focalizes his telling from the human perspective of those trying to spare Paul from the prophesied suffering.[91] The primary narrator of Luke-Acts has probably already suppressed an account available in his sources and in the other Synoptic Gospels that shows Peter trying in like manner to spare Jesus from prophesied suffering, only to be sharply rebuked by Jesus: "Get behind me, Satan. You are thinking not as God does, but as human beings do" (Mark 8:33, RNAB; cf. Matt. 16:23). In this case, the "we" narrator tells how Paul's steadfast clinging to God's will brought "us" around: "Since he would not be dissuaded we let the matter rest, saying, 'The Lord's will be done' " (21:14, RNAB).

The repeated mention of prophecies of Paul's arrest has been intensifying the plot's foreboding. (Acts 20:22–23 refers to many unnarrated earlier prophecies; see also Acts 21:4, 10–11). Finally the climax arrives in 21:15 as "we . . . went up to Jerusalem." The "we" narrator accompanies Paul up to his meeting with James. He prepares for the overall narrator of Acts to resume narrating by distinguishing Paul from "us": "The next day, Paul accompanied us on a visit to James . . . " (21:18, RNAB). The "we" narrator had prepared for his previous disappearance with a similar distinction in Acts 16:17, "[s]he began to follow Paul and us" (RNAB), which ultimately resulted in the imprisonment of Paul and Silas, but not of the "we" narrator, who therefore was not present and did not narrate their imprisonment.[92]

From this meeting with James, Paul's purification and consequent arrest, and throughout his years of trials under two governors in Jerusalem and Caesarea, the "we" narrator no longer signals his presence (Acts 21:19–26:32). He will first reappear in Acts 27:1, as Paul the prisoner is about to begin his voyage to Rome. Like Jesus, Paul has companions on his journey toward his imprisonments and trials, first to Philippi, then to Jerusalem, and finally to Rome. Like Jesus, Paul will also suffer his actual trials alone, without the companions who traveled with him. The exception is Silas, who becomes distinguished from the narrator's "we" party when he and Paul are arrested together at Philippi.[93]

The regular omniscient narrator takes over the account, showing Paul's meeting with James and the elders and their report of the slander that Paul is teaching Jews who live among the Gentiles to abandon Jewish law and practice. He shows Paul's compliance to their suggestion that Paul counter this slander by supporting four men as they terminate their Nazirite vows.

With irony, he shows again how human plans can be overturned: the very action that Paul undertakes to make himself more acceptable to the Jews is the action that leads to their seizing him. After showing the Jewish accusation that Paul was profaning the Temple, the narrator tells the audience in an aside that the Jews had seen the Gentile Trophimus with Paul and assumed (incorrectly and unjustly) that Paul had brought him into the Temple.

The narrator shows a vivid scene of turmoil, in which the mob tries to beat Paul to death; the Roman cohort commander intervenes, arrests Paul, and extricates him from the uproar. During this, the crowd shouts, "Away with him" (Acts 21:36, RNAB), reminiscent of the crowd shouting "Away with this man" against Jesus in Luke 23:18 (RNAB). He shows the commander's surprise that Paul speaks Greek; his confusion of Paul with an Egyptian revolutionary; Paul's answer that he is a Jew and citizen of Tarsus; his request to address the people (τὸν λαόν); and his addressing them "in Hebrew" (Acts 21:37–40). The narrator informs his audience that different languages are spoken, while presenting all the dialogue in the Greek they understand.

Thus he shows Paul speaking to the Jewish crowd, asking his audience to imagine that Paul's address (which he relates in Greek) is being spoken in Hebrew. Paul's defense speech uses not only the Greek language but Greek technical rhetorical terms like *defense* (ἀπολογία, Acts 22:1). He breaks into Paul's speech to note how the crowd quieted at hearing Hebrew (22:2), then shows the rest of the speech until the crowd interrupts to end it in Acts 22:22. This speech, which includes the second account of Paul's call, will be treated more fully in the chapter on character narrators. Its brief treatment here simply illustrates the overall pattern of different narrators in Luke and Acts, the topic of the current chapters.

The narrator shows the crowd listening to Paul recount his Jewish background, training, persecution of "this Way," call by the risen Jesus, healing and reception by Ananias, and further appearance of Jesus to him as he prayed in the Temple. When Paul reaches the point where Jesus sends him from Jerusalem to the Gentiles, the narrator shows the crowd angrily breaking up his speech (22:3–22). As noted previously, the narrator characteristically shows interruptions of speeches, when in fact all the information he wanted his audience to have has been included (as in Luke 4:28–30 and Acts 17:32).[94] Here he shows the crowd's outrage to be as violent as when they first seized Paul (22:22–23). He goes on to show Paul intimidating the commander with his Roman citizenship, so that he cannot be questioned under torture as the commander had ordered (22:24–29). Instead he shows the Roman attempting to get at the truth (τὸ ἀσφαλές, cf. Luke 1:4) by bringing Paul before the Sanhedrin the next day (22:30).

The narrator begins his account of Paul's trial before the Sanhedrin by showing the high priest Ananias having his attendants strike Paul, Paul responding in anger at Ananias, being corrected for reviling the high priest, and withdrawing his accusation with a quotation of Ex. 22:27 (Acts 23:1–5). At this point the narrator interjects several asides to his audience to explain Paul's strategy. In 23:6 he tells them that Paul was aware the Sanhedrin was divided between Pharisees and Sadducees. In 23:8 he explains that Sadducees and Pharisees disagree about resurrection and angels and spirits. In retrospect this confirms that the claim that Paul has just made, that he is "on trial for hope in the resurrection of the dead" (23:6, RNAB), is a deliberate attempt to provoke a split between the two parties. He shows a tumult over Paul in the official Sanhedrin similar to what had taken place among the mob in Acts 21–22, so that the commander again has to extricate Paul from their midst (23:7–10).

Without needing any overt comment, the disruptions shown by the narrator portray the Sanhedrin to be as disorderly and lawless against Paul as the mob had been. For Greco-Roman readers, the narrator's picture in

Acts 19 of riots over Paul by pagan idolaters in Ephesus, and by both a Jewish mob in Acts 21–22 and their chief court in Acts 23, makes all three groups appear equally ridiculous and lawless in the presence of Roman authorities.[95] He ends this section by omnisciently showing the Lord appearing to Paul at night and reassuring him that he shall similarly bear witness to Jesus' cause in Rome (23:11, RNAB).

The narrator shows the impasse over Paul finally broken by a plot on Paul's life, which necessitates his transfer from the tribune Claudius Lysias in Jerusalem to the governor Felix in Caesarea. From his omniscient perspective, he shows a secret plot by Jews against Paul, the discovery of this plot by Paul's nephew, and the nephew's report of it to the commander (Acts 23:12–22). He shows the tribune's preparations of a huge escort for Paul and the letter Lysias wrote to Felix (23:23–25).

The letter reviews some of the events that the narrator had shown, but with some self-serving inconsistencies from the narrator's account. As Tannehill comments, repetitious accounts of the same event by several narrators enable readers to see, by comparing what characters say to what the authoritative narrator has shown, human motivation at work.[96] Here Lysias implies that he rescued Paul because he knew he was a Roman citizen, but he is silent about the fact that he had almost tortured him. His main point, however, reemphasizes the narrator's central concern: to show through Roman testimony that accusations against Paul were rooted in intramural Jewish disputes and that Paul, therefore, was undeserving of death or imprisonment (23:26–30).

After showing the soldiers transferring Paul to Felix in Caesarea, the narrator shows Ananias and some elders five days later accusing Paul through a professional orator or advocate (ῥήτωρ), Tertullus (23:31–24:1). He depicts this as a formal trial, with Tertullus acting as prosecuting attorney (κατηγορεῖν) and Paul as his own defense attorney (ἀπολογεῖσθαι). After an artificial rhetorical attempt to create rapport with the judge (captatio benevolentiae), Tertullus accuses Paul of creating dissension and desecrating their Temple (24:2–6). Paul responds with a simpler captatio benevolentiae and defends himself against these charges (24:10–13). He then admits to the governor that "according to the Way . . . I worship the God of our ancestors . . . " (24:14, RNAB), and he demonstrates his innocence of every possible charge except his claim, " 'I am on trial before you today for the resurrection of the dead' " (24:21, RNAB).[97]

The omniscient narrator shows Felix postponing the trial and listening privately to Paul several times and tells his audience in an aside that Felix hoped for a bribe from him (24:22–26). Then he simply states that two years went by, after which Festus succeeded Felix. In a terse editorial comment that reflects his pro-Pauline point of view, he ends his treatment of Felix: "Wishing to ingratiate himself with the Jews, Felix left Paul in prison" (24:27, RNAB).[98]

NARRATORS IN ACTS 25:1–26:32:
TRIALS BEFORE
FESTUS AND AGRIPPA

In presenting a series of Paul's trials, the narrator chooses to hurry over some and focus in greater detail on others. Except for themes he wants emphasized, such as the repeated verdicts of innocent that Roman authorities give to Paul, he tends to leave unnarrated what would be repetitious from other trials. Therefore he puts less emphasis on the first Caesarean trial before Festus in Acts 25 than on the previous trial before Felix in Acts 24, or on the subsequent hearing before both Felix and Agrippa in Acts 26. After using his omniscient viewpoint to set the situation before Festus, which includes another plot to assassinate Paul on the way to Jerusalem, he merely summarizes the fact that the Jews brought many unprovable charges against Paul (25:1–7). Then he shows only Paul's basic plea in reply: "I have committed no crime either against the Jewish law or against the temple or against Caesar" (Acts 25:8, RNAB). With his omniscience, and from a pro-Pauline point of view, he tells his audience in an aside that the motive for Festus's next proposal was "to ingratiate himself with the Jews" (25:9, RNAB).[99] Paul refuses this motion of Festus to try him in Jerusalem, repeats his claim to innocence, and appeals for a hearing before the emperor (25:10–11). The trial ends dramatically with Festus's declaration: "You have appealed to Caesar. To Caesar you will go" (25:12, RNAB).

The narrator treats Paul's next hearing, before both Felix and Agrippa, as the climax of Paul's trials. In Acts 25:13–22, he lays elaborate narrative preparations. First he omnisciently shows the governor Festus consulting with King Agrippa and repeating, with even greater elaboration, what the narrator had reported about Paul's first trial before him. The information from Festus that the narrator's original account had not mentioned includes Paul's claim that the dead Jesus is again alive. By having Festus provide his own viewpoint on what happened, the narrator furnishes his audience with two quite different perspectives on the same event. The narrator's own perspective gave little detail, but merely emphasized that Festus was ingratiating himself with Paul's accusers. Festus's version delineates more clearly the debate over Jesus' resurrection and the confusion of Festus over what looked to him like intramural Jewish issues.

The narrator builds an elaborate scene for Paul's climactic defense speech before Agrippa and Felix, exhibiting Agrippa's ceremony and the large audience of leading figures. He shows Festus repeating still again both the charges against Paul and his finding Paul not guilty, as well as Paul's appeal to the emperor (Acts 25:23–25). He shows Festus explaining to Agrippa that the reason he sought this hearing was to have something definite (ἀσφαλές τι, cf. Luke 1:4) to write to Caesar about the charges against Paul (25:26–27). Finally he shows Agrippa inviting Paul to speak and Paul making an elaborate defense speech (ἀπελογεῖτο, 26:1).

In Paul's speech, the primary narrator presents Paul as a narrator within the story telling his tale to Agrippa and Felix. Paul's defense in Acts 26 marks the second time he narrates the incident of his conversion and call. Paul's first narration of that event was from the perspective of a zealous Pharisee. Here he focalizes his account retrospectively from his later Christian point of view. His emphasis is on the present: "But now I am standing trial because of my hope in the promise made by God to our ancestors" (26:6, RNAB). Paul goes on to narrate his past persecution of Christians, whom he calls from his present vantage point "many of the holy ones" (πολλούς τε τῶν ἁγίων, 26:10). (The use of the Christian term "holy ones" for Christians seems appropriate for the retrospective viewpoint of the narrator Paul, but less suited to the narratee Agrippa to whom he is telling the story.) As a special instance of Paul's general persecuting activity, he next tells of his trip to Damascus and Jesus' appearance to him on the way. He clearly remains in the telling rather than showing mode of narration, explicitly addressing Agrippa as "O King" or "King" four times throughout the speech (vv. 2, 7, 13, 19, RNAB), and again in the interchange after the speech (v. 27).

Paul's account reflects his present situation of speaking in Greek to Agrippa: though he mentions that Jesus spoke to him in Hebrew, he adds a Greek proverb to what the previous versions in Acts 9 and 22 had shown Jesus saying to him (Acts 26:14). This same later perspective collapses Jesus' first appearance to Paul with what Acts 9 and 22 had described as later commissionings and visions through Ananias (9:15–16, 22:15) or in the Temple (22:17–21). Scholars have noted this tendency to collapse a process-with several steps into the single primary call experience, and the consequent apparent discrepancies with Acts 9 and 22.[100] Such a tendency corresponds both to the limits created by setting an apologetic autobiography in a juridical defense and to a normal aspect of some retrospective narrative.[101] The retrospective focus of this narrative may also partially account for its substitution of the conversion language dualisms—sight/blindness, light/darkness, God/Satan—for Paul's literal blindness and sight through Ananias in Acts 9 and 22 (Acts 26:17–18).

Finally, Paul's account moves quickly through his missionary career to his capture in the Temple, focusing on his preaching of repentance. The climax of his narration comes with his claim that his message is simply that of the prophets and Moses—"that the Messiah must suffer and that, as the first to rise from the dead, he would proclaim light both to our people and to the Gentiles" (26:23, RNAB). Paul's narrative thus culminates in an explicit proof from biblical prophecy of the death, resurrection, and proclamation of the Messiah to the Gentiles, which is one of the ways Luke-Acts demonstrates "the certainty [ἀσφάλεια] of the teachings you have received" (Luke 1:4, RNAB).[102]

The original narrator of Acts now shows Festus interrupting Paul's defense, repeating the pattern of interruption of virtually complete speeches throughout Luke and Acts (as in Luke 4, Acts 4, 17, and 22). The following interchange discloses that Paul's defense appears to be madness to the Roman Festus but quite reasonable to Agrippa, who understands Jewish customs and controversies (26:24–26, cf. 26:3). The claim of Paul to Agrippa exemplifies one of the goals of the narrator of Acts, to demonstrate that "this was not done in a corner" (26:26, RNAB).[103]

The narrator concludes this episode with a reiteration of Paul's innocence. With his omniscience, he shows the king and governor withdrawing and declaring privately to each other, "This man is doing nothing [at all] that deserves death or imprisonment" (26:31, RNAB). He ends by letting his audience see how Paul could both be innocent and yet be sent to Rome for trial, through showing Agrippa's verdict: "This man could have been set free if he had not appealed to Caesar" (26:32, RNAB).

NARRATORS IN ACTS 27:1–28:16: JOURNEY TO ROME

Again without warning, the "we" narrator takes over and gives his audience a vivid report of the sea voyage to Rome and shipwreck on Malta. This account also will be analyzed more fully in the chapter on the "we" narrator, so only a summary of how it fits into the narration of Acts as a whole is needed here. The "we" narrator speaks from the point of view of a marginal participant in and observer of the events on the voyage. He uses the first-person "we" and "us" flexibly, sometimes to include all on board ship, at other times to distinguish Paul's companions from the sailors or others. This narrator tells the audience about the stops and routes in summary fashion and about individual episodes between Paul and the centurion or crew in vivid scenic detail.

His account is focalized from his own perspective as a witness and companion of Paul, from a point of view loyal to Paul and spontaneously sympathetic to Paul's side of disagreements. Thus he implies that the centurion was foolish to listen to the pilot and owner of the ship, rather than to Paul's warning that travel now would risk the ship and their lives. Such a point of view might not be surprising in a follower of Paul, but most impartial narrators would expect the centurion to listen to the ship's pilot and owner rather than to a warning by a prisoner with no navigational skill.[104]

The report of the storm and of the crew's responses to it is full of vivid detail, climaxing in a candid admission of despair: "Finally, all hope of our surviving was taken away" (27:20, RNAB). Fully taking Paul's side, the "we" narrator tells how Paul admonishes the others for not heeding his warning but encourages them with a promise from an angel that, despite running aground, all lives would be saved (27:21–26). Then the "we" narrator slows the pace of narration by going into greater detail about the sailors testing for depth and trying to escape (27:27–32).

In his report of the ship's company finally eating in response to Paul's example, the narrator surprisingly does not use "we" and thus include Paul's companions in that act (27:36). Only belatedly does he tell his audience: "In all, there were two hundred seventy-six of us on the ship" (27:37, RNAB). In vivid scenic detail, he finishes the narrative to the point where they reached shore (27:38–44), presumably basing his knowledge of the soldiers' hidden intentions of killing the prisoners on hindsight.

Since the "we" narrator is a participant, he does not have the omniscience of the regular narrator of Acts; therefore, he can only name the island by using information they received afterward (Acts 28:1). A participant's perspective focuses the whole report: the natives' hospitality is described with the gratitude of one who received it; Paul's snakebite and the natives' commentary are narrated from the viewpoint of someone sitting around the fire. The narrator does not tell his audience how he understood speech in the native language or their unspoken expectations in 28:2–6. His knowledge must be credited to observation of their actions and imputing to them thoughts that would correspond to their behavior, since an observer would not have access to the thoughts of those he observed.[105]

The "we" narrator then switches to another locale on the island, telling of Publius's receiving "us," of Paul's healings, and of how the natives honored "us" and gave us provisions. The "we" narrator then quickens the pace to a summary report of their travels and stations on the way to Rome but maintains the Christian perspective, as when he calls fellow Christians "brothers" (28:7–16).

NARRATORS OF THE END, ACTS 28:17–31

Once Paul is under guard, the "we" narration stops, and the regular narrator finishes the Acts narrative. The implication is that Paul no longer has the companionship of those who traveled to Rome with him and told the audience of the journey and shipwreck and stay at Malta. The regular narrator resumes his omniscient, showing mode of narration, without direct comments to the audience. He shows Paul three days later inviting the leaders of the Jews and addressing them briefly about his capture, his trials, his innocence, why he had to appeal to Caesar and how he did so without accusing his own nation (ἔθνος). Paul tells them he is chained because of "the hope of Israel" (28:20, RNAB).

The narrator shows their answer, then a later meeting in which Paul spent all day "trying to convince them about Jesus from the law of Moses and the prophets" (28:23, RNAB). When the Jews are divided, some believing and some not believing, he shows Paul's final statement, a long quotation from Isa. 6:9–10 LXX, which he had earlier alluded to in Luke 8:10. After the quotation, which explains the people's lack of faith, he shows Paul ending: "Let it be known to you that this salvation of God has been sent to the Gentiles; they will listen" (28:28, RNAB). This is Paul's third and final, climactic statement about turning from Jews to Gentiles (also Acts 13:46, 18:6). These are the last words the narrator quotes Paul saying, and their climactic position makes them ominous.

But the narrator ends the two volumes on a higher note, withdrawing from his close scenic account of Paul's conversation with Jewish leaders to provide a summary overview from a greater distance of both space and time. He shows Paul for two full years receiving all who came, proclaiming God's kingdom and teaching about Jesus with great boldness and without hindrance (μετὰ πάσης παρρησίας ἀκωλύτως). By referring to "two full years" the narrator implies he knows what happened at the end of this time (i.e., Paul's release or death), but he does not inform his audience. On this high note of unhindered bold preaching of the word, the narrator ends his account. His theme of unstoppable growth and spread of God's word, no matter what the human opposition, plays itself out to the very end of his narrative.[106]

The use of narrators in Acts has proven more complex than in the Gospel of Luke. Though both volumes share the same two narrators, the first-person singular narrator in both prologues and the third-person omniscient narrator for the greater part of the narrative, the added introduction of two intradiegetic narrators within the story of Acts has caused some confusion and raised further issues. Of the latter, the first-person plural character narrator ("we") in selected sections after Acts 16:10 has proven to be the most significant and problematic intradiegetic narrator. Whereas most of the story is filtered from without by the overall extradiegetic Acts narrator, the "we" sections are focalized from the

perspective of a marginal participant in and observer of the events recounted.[107] This has led to many historical questions about whether the
author of Acts was a sometime companion of Paul. The second kind of
intradiegetic narrator is the use of characters within the plot to narrate
stories within the story, as when Paul retells his own conversion story in
Acts 22 and 26, which the extradiegetic narrator had recounted in Acts 9.

With greater freedom than in the Gospel from restrictions of sources
and previous versions of the story, the narrators in Acts are able to provide a less episodic and more elaborated plot, where one incident flows
into the next. With fewer traditional sayings of the apostles than of Jesus,
the narrator of Acts is freer to formulate appropriate speeches for the
characters. Also, the narrator of the Gospel showed only assertions by
Jesus that the Christ must suffer according to the scriptures, thus leaving
the implied readers in the dark as to which scriptures. It is the Acts
narrator who shows the apostles revealing both to other characters and to
readers what particular scriptures taught about the suffering and glorification of the Christ.

The Acts narrator also makes fuller use of *exempla* than in the Gospel
(such as the positive and negative examples respectively of Barnabas and
Ananias and Sapphira). By framing and irony he shows the unstoppable
spread of the word despite the machinations of opponents like Saul, who
becomes one of its chief proponents. The Acts narrator interweaves scenic
passages like the conversion of Cornelius with summary passages about
the spread of the word, to generalize trends from specific examples. As in
the Gospel, he builds a sense of foreboding through characters' prophecies
of suffering.

Because of the special issues raised by the "we" and character narrators, they were only treated in passing in plot context in this chapter. The
next two chapters will be devoted to these narrators within the story:
chapter 7 to the "we" narrator, chapter 8 to the character narrator Paul.

7 Narrative Claims of "We" in Acts

I n the previous two chapters, we followed the varying uses of Lukan narrators throughout the Gospel and Acts. In Acts we noted the use of a marginal character narrator in the first person ("we," "us") in some of the incidents from Acts 16:10 and following. In this chapter, let us probe further this somewhat peculiar variant narrator and its functions within the Acts narrative. Since there is so much debate about these "we" accounts, we will begin with a recapitulation and critique of previous approaches. Then we will study the narrative claims being made by the use of this "we" narrator: the limited perspective it enjoys compared to the omniscient narrator; the expansions and contractions of the group included under "we"; the inclusion or exclusion of Paul among the "we" group; distinctions among Paul's "we" companions; the lack of a presence claim in the absence of "we"; and the narrative importance of "we" claims. Though not primarily a narrative literary question, we will add a brief discussion of the historical value of these "we" claims, because the historical issues so often distract attention from the narrative functions of the "we" narrator.

BACKGROUND: APPROACHES TO "WE" AND NEED FOR NEW SOLUTION

PRAEDER'S CRITICISM OF REDACTIONAL AND COMPARATIVE APPROACHES

Historical treatments of the "we" sections of Acts have resulted in a stalemate between conflicting explanations, to which narrative approaches promise a solution. In 1987, Susan Marie Praeder added her critiques of the redactional and comparative procedures to the now common objections against the traditional and source explanations of the "we" sections. She found that the increasingly prevailing solutions based on comparative studies of sea voyages in historiography and literature around the first century are simply not based in fact. The evidence in Acts and comparative literature does not confirm an alleged obligatory shift to first-person narration for sea voyages. For example, Acts 13:4–5, 14:20b–28, and 18:18–23 are third-person sea voyages, sometimes quite ranging, and first-person passages include both land travels and land scenes.[1] Nor do the alleged comparisons account for the peculiarities of Lukan use, especially the exclusive plural. In all parallels, "first-person narrators of any importance in the history or story always refer to themselves as first-person singular participants."[2]

Both redactional and comparative solutions leave four features of first-person narration in Acts unexplained: "the *anonymity* of the first-person narrator, *plurality* of the first-person participants, occurrence of first-person narration *only in 16:10–17, 20:5–15, 21:1–18, and 27:1–28:16,* and *first- and third-person sections* in the first-person passages."[3] This narrative approach will try to take into account all four of these concerns.

The impasse in previous explanations of "we" passages is linked to historical and theological questions about which no consensus has been possible. Before addressing such questions and risking entanglement in the same impasse, let us carefully specify what narrative claims are made by the text in its final form.

CLAIMED PRESENCE OF NARRATOR/IMPLIED AUTHOR AS OBSERVER OF PAUL

The very fact that for centuries the "we" passages in the later parts of Acts have been interpreted as including the author Luke is evidence that readers naturally identify these expressions as claims to be present at the scene narrated. Virtually all scholars who have addressed this question agree that there is such a claim in the use of the first person, but they disagree over the historicity of this claim and whether it is best applied to the author or his sources.[4]

The reversion to "we" in Acts 16:10 after Paul's dream of the Macedonian begging for his help is without warning or preparation. In the first sixteen chapters of Acts, the narrator had been extrinsic to the narrative, "extradiegetic"; suddenly the narrator is a character within the account, "intradiegetic." No longer attending to someone outside the story, the readers or listeners are now hearing the account of someone who had participated in the event. The account is thereby made more immediate and vivid, giving the audience a sense of privileged access to the event through a participant.

This heightened sense of immediacy cannot help but imply that the narrator was present, which in turn infers an eyewitness authority. Many contemporary actual readers are reluctant to grant such eyewitness authority to the narrator, even if ancient implied readers were expected to do so. The main reasons for modern reluctance seem to be doubts about the historicity of what is described. These doubts are extensively influenced by a post-enlightenment a priori skepticism about the miraculous interventions described in these first-person accounts. They are also influenced by perceived differences in the portrait of Paul and his theology from what he himself describes in his letters. This means that some contemporary readers are not able to accept the role of the readers originally implied by the narrative.[5] But study of a narrative must begin with what is implied within the narrative itself. The claims of the "we" narrator on implied readers are clear, but they are unacceptable to many contemporary real readers.

However, though the change to first person automatically implies presence and therefore witness, Acts' exclusive use of "we" instead of "I" suggests minimized concern with historical credibility. The emphasis, rather, seems to be on the narrative's immediacy and vividness. The reader, for the sake of historical reliability, does not remain an uninvolved, second-hand observer but is drawn into what Tannehill called "imaginative participation in the narrative."[6]

LIMITATIONS ON PERSPECTIVE OF NARRATOR AS CHARACTER

Not only are the credibility claims of the "we" passages minimal, but the perspective of the narrator is also limited. E.g., in the episode recounted in Acts 20:7–12, the narrator is only peripherally involved; he is not, as in other parts of Acts, omniscient. Because his point of view is limited to that of an onlooker, it is not self-evident to readers whether or not the boy who fell really had died before Paul embraced him and returned him "alive" to the community. Though the narrator's presence at the event adds to the readers' vivid experience of the scene, it reduces the reader to the same ambiguities any original witnesses would have encountered.[7] Most readers would assume, as did the original onlookers, that the boy was dead. The narrator, however, does not answer possible queries whether the boy was only apparently dead.

Tannehill observes a similar limitation of the narrator's perspective in Acts 21:10–14. There Paul's companions (including the "we" narrator) and

and local Christians urge Paul not to go to Jerusalem,[8] which is a sign "that the 'we' narrator is not omniscient but shares the limited insight of Paul's companions."[9] The narrator is part of a group of characters who do not have the perspective of God's plan from which most of Acts is told. Along with the Christians at Caesarea, "we" initially seem to resist a prophecy of the Spirit and only after Paul's rebuke accept the Lord's will (21:12–14).

EXPANSIONS AND CONTRACTIONS OF THE "WE" GROUP

One of the problems with an anonymous "we" group is the changing extension of who is included in the party. There is often no easy way to know how many and who are included within the "we." One of the most problematic variations in the inclusivity of "we" occurs in the episode of the storm at sea in Acts 27–28. The "we" had been absent from the time of Paul's meeting with James and throughout the imprisonment and trials that followed in Acts 21–26. The group suddenly reappears in Acts 27:1, where its extent is quite unclear: "When it was decided that *we* should sail to Italy, they handed Paul and some other prisoners over to a centurion named Julius of the Cohort Augusta" (RNAB, my emphasis). Most of the commentators as well as many manuscript copyists notice the awkwardness here, for some manuscripts read "those around Paul" in place of "we."[10] Kirsopp Lake and Henry J. Cadbury in their commentary and James Ropes in his study of the variant textual traditions of Acts show that the Western Codex Bezae removes the "we": "And thus the governor decided to send him to Caesar, and the next day he called a centurion named Julius . . . and handed over to him Paul with other prisoners."[11]

The context implies that the decision to sail to Italy is not the travelers' personal choice but is made for them by others. The decision therefore suggests that the travelers are prisoners rather than people freely choosing to travel. Yet "we" do not seem to be fellow prisoners with Paul on this trip, since at its end in Rome only Paul is kept under house arrest. The statement in the following verse, "Aristarchus . . . was with us" (27:2, RNAB), which adds to the impression that "we" are Christians freely voyaging on the same ship as Paul,[12] excludes Aristarchus from the first-person plural. But in the verses immediately following, "we" seems to include him and all aboard ship, as in 27:3: "On the following day we put in at Sidon where Julius was kind enough to allow Paul to visit his friends who took care of him" (RNAB). The "we" group are remarkably passive on this voyage, doing little more than observing and reporting the experience that they share with Paul and their other shipmates.

The next two verses, 27:4–5, show the "we" group putting out to sea, sailing around Cyprus, and arriving at Myra in Lycia. Here the "we" term encompasses all on board ship. Acts 27:6 may have similar problems of point of view as 27:1: "There the centurion found an Alexandrian ship that was sailing to Italy and put *us* on board" (27:6, RNAB; my emphasis). In 27:1, the first-person pronoun seems to apply properly to prisoners, whose fate is decided for them. In 27:6 the pronoun includes Paul's companions among those who are put on board.[13] Yet the "we" group seems not to be prisoners but companions freely choosing to accompany Paul to Rome.[14] Perhaps the inconsistency is only apparent in this second case, since it is possible when speaking of the centurion putting "us" on board to mean simply that the centurion is in charge of the overall boarding of the ship, including those who follow his directions freely. This apparent inconsistency may have contributed to Allen James Walworth's judgment that the sudden shifts between "we" and "they" constitute a flaw in the narrative strategy of Acts.[15]

The following verses, Acts 27:7–8, revert to a "we" inclusive of all on board: "For many days we made little headway, . . . because the wind would not permit us to continue our course we sailed for the sheltered side of Crete. . . . We sailed past it with difficulty and reached a place called Fair Havens . . . " (RNAB). In Acts 27:9–12 the narrator focuses exclusively on Paul's unsuccessful attempt to dissuade those in charge from sailing further at this dangerous time of year. There is no occasion to mention the narrator's own presence via "we."

Acts 27:13–14 continues from vv. 9–12 the third-person focus on others' actions: "thinking they had attained their objective, they weighed anchor and sailed. . . . Before long . . . a 'Northeaster' struck" (RNAB). The "we" indicate no participation in the decision to leave port but do share in the results of this poor decision, even though some of the actions more properly apply to the sailors: " . . . we gave way and let ourselves be driven. We passed along the sheltered side of an island . . . " (RNAB). Verse 17 describes the sailors' actions as distinct from those of the "we" group. Therefore it uses the third person, so that the same expression for being carried along (ἐφέροντο, cf. v. 15 ἐφερόμεθα), which literally would include all on board, is kept in the third person for the sailors. But v. 18 switches back and forth: "We were being pounded by the storm so violently that the next day they jettisoned some cargo" (RNAB). The lack of hope in v. 20 applies again to all on board: "Finally, all hope of our surviving was taken away" (RNAB). The narrator is obviously trying to suit his use of first- or third-person verbs to the context, but not with complete success, as Walworth had complained.[16]

Acts 27:21–26 reports Paul's exhortation to eat, based on the promise he received from God's angel that all on board would be saved. There is no reference to the narrator's group: "When many would no longer eat, Paul stood among them and said . . . " (27:21, RNAB). But we are reminded of the narrator's presence immediately after these verses: "On the fourteenth night, as we were still being driven about . . . the sailors began to suspect that they were nearing land" (27:27, RNAB). Verse 28 reports in the third person the sailors' soundings. Verse 29 recalls the narrator's presence: "Fearing that we [inclusive of all on board] would run aground . . . they . . . prayed for day to come." Verses 30–32 recount, with no need to aver to the narrator's presence through "we," the sailors' attempt to flee the ship in a dinghy, Paul's warning, and the soldiers cutting the dinghy adrift.

Acts 27:33–35 relates in the third person how Paul encourages all to eat by his own example of taking nourishment, an act described in terms highly reminiscent of the Eucharist: "They were all encouraged, and took some food themselves" (27:36, RNAB).[17] The narrator reverts to first person in Acts 27:37 to say how many "all" are. Tannehill remarks, "The 'we' in the voyage to Rome generally refers to a small group of Christians. Here, however, the entire ship's company becomes a single 'we' as the narrator numbers the company. . . . "[18] However, the following verses continue exclusively in the third person, focusing almost solely on the sailors' actions.

> After they had eaten enough, they lightened the ship. . . . When day came they did not recognize the land. . . . They planned to run the ship ashore. . . . So they cast off the anchors. . . . But they . . . ran the ship aground. . . . The soldiers planned to kill the prisoners so that none might swim away and escape, but the centurion wanted to save Paul. . . . In this way, all reached shore safely. (27:38–44, RNAB)

The last sentence in Acts 27:44 refers to all on ship but does not revert to the first person to include reference to the narrator, though one could have expected this from v. 37: "there were two hundred seventy-six of us on the ship" (RNAB). The use of the inclusive "we" also in the following verse, Acts 28:1, would confirm expectations for the first person in 27:44: "Once we had reached safety we learned that the island was called Malta" (28:1, RNAB).[19]

The "we" narration continues in Acts 28:1–10 for the winter in Malta. It is not clear who is included in the "we" group—all the survivors of the shipwreck (the impression in 28:1–6) or just Paul and his Christian companions (the impression in the Publius episode in 28:7–10).

The narrator's point of view in the incident of the viper in 28:1–6 is vividly focalized, the perspective of an observer seated around the fire. The fact that the Greek narrator quotes a statement made in a "barbarian" language, as well as the natives' change of mind from whether the goddess Dikē was pursuing Paul to whether Paul himself was a god, indicate knowledge from hindsight, rather than omniscience frequently found in biblical narrators. It also represents common Hellenistic preconceptions about the ignorance of natives more than striking new insight into others' minds.[20] The narrator simply reports the mistaken views of the pagans without explicit comment, but seems to find their opinions amusing.[21]

The last episode with the first-person narrator, Acts 28:11–16, recounts the trip from Malta to Rome. At first the "we" group includes the entire party on board: "Three months later we set sail on a ship. . . . We put in at Syracuse . . . and from there we sailed around the coast and arrived at Rhegium. After a day, a south wind came up and in two days we reached Puteoli" (28:11–13, RNAB). In vv. 14–15 the "we" seem to contract to include only Christians. "There we found some brothers. . . . And thus we came to Rome. [The "we" is ambiguous: either Christians from the context or all the party.] The brothers from there [Rome] heard about us [probably only the Christians] and came . . . to meet us" (RNAB). This is the last mention of the "we" party, the narrator of which is presumably still speaking in v. 15b: "On seeing them, Paul gave thanks to God and took courage" (RNAB). Verses 16 to the end of Acts report in the third person Paul's imprisonment, with no longer any implication that the narrator was with him.

PAUL INCLUDED AMONG THE "WE"

A more specific instance of this expansion and contraction of the "we" group is the inclusion or exclusion of Paul among their number. When the "we" are first introduced in Acts 16:10, the group obviously includes Paul. The narrator interposes himself into Paul's searching for passage to Macedonia and perceived mission to preach the good news there. Whether there were other companions has to be determined from the context.

The passages leading up to Acts 16:10 have some curious uses of singular and plural verbs, all in the third person. From 15:40–16:3 the narrator describes Paul's and Silas's travels, using third-person verbs in the singular, with exclusive focus on Paul: "But Paul, having chosen Silas, departed . . . and traveled through Syria and Cilicia . . . " (15:40–41, my translation).[22] The singular verbs continue when Paul (with Silas) arrives at Derbe and adds Timothy as another companion (16:1–3). But the next verse, 16:4, switches to the plural to include Timothy, almost as if Silas's presence had not counted.[23]

Third-person plural narration continues in 16:6–8, but reverts in 16:9 to the singular to describe Paul's night vision of the Macedonian asking him (singular) to help them. The third-person singular continues in 16:10, until the abrupt introduction of the first-person plural: "When he [Paul] had seen the vision, we sought passage . . . concluding that God had called us . . . " (RNAB).

The unknown identity of this "we" creates a gap in the text. For the first time and without warning it includes the narrator among Paul and his companions. But is the narrator some previously unmentioned companion who first joins Paul in Troas, or one of the people, Silas and Timothy, who had accompanied Paul to Troas?[24] The fact that later in 20:4–5 the narrator seems to mention Timothy in a group distinct from the "us" to which the narrator belongs would appear to eliminate Timothy from the "we."[25] Because Silas is not mentioned there, he could remain a possibility.[26]

The "we" group in Acts 16:10–17 participates as companions in Paul's mission and journeys, with intermediate stops, to Macedonia. They go together to evangelize at the place of prayer and meet and stay with Lydia. The use of "we" here makes no distinctions among Paul's companions, who are easiest to imagine as few in number.

In Acts 16:11–15, the "we" group includes Paul, though within this "we" the narrator is clearly distinct from Paul (vs. Conzelmann). "We set sail from Troas . . . to Philippi. . . . We spent some time in that city. . . . We went outside the city gate. . . . We sat and spoke with the women. . . . One of them, a woman named Lydia . . . listened, and the Lord opened her heart to pay attention to what Paul was saying. . . . She offered us an invitation . . . and she prevailed on us" (RNAB).

The "we" passage in 21:1–18 makes no distinctions among Paul's companions or between them and Paul. Only in 21:18 does the narrator distinguish between Paul and the "we" group, in obvious preparation for the transition away from first-person narration in 21:19. "The next day, Paul accompanied us on a visit to James. . . . " (21:18, RNAB). The next several chapters, from Acts 21:19 to Acts 26:32, return to the usual Lukan third-person omniscient narrator, which is also the most common kind of narrator in Luke's Greek Bible.[27]

DISTINCTIONS BETWEEN "WE" GROUP AND PAUL

However, in the pericope immediately following the Lydia conversion, the first-person narrating group is distinguished from Paul, in preparation for a passage recounting the arrest and imprisonment of Paul and Silas narrated in the third person. As the passage begins, "we" includes Paul: "As we were going to the place of prayer, we met a slave girl with an oracular spirit . . . " (16:16, RNAB). The distinction is then made: "She began to follow Paul and us . . . " (16:17, RNAB). From this point on, the narration is focalized in the third person wholly on Paul and eventually also on Silas: Paul became annoyed, exorcized the spirit, and he and Silas were seized by the girl's irate owners (16:18–19). The narrator implies he was with the group who met the slave girl and heard her words. It is not clear whether he claims that he was present some days later when Paul finally exorcized the spirit. The third-person verbs and context suggest that the narrator was not with Paul and Silas later during their arrest and imprisonment.

To prepare for a return from first- to third-person narrator by distinguishing Paul from the "we" group is a Lukan stylistic pattern.[28] A similar separation of Paul from the "we" group occurs toward the end of the third "we" passage in Acts 21:18: "The next day Paul accompanied us on a visit to James . . . " (RNAB). The rest of the episode has a third-person narrator.

In Acts 20:5–15, the "we" passage also distinguishes Paul from the "we" group before returning to third-person narration, but the distinction is based on "we" and Paul taking different routes to the same destination. Acts 20:13–14 relates "We went ahead to the ship and set sail for Assos where we were to take Paul on board . . . since he was going overland. When he met us in Assos, we took him aboard and went on to Mitylene" (RNAB). The next verse, 20:15, includes Paul again in the "we" who sailed to Miletus, but after v. 16 the focus is exclusively on Paul, with narration of his farewell speech in the third person until Acts 20:38b: "Then they escorted him to the ship." The next verse reverts to first person: "When we had taken leave of them we set sail. . . . (21:1, RNAB). The distinctions between first- and third-person narration depict the "we" group going ahead by boat and taking Paul on board at Assos, then sailing together with Paul to Miletus. There a third-person narrator focuses exclusively on Paul's decision to avoid Ephesus but to send for their elders, and his farewell speech to them. It is as if the "we" group stayed on board ship waiting for Paul, then incorporated him again after the elders escorted Paul to the ship (20:38b), when "we" took leave of the elders and sailed on for Cos (21:1). The narrator unquestionably represents himself as part of a group that sometimes traveled with Paul and sometimes met or waited for him. The narrator is a minor character and observer in the events narrated.[29]

The end of the last "we" section, in Acts 28:15–16, does not explicitly distinguish Paul from "us," as in these earlier cases. The narrative now focuses exclusively on Paul, and the "we" group that has to this point been narrating simply ceases to call attention to itself and drops out of consideration. "The brothers from there heard about us and came . . . to meet us. On seeing them, Paul gave thanks. . . . Paul was allowed to live by himself, with the soldier who was guarding him" (RNAB). The rest of the book is recounted in the third person by a narrator who is extrinsic to the story.

DISTINCTIONS AMONG PAUL'S "WE" COMPANIONS

Not only do the boundaries and extent of the "we" group expand and contract in number, sometimes including and sometimes excluding Paul. In Acts 20:5–15, further distinctions are sometimes made among Paul's companions, distinctions that clearly illustrate their roles in the account that one of them narrates. Paul had planned to travel to Syria by ship, but because of a Jewish plot he decided to begin his return overland through Macedonia. Some named companions went with him. Others, apparently unnoticed by the Jewish plotters, were able to go by ship, as Paul had originally planned to do. Sopater, Aristarchus, Secundus, Gaius, Timothy, Tychicus, and Trophimus accompanied Paul overland from Greece through Macedonia to Troas, where they waited for "us" (20:5).[30] "We sailed from Philippi . . . and rejoined them five days later in Troas, where we spent a week" (20:6, RNAB). The group in 20:6 that rejoins Paul, Sopater, and the others after a sea journey from Philippi to Troas includes the narrator and is distinct from the seven companions named in 20:4. However, during their stay in Troas (20:6b) the "we" group contains both groups: the narrator and others who sailed to Troas and those who traveled there with Paul by land.

In the following Eutychus episode at Troas, the narrator identifies closely with Paul's perspective, hearing what he says to the Christians of Troas but not considering it addressed to himself and to Paul's other traveling companions. The narrator's focus remains exclusively on Paul, the local Christians, and the boy who fell, until the end of the episode in v. 12. He only mentions the "we" group again in the resumption of the journey in v. 13: "We went ahead to the ship and set sail for Assos, where we were to take Paul on board" (RNAB). But here the people connoted by "we" are distinguished temporarily from Paul.

NO PRESENCE CLAIM WHEN NO "WE"

The obvious corollary to a narrator's claim to be present when using "we" is the lack of such a claim when "we" is not used. Just as readers automatically imagine the narrator present when "we" is utilized, they tend not to imagine his presence in sections where it is missing. Though this observation may seem pedestrian, it makes a difference in how an audience visualizes a narrative. Non-use of the "we" narrator influences readers' imaginations as significantly as its use. For example, the absence of "we" in Acts 17:1–20:4 suggests that the narrating member of the "we" group remains at Philippi during those journeys of Paul. When the "we" account resumes at 20:5, the implication is that "we" rejoin Paul's party from Philippi.

"WE"/THE TWELVE: COMPANIONS TO JERUSALEM OR ROME, ABSENT AT TRIALS

Another striking example is the absence of the "we" group during Paul's trials and imprisonments, even when they had accompanied Paul to the place of trial and imprisonment. Thus "we" were with Paul in Philippi during the slave girl incident but not during his imprisonment there. "We" traveled with Paul to Jerusalem but disappeared during his arrest and defense before the Roman magistrate. "We" accompanied Paul on his shipwreck and journey to Rome, but Paul is alone with a guard during his house arrest.

In this sense, the "we" group that includes the narrator is similar to the Twelve in the Gospel. "We" accompany Paul to Jerusalem and to Rome as the Twelve had accompanied Jesus to Jerusalem until the time of Jesus' arrest. Just as Jesus had companions on his journey to suffering but not during the trials themselves, so did Paul have the "we" companions on the way to Philippi and Jerusalem and Rome, but not during his trials and imprisonments in those places. Both Jesus and Paul had to face their actual trials and suffering alone.

NARRATIVE IMPORTANCE OF "WE" CLAIMS

The "we" claims not only provide a thematic parallelism between Jesus and Paul, but they also imply the narrator's presence as eyewitness at some of the later events in Paul's life. His presence at such Pauline incidents provides evidence for the debate about an ambiguous claim in the Lukan prologue to have followed (παρηκολουθηκότι) all things closely (Luke 1:3).[31] The narrator's claimed presence supports those like Henry J. Cadbury and A. J. B. Higgins who see at least a double meaning of physical presence at some of the events as well as accurate investigation.[32]

HISTORICAL VALUE OF "WE" CLAIMS

Many scholars hesitate to admit the presence of "we" during some of Paul's later journeys because of questions about the historicity of these claims. For this reason we have bracketed historical discussions while examining these claims. On the purely narrative level, it seems difficult to disallow that these unexpected changes to "we" narration constitute an implicit claim to have participated in the events recounted.

Though this is primarily a narrative and not a historical study, a brief review of some historical evidence concerning these claims might be helpful in dealing with obstacles for many even to consider these claims. For this limited purpose, the treatment of Joseph Fitzmyer of the authorship of Luke-Acts in his commentary on Luke, with his additional reflections in his later book, *Luke the Theologian*, can be our primary guide to the issues.[33]

Fitzmyer acknowledges the differences in theology between Acts and Paul and attributes them partially to the fact that the "we" claims of accompanying Paul begin late in the story of Paul's career, after the Jerusalem Conference in Acts 15. Nor did "we" accompany Paul after the Philippi visit in his second mission (ca. 49–52 CE) until Paul returned to Philippi at the end of his third mission (ca. 54–57CE). Using standard chronologies, Fitzmyer dates the meeting of the "we" party with Paul at Troas in Acts 20:6 to about spring of 58 CE, a gap of some eight years after the Philippi incident in Acts 16, during which Paul's most important letters were written. Irenaeus read too much into the "we" passages when he called the author an "inseparable" companion of Paul. The "we" passages reveal rather that the narrator was not with Paul during most of his missionary activity, nor when his most important letters were written, nor during the crises of Judaizing, Corinthian factions, and the Thessalonian questions. Many of the historical inconsistencies between Acts and Paul refer to Paul's early career and times when there is no "we" claim to presence with Paul.[34]

In his later reflections on problems in the second-century tradition, Fitzmyer argues plausibly that Irenaeus was probably trying to bolster an existing tradition about Luke as author. For the second-century fathers, all the Pauline correspondence, including letters that today are judged not to stem from Paul, would have been consulted for evidence of which companion of Paul might be responsible for the "we" passages. In that event, the statement in 2 Tim. 4:11 that Luke was the only one with Paul would not have indicated that Luke could be the *only* candidate for author of Acts.[35] Besides the Muratorian Canon, the late dating of which Fitzmyer challenges, the Egyptian papyrus Bodmer XIV provides new evidence (published only in 1961) in its title, *Gospel According to Luke*. The attestation of this late second-century codex is independent of Irenaeus and Tertullian, who also attribute this Gospel to Luke. It witnesses to a late second-century tradition of the Egyptian church. All this adds up to second-century traditions in several parts of the Christian world attributing the Gospel of Luke and Acts of the Apostles to Luke. Luke in turn is such a minor personality in the New Testament that the most plausible explanation for this widespread attribution to him is that it is factual.[36]

Besides problems of theology and Paul's biography, many authors also have a hard time accepting that a participant created the novelistic account of the voyage to Rome and shipwreck in Acts 27–28, in which Paul's role seems exaggerated.[37] But the description of an (admittedly partial) companion can hardly be presumed to be impossible if Paul in fact did have the good relationship with the centurion Julius that Acts claims he had. One can allow for exaggerations without rejecting the text in its entirety. As a matter of fact, true accounts can sometimes seem too implausible to be appropriate for fiction. Paul himself claims to have survived not one but three shipwrecks (2 Cor. 11:25).

On a merely narrative level, the implicit claims to participation made by the "we" passages in those events are manifest. The arguments of Fitzmyer and others suggest that these claims may also have historical plausibility, and need not be rejected a priori. Whether or not one identifies the narrator in the "we" passages with Luke, there seems genuine plausibility to the claims that the author of Acts was a companion of Paul and a peripheral participant during some of Paul's later journeys and experiences.

As enumerated by Susan Marie Praeder, four features of first-person narration in Acts that are left unexplained by both redactional and comparative solutions find a clarification in a narrative approach.[38] (1) "The *anonymity* of the first-person narrator" indicates a self-effacing narrator who draws attention not to his own identity but simply to his presence and participation in the events. The priority is not on the narrator as historical witness, but on drawing the intended readers into a vivid presentation of the episodes. The anonymity can also convey that the implied readers knew the author's identity, as would Theophilus to whom the work is addressed.

(2) The "*plurality* of the first-person participants" is most unusual for the first-person narration, which is normally in the singular, as are the prologues to Luke and Acts. The exclusive use of the plural in the "we" passages is closely related to the anonymity of the first-person narrator. By keeping the plural, the narrator "hides behind a crowd" and refuses any special attention to himself. The identity that the narrator reveals is never his individual identity but always a group identity as a member of a

community. In this respect the "we" companions of some Pauline journeys are similar to lesser members of the Twelve who never receive individual attention (except when the names of all twelve are listed).

(3) The "occurrence of first-person narration *only in 16:10–17,
20:5–15, 21:1–18, and 27:1–28:16*" functions in the narrative as making
selective claims to the narrator's presence at only some Pauline episodes.
For the vast majority of Paul's adventures the narrator makes no such
claims, and his absence can be presumed. As a result, the "we" narrator
appears to have remained in Philippi between Paul's return to Jerusalem
and his reappearance there much later. Nor do the "we" companions
accompany Paul and Silas to prison in Philippi in Acts 16, participate in
Paul's farewell to the Ephesian elders in Acts 20, nor share in his arrest
and trials from the middle of Acts 21 to Acts 26 and at the end of Acts. As
Jesus had the Twelve as companions on his journey to Jerusalem where he
had to suffer alone, so Paul had companions on his journeys but had to
suffer alone (or at Philippi with only Silas).[39]

(4) The "*first- and third-person sections* in the first-person passages"
sometimes are confusing, as in parts of the sea voyage, when they are
open to the charge of careless writing. But they more often have a purpose. The alternations serve to make distinctions (as between Paul and his
companions and among his companions) or show differing focuses on the
group inclusively ("we") or on the sailors or others acting separately
("they"). This alternation between first- and third-person narration in the
"we" passages is a major obstacle to Vernon K. Robbins' thesis that first-
person narration is de rigueur and thus quasi-automatic style for sea
voyages.[40]

In the next chapter, we turn to another kind of character narrator
within Acts, using Paul's retellings of his conversion and call as examples.

8 Influence of Variant Narrators on Repeated Acts Narratives

T he previous chapter investigated the effect of a narrator who was a peripheral character and observer, a member of the "we" group who relates some incidents on the later journeys of Paul in Acts 16–28. This chapter will focus on the effects of having a narrator who participates in the story tell an imbedded narrative or story within the story. The clearest instances of such narrative occur in the speeches in Acts. The story of Paul's conversion, for example, is told once by the overall narrator of Acts and twice (to different audiences) by Paul, a character within Acts. It therefore provides an excellent example of the factors involved in having narrators both from outside and from within the narrative recount the same incident. Space restrictions limit this study of narrators only to the repeated narratives of Paul's call in Acts 9, 22, and 26.[1]

After studying the narrator's version of Paul's call in Acts 9 as a kind of experimental control case, we will compare and contrast the accounts by the character Paul in Acts 22 and 26. In Acts 9 we will see the effects of having a general narrator who is not part of but outside the story and who enjoys an omniscient point of view. Acts 22 and 26 will demonstrate the results of having a narrator who is a character within the story and who works out of an ideological (and non-omniscient), telling point of view that is subordinate to the narrator's omniscient perspective. It will study the results of different focalizations of the story through Paul instead of through the general narrator, or through Paul's pre-Christian perspective (Acts 22) or later retrospection (Acts 26). The focus on character narrators will be correlated to the ancient rhetorical practice of *prosopopoeia*, creating speeches suited to particular speakers, occasions, and audiences.[2] The reader can then make similar observations about other repeated narratives like the Peter-Cornelius incident, whose viewpoints vary from the

125

omniscient general narrator to Peter and Cornelius (note the increasingly later retrospective points of view of the latter two versions).

Many redactional inquiries have studied how the narratives of Paul's call in Acts 9, 22, and 26 adjust to different audiences. Whereas those analyses emphasized the effects of audience reception on narratives, this narrative examination reverses that perspective, with the complementary emphasis on how different narrators with their distinct points of view influence variations in the narratives.[3] Both perspectives are needed for a complete investigation.

To most critics, the minor contradictions in Acts 9, 22, and 26, between what Saul's companions saw or heard, seem careless Lukan redaction at best; he either did not notice differences in his sources or was inconsistent with his own previous versions. Thus Acts 9:7 says his companions heard the voice but saw no one, but Acts 22:9 states that they saw the light but did not hear the voice. Acts 9:7 has the companions standing speechless, but Acts 26:14 has them falling to the ground with Saul.[4]

Luke's use of different narrators can provide a way to explain such discrepancies without having to accuse him of carelessness. My main thesis is that the extradiegetic narrator of Acts 9 enjoys an omniscience that Paul in Acts 22 and 26 does not have, even though he is the protagonist in the event. Therefore, the Acts 9 narrative is authoritative for Acts, and the other Acts versions can be explained as intradiegetic and subordinate versions from Paul's limited and personal point of view.[5]

EXTRADIEGETIC OMNISCIENT NARRATOR IN ACTS 9

The narrator of most of Luke-Acts, through whom the reader first hears the story of Saul's call, uses a "showing" point of view, presenting the account as an unobtrusive narrator without drawing attention to his presence or influence.[6] As an omniscient narrator, he can describe individual, interior viewpoints of Ananias and Paul, as well as simultaneous but different events each experiences, until Ananias comes to Saul in 9:17–18. (A character narrator like Paul in Acts 22 can only follow what is happening to himself, not what is concurrently befalling Ananias.) Omniscient narration also enjoys the literary presumption of accuracy in details: in conflicting minor details (such as what Saul's companions saw or heard), the narrator's version can be judged more reliable than Paul's versions.

Thus, the narrator's description of Saul's blindness in 9:8 is focalized through an observer's rather than Saul's perspective: "he could see nothing; so they led him by the hand. . . . " In 9:15–16, the Lord's report to Ananias of Saul's commission gives the report a kind of objectivity: "Go, for he is a chosen instrument of mine to carry my name before the Gentiles and kings and the sons of Israel; for I will show him how much he must suffer for the sake of my name."

The literary omniscience of the narrator in Acts 9 is not temporally or spatially restricted to the main event on the road to Damascus, but it includes its cause, Saul's previous acquisition of letters against the disciples, as well as the letters' contents. His use of the particles δέ and ἔτι links this incident yet further back to the one narrated at Acts 8:3: "But Saul was ravaging (ἐλυμαίνετο) the church, and entering house after house, he dragged off men and women and committed them to prison." Here the narrator shifts abruptly into free indirect speech from the perspective of the focalizing letters of Saul, "so that if he found any belonging to the Way, men or women, he might bring them bound to Jerusalem" (9:2).[7] (The phrase "men or women" in 9:2 echoes Saul's dragging off "men and women" in 8:3.)

The narrator continues to use omniscient narration as he describes the epiphany of the risen Lord Jesus to Saul, of which the narrator reports that only Saul saw Jesus though his companions heard the voice.[8]

The omniscient narration next describes "the Lord's" appearance in a vision to Ananias and their prayer conversation, which would not have been overheard by ordinary observers (9:10–11). An even more striking example of omniscience is the description of the double vision—Jesus tells Ananias that Paul in his prayer has seen "a man named Ananias" lay hands on him (9:12).[9] The perspective gets convoluted here, and the reference to "a man named Ananias" is focalized from the perspective of Saul, to whom Ananias is a stranger. Several levels of narratives are imbedded here: (1) the narrator relates (2) that the Lord recounts to Ananias Saul's vision (3) in which is narrated (in indirect speech) Ananias coming to Saul.[10] His omniscient stance starkly contrasts with the limitations of the narrator Paul's version of this event in Acts 22, which narrates none of Ananias' prayer experience because none of it was accessible to him.

By his omniscient description of Ananias's objections to Saul and how the Lord himself overruled them (9:13–16), the narrator is giving the strongest possible apologetic for Paul: "Go, for he is a chosen instrument of mine to carry my name before the Gentiles and kings and the sons of Israel; for I will show him how much he must suffer for the sake of my name" (9:15–16). The perspective is obviously Christian: the narrator calls Jesus "the Lord"; Jesus calls Paul his "chosen instrument," σκεῦος ἐκλογῆς.[11] Further, the Lord's prediction about Saul functions as a kind of table of contents for the rest of the Acts narrative about him. In the narrative, the Lord's supernatural omniscience about the future undergirds the narrator's functional omniscience and foreshadows what is to be narrated.[12]

Only the Acts 9 narrator mentions Paul's reception of the Holy Spirit at the hands of Ananias (9:17). In Acts 22:13, Paul merely mentions his cure from blindness. In Acts 26, Paul does not mention Ananias at all. Only the Acts 9 narrator mentions something like scales (ὡς λεπίδες) falling from Saul's eyes, which in Greek seems to allude to Tobit 11:12 LXX: "and the cataracts peeled off (ἐλεπίσθη) from the corners of his eyes." The narrator recounts the event from within the biblical worldview with scriptural allusions to Tobit's cure from blindness, adding an intertextual depth to his report.[13]

On the other hand, the almost identical accounts of the essence of Jesus' appearance to Saul in 9:3–6 and 22:6–10, despite the different narrators, can be attributed to the fact that both are focalized through Saul's experience (rather than through that of the risen Jesus, for example). From his privileged omniscience the extradiegetic narrator has, as it were, entered within Saul's experience to provide as clear and personally focused an account as Paul himself later supplies as narrator in Acts 22.

INTRADIEGETIC CHARACTER NARRATOR PAUL IN ACTS 22 AND 26

Intradiegetic narration corresponds to what the ancient rhetorician Theon described as *prosopopoeia,* the rhetorical practice of assuming some persona and then giving a speech as if that person.[14] In Acts 22 and 26, the real author exercises *prosopopoeia* when he creates a speech for Paul that would be appropriate to what Paul would have said on that occasion.[15] Described in contemporary literary terms, the extradiegetic narrator continues to narrate the principal story of Acts, in which he *shows* a character Paul *telling* his imbedded narrative.

This intradiegetic narrator uses a "telling" point of view, acting as an *obtrusive narrator* whose influence on the narration is made explicit. Paul is obviously telling his story to the Jews in Acts 2 or to Agrippa and Felix in Acts 26, interacting with his narratees, addressing and making comments to them, and finally being interrupted by them (22:22 and 26:24). Thus Paul directly addresses Agrippa ("King Agrippa," 26:2, "O King," 26:7, 13) and interrupts his narrative with questions to him ("Why is it thought unbelievable among you that God raises the dead?" 26:8, RNAB).

As an intradiegetic character narrator, Paul's ideological point of view and standards of judgment are subordinate to the main narrator's. Whereas Acts 9 shows that the main narrator's ideological point of view is Christian, the character narrator Paul's in Acts 22 is Jewish. Thus in Acts 22:3 he cites his persecution of Christians to illustrate how he was "zealous for God" (ζηλωτὴς ὑπάρχων τοῦ θεοῦ). He treats his persecuting activity as an important credential that makes him worthy of a hearing from his Jewish listeners:"I persecuted this Way to the death . . . as the high priest and the whole council of elders bear me witness" (22:4–5). Paul's Jewish ideological point of view reappears in 22:5, where he refers to the recipients of his letters as "the brethren," compared to the more objective "synagogues" in 9:2.[16]

The ideological point of view that treats persecution of Christians as an act of serving God is unreliable, even though expressed by Paul.[17] Since it does not accord with that of the narrator of Acts as a whole, readers tend to view it as part of the character Paul's attempt to win over his Jewish audience, not as truly the viewpoint of the Paul who gave his farewell address to the Ephesian Christian elders in Acts 20. As such a *captatio benevolentiae*, it strikes the implied readers as ironic.

FOCALIZATION THROUGH THE CHARACTER PAUL

The narration in both Acts 22 and 26 is focalized biographically through the character Saul rather than historically through the general narrator.[18] Paul's experience focalizes the account: "when I could not see . . . I was led . . . " (2:11). "I received my sight and saw him" (22:13–14). In contrast, the narrator focalizes the parallel in 9:8 through the perspective of Paul's companions: "he could see nothing; so they led him by the hand. . . . " Focalization through Paul of his own commission in Acts 22 gives it a more personal significance than the objective version in Acts 9.

Limits From Focalization Through the Character Paul

Focalization through Paul puts *limits* on what is narrated. Due to Saul's preoccupation with his own overwhelming experience, as a narrator in Acts 22 and 26 he would have a less reliable awareness of what his companions underwent than the extradiegetic and omniscient narrator in Acts 9. In Acts 9:7, the narrator focalizes the account through a bird's-eye view, which has as good a perception of what is happening to the companions as it does of what is happening to Saul. "The men who were traveling with him stood speechless, for they heard the voice but could see no one" (9:7, RNAB). The narrator's superior perspective in Acts 9 to that of Paul as narrator in Acts 22 can sufficiently account for discrepancies between Acts 9 and 22 about what Saul's companions saw or heard.

The most obvious limitation of focalization through Paul concerns Ananias. Because Paul is narrating in Acts 22 from his own limited perspective, he does not mention Ananias' vision of Christ described in 9:10–16. He evaluates the whole incident as an external observer of Ananias without access to his inner thoughts. In 22:12–13 Paul can only report how Ananias was devout and well spoken of by the Jews and how Ananias interacted with him.

Variations in Character Focalization

Paul's intradiegetic narration also varies its focalization between the pre-Christian perspective of Saul the persecutor and the retrospective focalization of Paul the speaker.[19] The phrase, "to be punished," in Acts 22:5, which implies Paul's approval of the Christians' capture, exemplifies Saul's pre-Christian perspective.[20] So does his statement in 26:9: "I myself was convinced ('Εγὼ μὲν οὖν ἔδοξα ἐμαυτῷ) that I ought to do many things in exposing the name of Jesus of Nazareth."[21]

Paul's substitution of conversion language in Acts 26:17–18 in place of previous narration about Ananias and Paul's blindness illustrates a special focalization. Because this is an autobiographical apology before the Hellenistic rulers Agrippa and Felix, he omits the irrelevant details of his blindness and Ananias and merges them into his commission to convert Gentiles.[22] From the perspective of his Christian hindsight, the intradiegetic narrator Paul collapses all the elements of his commission by the risen Jesus, which in Acts 22 he had attributed to the medium of Ananias and to a later vision in the Temple, into his first experience of Christ (26:16–18). He ignores Ananias and his own blinding from the earlier accounts and instead uses the blindness motif as missionary and conversion language: "to whom I send you to open their eyes, that they may turn from darkness to light and from the power of Satan to God . . ." (26:17–18). All these adjustments fit the point of view of the intradiegetic narrator Paul having to summarize his narrative in an autobiographical apology before a ruler, and the focalization of his later Christian perspective.[23]

Since Acts 22 features the Jewish Paul talking to the Jewish mob, it has a theocentric rather than christocentric perspective. Paul was "zealous for God, just as all of you are today" (22:3, RNAB). Ananias tells the narrator Paul that "The God of our ancestors designated you to know his will, to see the Righteous One, and to hear the sound of his voice" (22:14, RNAB).[24] This contrasts with the christocentric perspective of Acts 9:10–16, when the Lord Jesus appears to Ananias and insists that he go to Saul. When he arrives, Ananias does not mention God appointing Saul to see the Just One, but the Lord Jesus sending him that he may regain his sight and be filled with the Spirit (9:17).

Redaction critics had attributed the differences between the three versions of Saul's call narrative primarily to the different audiences to which they were addressed. Some had discussed the Lukan use of the ancient rhetorical process of *prosopopoeia* in fashioning the two versions in the Pauline speeches in Acts 22 and 26, according to how Paul would have expressed them to his differing audiences—a Jewish mob and the rulers Agrippa and Felix. To these insights our narrative approach has added how different narrators affect these discrepancies.

Comparison of narrators resolved minor contradictions in Acts 9, 22, and 26 in favor of the authoritative version of the extradiegetic narrator in Acts 9. His omniscient point of view enabled him to see what was unavailable to the limited point of view of Paul. For as a particular character, Paul was not privy to what happened within Ananias' experience, nor was he very aware of what was happening to his companions while he was seeing the risen Jesus. Our comparison of narrators and their different points of view also helped explain the change from a christocentric focus in Acts 9 to a theocentric one in Acts 22.

Whereas the version of Paul's commission in Acts 9 found increased objectivity by presenting it in Jesus' words to the third party Ananias, the further commission to Paul himself in the Temple (22:17–21) after his initial commission through Ananias (Acts 22:14–16) adds a subjective and personal perspective, which becomes totally personal in the hindsight and capsulized recapitulation of Acts 26:16–18. This recapitulation illustrates how Paul's retrospective point of view makes it easier to combine in Acts 26 what Acts 22 had described as two separate moments in his call and commissioning.

Similar analyses can be made of the Peter-Cornelius incident and other places in Acts where characters narrate an event from their own limited points of view, which are subordinate to the general narrator's omniscient perspective. This close analysis of one important example of that Lukan practice provides principles that, with attention to individual differences, can be generalized to apply to other examples as well.

In the previous five chapters we have applied methods of narrative analysis to the predominant figure of the narrator, showing his influence throughout the prologues, the Gospel, and Acts, and observing the two special kinds of character narrators, the "we" narrator in Acts 16–28 and a character narrator (in this case, Paul) telling a story within the story. In the next chapter, we will look at two ways the narrator provides implicit commentary on the events recounted, through irony and the motif of misunderstanding.

3

Applications:
Implicit
Commentary

9 Implicit Commentary in Luke-Acts

The preceding applications of narrative approaches to the kinds of narrators within the Gospel and Acts lead easily into treatment of implicit commentary, which is closely associated with and proceeds from the narrator's point of view. This chapter will concentrate on two kinds of implicit commentary, misunderstanding and irony, which are normally filtered through the narrator. It will investigate how the first, irony, is sometimes based on knowledge shared among demonic forces and the readers, sometimes on questions about Jesus' identity, sometimes on irony in parables; major ironies occur in the passion of Jesus and its retrospections in Luke 24 and Acts. In Acts, a principal irony concerns how attempts to repress evangelization result instead in the spread of the word. Another kind of irony involves mocking of Jewish exorcists and of magic and pagan superstitions.

Regarding the second kind of implicit commentary, misunderstanding, we will ask whether James M. Dawsey's thesis of conflicting views between the narrator and Jesus in Luke's Gospel is the best explanation of the evidence. Then we will look at misunderstanding as portrayed in the Lukan ignorance theme, then at other miscellaneous examples of misunderstanding in Luke and Acts. Another major example of misunderstanding (overlapping somewhat with irony) is the mockery and polemic in Acts against magic and pagan misunderstanding. We shall conclude this chapter by analyzing the final and climactic instance of the motif of misunderstanding, the citation of Isa. 6:9–10 at the end of Acts.

The fruitfulness of Alan Culpepper's treatment of implicit commentary through irony, misunderstanding, and symbolism in the Fourth Gospel recommends trying a similar approach to Luke-Acts, but one modified in view of the manifest differences in the two narratives.[1] Both John and Luke-Acts make dramatic use of irony as a form of implicit commentary.

Both also make indirect comments through the motif of misunderstanding, though the Fourth Gospel's use of misunderstanding is far more pronounced and thematic than in Luke-Acts. Irony and misunderstanding are also closely related to each other, together illustrating indirect but important ways of communicating with the Lukan audience.

However, whereas the Johannine use of symbolism is quite explicit and extensive, Lukan symbolism is far less thematic and original to Luke-Acts. And most Lukan symbolism has already received ample treatment. Thus the heavy Lukan reliance on parallelism for implicit commentary—as between the Baptist and Jesus in Luke 1–2 and among Jesus and Peter and Paul in Luke and Acts—is well known.[2] So also are examples of symbolism like the boy Jesus' three days in the Temple in Luke 2; catching humans after catching fish in Luke 5:1–11; and the eucharistic symbolism of Paul breaking bread and eating during the storm at sea in Acts 27:35.[3] One could also note Lukan commentary through the use of double meanings: the moral of the parable of the rich man and Lazarus implicitly refers also to Jesus' resurrection and Acts—"If they will not listen to Moses and the prophets, neither will they be persuaded if someone should rise from the dead" (Luke 16:31, RNAB). The fate of the "beloved son" in the parable of the tenant farmers clearly alludes to Jesus' passion (Luke 20:9–18). Acts 3:22 (with 3:26) and 7:37 pun on "raise up" and "resurrect" (ἀναστήσει) in quotations from Deut. 18:15–20—"A prophet like me will the Lord, your God, raise up [ἀναστήσει] for you . . . " (Acts 3:22, RNAB). And the meaning of "at the feet of the apostles" receives an ironic double import in the contrast between placing proceeds of property sales "at the feet of the apostles" (4:35, 37; 5:2) and Sapphira's death there (5:10). More typical and illustrative of implicit commentary in Luke-Acts are the uses of irony and the motif of misunderstanding, to which we now turn.

IRONY

The key to irony in Luke-Acts is to approach the narrative on two levels: on a higher level, the readers share with the implied author and his narrator insight and information lacking to dramatis personae on the lower level of the plot line within the account. The audience can watch from a vantage point of superior knowledge as individuals in the narrative display their ignorance of or hostility to this higher perspective.[4] This makes the audience part of an inner circle sharing knowledge that some outsiders within the narrative lack. Irony is thus closely linked with the point of view both of the narrator and of intended readers. Contemporary literary-critical studies have underscored how closely irony is also connected to worldview. Because of the Christian worldview of Luke-Acts, and of my interpretation, the irony in Luke-Acts will be expounded as stable irony, even though a deconstructionist worldview would treat it as unstable irony, with "no fixed standpoint which is not undercut by further ironies."[5] Irony of this stable variety functions more to include the readers in the author's inner circle and to invite them to share the author's ideological point of view than to exclude victims of the irony, who are not the intended audience but primarily characters in a narrative about the past.[6]

That the irony in Luke-Acts is meant to be inclusive for the audience at the expense of characters from the past is especially evident in the Lukan motif of God working out his saving plan through human blindness.[7] As Tannehill notes, the God of Luke-Acts is a God of irony. He accomplishes his plan through the very rejection of his plan and of its messiah and messengers.[8] To the extent that the narrator is able to convince his audience of this basic irony of history, he is succeeding in his goal that they may "know the certainty [ἀσφάλειαν] of the reports [λόγων] about which they had been informed" (Luke 1:4, my translation). He can thus win them over to his interpretation of the "events that have been fulfilled among us" (Luke 1:1, RNAB) as accomplishing God's plan of salvation.

Both in the Gospel and in the speeches of Acts the Lukan narrator depicts the very rejection of Jesus as opening the way of salvation to those who rejected him. The scattering of the Jerusalem disciples through persecuting attempts to suppress the word ironically leads to the further spread of that word (Acts 8:1, 4–5; 11:19–21).[9] Thus, Saul's persecution of the word eventually leads to the word being preached in Syrian Antioch, where the converted Paul is brought (in an ironic full circle) to minister to the new disciples (Acts 8:1, 4–5; 11:25–26).

In both the Gospel and Acts, Pharisees who oppose Jesus and the apostles speak God's perspective unwittingly: "Who can forgive sins but God alone?" (Luke 5:21); "If this man were a prophet, he would know what kind of woman was touching him" (Luke 7:39); Gamaliel: "But if it [this activity] comes from God, . . . you may even find yourselves fighting against God" (θεομάχοι, Acts 5:39, RNAB). Throughout much of Acts, the narrator also directs a caustic irony bordering on sarcasm and mockery against inappropriate pagan responses to signs and wonders of Jesus' followers, but since this is based on the motif of misunderstanding, it will be treated under that rubric (e.g., see Acts 8:18–24; 14:11–18; 19:15). Let us test how specific examples of irony in Luke-Acts function as implicit commentary to the audience.

THE SHARING OF HIDDEN KNOWLEDGE BETWEEN DEMONIC FORCES AND READERS

Demonic Knowledge of Jesus as "Son of God"

An irony that the Gospel of Luke shares with the other Synoptic Gospels is that demonic forces recognize Jesus as Messiah and Son of God before most human participants in the story are aware of that truth. While human observers of Jesus' actions are acclaiming him as a prophet, devils are "proclaiming" Jesus by his true identity. In Luke 4:31–35, after the people at Nazareth had rejected Jesus' claim to be the Messiah anointed by the Holy Spirit (4:18–19), a demon in Capernaum accosts Jesus: "I know who you are—the Holy One of God" (4:34, RNAB). The readers know that the demon is correct, even though the observers in the story who see Jesus silencing it do not realize this, but are only amazed at his display of power (4:36). Only a few verses later, the narrator again shows Jesus being recognized by demons and forbidding them to speak: "And demons also came out from many, shouting, 'You are the Son of God.' But he rebuked them and did not allow them to speak because they knew that he was the Messiah" (4:41, RNAB). By showing that the demons know Jesus as Son of God and Messiah, the narrator gives the audience a sense of being privy to inside, even supernatural, information not shared by the people of Capernaum.

Acts 16:17—Spirits' Knowledge of Paul as "Servant of God"

The "we" narrator in Acts 16 reports a similar ironic situation of demonic witness to the true identity of Jesus' followers. In Philippi a slave girl with an oracular spirit keeps following "Paul and us" and proclaiming, "these people are servants of the most high God, who proclaim to you the way of salvation" (Acts 16:17). After several days of this, Paul in annoyance expels the spirit from her. From its inside perspective, the audience realizes that the oracular spirit's proclamation about Paul and his companions is literally true, as had been the demons' shouting about Jesus, "You are the Son of God," in Luke 4:41. Just as Jesus silenced that "confession," so Paul silences this spirit by expelling it. The similar irony in both cases confirms the audience's sense of knowing the inside story, which the original observers had missed.

IRONIC FUNCTIONS OF QUESTIONS ABOUT JESUS' IDENTITY

Questions too can have an ironic impact. When characters in the story ask questions whose answers the audience knows, the effect is reassuring for the audience. It confirms their sense of superior insight into the inner meaning of the narrated events, which eludes the original observers. For example, after Jesus calmed the storm that had terrified the disciples in the boat with him, "they were filled with awe and amazed and said to one another, 'Who then is this, who commands even the winds and the sea, and they obey him' " (Luke 8:25, RNAB).[10] The audience knows.

This is part of a series of similar questions about Jesus' identity that punctuates chapters 4–9 of the Gospel. In Luke 4:34 a demon says, "I know who you are, the Holy One of God." Two verses later (4:36), the people of Capernaum ask, "What is this word . . . he commands unclean spirits. . . . " In 5:21 the Pharisees ask, "Who can forgive sins but God alone?" In 7:39 a Pharisee thinks, "If this were a prophet, he would know who and what sort of woman this is who is touching him. . . . " In 7:49 those at table ask, "Who is this who even forgives sins?" In 8:25 the disciples ask, "Who then is this, that he commands the wind and water . . . ?" In 9:9 Herod wonders, "John I beheaded; but who is this about whom I hear such things?"[11] The effect of such a series of questions is to deepen the ironic sense of superiority of the audience over those asking the questions. Such ironic questions invite a spontaneous response like "I know who he is." The readers tend to identify with the narrator in providing the answers, thus emphasizing and deepening their own awareness of Jesus' true identity and its implications.

IRONY OF THE VINEYARD PARABLE IN LUKE 20:9–19

The parable of the vineyard and tenant farmers in Luke 20:9–19 turns on the primary irony behind the entire Lukan passion narrative and makes a good introduction to that passion irony. Although this parable is part of the tradition that the Gospel inherited and is common to all three Synoptic Gospels, the narrator's special touches highlight the Lukan ironic perspective on Jesus' death.[12]

First, the narrator specifies at the outset that Jesus speaks this parable to "the people" (i.e., of God, πρὸς τὸν λαὸν, Luke 20:9). And he ends the pericope by specifying that it is the scribes and high priests who want to seize him, "for they knew that he had addressed this parable to them" (20:19, RNAB). Thus he accentuates the public nature (in the presence of God's people) of Jesus' attack on the leaders of the people in this parable.

Second, in Jesus' mouth he varies the steps of the parable as probably found in his source so that the tenant farmers mistreat the slaves in diverse ways but slay only the owner's son. This progression and contrast emphasize the enormity of the crime of killing the son.

Third, by shifting the statement from indirect discourse in the probable Markan source to direct discourse, he has the owner echoing the exact words, "my beloved son" (20:13), that God had spoken about Jesus in Luke 3:22. He thus underscores the application of the parable to Jesus.

Fourth, differently from Mark (though as in Matthew) the tenants throw the son outside the vineyard before killing him, which corresponds to the pattern of Jesus' actual death outside the city, of the Nazareth foreshadowing of that death in Luke 4, and of the resonances to that death in Stephen's martyrdom in Acts 7.

Fifth, the narrator shows Jesus shortening the citation of Ps. 118:22 about the rejected stone to include only the pivotal contrast between the rejected stone and the keystone. Only in Luke does Jesus then specify this contrast further with the threat, "Everyone who falls on that stone will be dashed to pieces; and it will crush anyone on whom it falls" (20:18, RNAB). This corresponds to the peculiarly Lukan emphasis on the punishment of Jerusalem (Luke 13:34–35, 19:41–44, 21:5–6, 20–24, 23:28–31, Acts 6:14) and of those who rejected Jesus after his confirmation as "keystone" (Acts 3:23, 13:40–41).[13]

DIVINE WORKING THROUGH HUMAN BLINDNESS

A special emphasis of the Lukan passion account, even though it is found in the pre-Lukan traditional passion materials and in their Old Testament referents, is how God works through human blindness.[14] A particularly Lukan angle is emphasis on the Jews not recognizing the savior whom they read about in their scriptures, which recalls the motif of non-recognition and recognition (ἀναγνώρισις) in Greek literature (e.g., Homer's *Odyssey*) and drama (e.g., Sophocles' *Oedipus Rex*), as discussed in Aristotle's *Poetics*.[15] This theme of non-recognition heightens the audience's sense of irony as readers observe people in the narrative blindly fulfilling God's plan by rejecting the messengers God sends them.

Passion: Jewish Non-recognition, Fulfillment of Scriptures

Regardless of which follower of the risen Jesus is the ostensible speaker of the missionary speeches in Acts, together they function in Luke-Acts as intrinsic Lukan commentary elaborating the theological meaning of the Lukan passion account.[16] Acts 13:27 clearly articulates one of the central ironies of the passion: "The inhabitants of Jerusalem and their leaders failed to recognize [ἀγνοήσαντες] him [Jesus as Messiah], and by condemning him they fulfilled the oracles of the prophets that are read sabbath after sabbath"[17] (RNAB). This interpretation of the Lukan passion is also bolstered by the speech in Acts 3: "Now I know, brothers, that you acted out of ignorance [ἄγνοιαν], just as your leaders did; but God has thus brought to fulfillment what he had announced beforehand through the mouth of all

the prophets, that his Messiah would suffer" (Acts 3:17, RNAB).[18] The effect
of these two speeches on the audience is to ground this ironic interpretation
of the Passion in both Petrine and Pauline preaching.

Acts 2–3: Releasing a Murderer, Killing the Innocent

Another irony of the Lukan passion account underscored in the
speeches of Acts is the contrast between releasing the murderer Barabbas
and killing the innocent Jesus. In Luke 23:25 the narrator recapitulates
what he had recounted in 23:18–24: "So he released the man who had
been imprisoned for rebellion and murder, for whom they asked, and he
handed Jesus over to them to deal with as they wished" (RNAB). This
explicit contrast of Barabbas, imprisoned for murder (23:19), and Jesus, in
whom Pilate (23:14, 22) and Herod (23:15) had found no guilt, interprets
the Barabbas incident ironically.

Nonetheless, Acts 3:13–15 lays even further emphasis on this irony,
chiefly through repetition, and adds an explicitly theological interpretation. "The God of Abraham . . . has glorified his servant Jesus whom you
handed over and denied in Pilate's presence, . . . You denied the Holy and
Righteous One and asked that a murderer be released to you. The author
of life you put to death, but God raised him from the dead . . . " (RNAB).
This set of theological contrasts ironically juxtaposes the vindication of
Jesus by the God of Abraham ("their God"), with their own denial of
him. It accentuates the unrighteousness of their choice of Barabbas, a
murderer, over Jesus, the Holy and Righteous One. It finally underscores
the contradiction between their execution of the author of life (ἀρχηγὸν
τῆς ζωῆς) and God's raising him from the dead.[19] Acts 3:13–15 proclaim
that their choice and action against Jesus has been contradicted and overturned by God himself.

Luke 23:35–39: Mocking of Jesus on the Cross

All the synoptic passion accounts of the mocking of the crucified Jesus
are built on a foundation of irony. The Lukan version avoids distraction
from any other issues to focus the irony exclusively on the blindness of
diverse groups to Jesus' true identity.[20] The first group, the rulers, ironically mocks Jesus with, "let him save himself if he is the chosen one, the
Messiah of God [ὁ χριστὸς τοῦ θεοῦ ὁ ἐκλεκτός]" (23:35b, RNAB). The
audience hears the double irony in this mockery: that Jesus is truly the
savior (Luke 2:11, to be confirmed in Acts 5:30–31, 13:23); chosen one
(Luke 9:35); and God's Messiah (Luke 9:20); all of which titles the rulers
of God's people treat with unbelieving sarcasm.

The second group, the soldiers, also mock Jesus for being what the readers know he is, in this case "the king of the Jews" (23:37). The narrator intervenes at this point to call attention to the inscription, also obviously ironic, to which the soldiers' mocking relates: "This is the King of the Jews" (23:38, RNAB).

The third ironic mocking comes from one of the criminals being crucified next to Jesus. The narrator draws attention to the irony of this mockery by calling it blasphemy (ἐβλασφήμει αὐτον). And he describes the blasphemer not as one *crucified* but as *hung* (κρεμασθέντων), which bears intertextual allusions to the curse of Deut. 21:23, "cursed by God is everyone hung on a tree" (πᾶς κρεμάμενος ἐπὶ ξύλου). The speeches in Acts 5:30 and 10:39 confirm the Deuteronomic curse allusions here. Both speeches describe Jesus' crucifixion in undoubtedly Deuteronomic language as "hanging him on a tree" (κρεμάσαντες ἐπὶ ξύλου). Thus, not only is there verbal irony in the criminal mocking Jesus as Messiah. There is also dramatic irony in one who is himself cursed blaspheming someone else. The narrator shows the other criminal explicating this irony: a cursed person is hardly in a position to blaspheme someone else, especially when he is "subject to the same condemnation" (Luke 23:40, RNAB) and when his condemnation, unlike Jesus', is justly deserved (23:41).

Acts 7: Double Rejection of Moses and the Prophet Like Moses

Perhaps the most forceful picture of human blindness ironically furthering God's plan is the Lukan pattern of the rejection of Jesus—not just once, but twice. This double rejection by God's people of the man sent to save that people structures the Mosaic core of the Stephen speech in Acts 7.[21] The speech as a whole applies the Lukan pattern of periodization (as in Luke 21) to God's history of saving his people, from Abraham through Moses to the killing of the prophets.[22] It introduces this Moses section in Acts 7:17–43 as the time of promised salvation: "When the time [χρόνος] drew near for the fulfillment of the promise that God had pledged to Abraham . . ." (7:17, RNAB). At the time of Pharaoh's oppression, Moses is born and (ironically) raised by Pharaoh's daughter (7:20–22). The speech applies the pattern of periodization to Moses' life, divided into periods of forty years. Moses' first rejection came "when the time [χρόνος] of the fortieth year was fulfilled [ἐπληροῦτο] for him" (7:23, literal translation). When Moses tried to help the Hebrews, "He assumed [his] kinsfolk would understand that God was offering them deliverance [σωτηρίαν] through him, but they did not understand" (7:25, RNAB), and he fled to Midian from the charge of murder (7:28–29).

"And when forty years were fulfilled [Καὶ πληρωθέντων ἐτῶν τεσσερ-

ἄκοντα]" (7:30, literal translation) an angel appeared to him in the burning bush, sending him back a second time to save his oppressed people
(7:30–34). Stephen, the narrator within the story, underlines the irony of
this situation: "This Moses, whom they had rejected with the words,
'Who appointed you ruler and judge?' God sent as [both] ruler and deliverer . . . " (7:35, RNAB). After recounting Moses' saving wonders and signs
(7:36), he lays the foundation for applying that same ironic pattern to
Jesus: "It was this Moses who said to the Israelites, 'God will raise up
[ἀναστήσει] for you, from among your own kinsfolk, a prophet like me' "
(7:37, RNAB). The speech goes on to recount the people's second rejection
of Moses in Acts 7:39–41 and God's consequent rejection of them (7:42–
43, citing Amos 5:25–27 LXX).

The double rejection of Jesus (the prophet like Moses of Acts 7:37) had
already been presented in Peter's speech after the healing in Acts 3:22–23:
"For Moses said, 'A prophet like me will the Lord, your God, raise up
[ἀναστήσει] for you from among your own kinsmen. . . . Everyone who
does not listen to that prophet will be cut off from the people" (RNAB). The
speeches of Acts 2–3 had already accused the people of Jerusalem of
rejecting Jesus once at his crucifixion.

Acts 3 and 7 also threaten that those who reject Jesus, the resurrected
prophet like Moses (a second time), will be cut off from the people, as
those who rejected Moses (a second time) in the desert had been cut off to
die there. By echoing the same prophecy of Deut. 18:15 that Acts 3:22–
23 had cited, about the prophet like Moses who will be "raised up," Acts
7:37–43 clearly alludes to the identical pattern of double rejection experienced by Moses (Acts 7) and by Jesus (Acts 3). God's plan continues to
accommodate ironically the pattern of his people's incredible blindness,
even to their double rejection both of Moses and the prophet like
Moses.[23]

LUKE 24:15–24: IRONY ABOUT JESUS IN THE EMMAUS INCIDENT

The irony of the Emmaus story is a striking example of the Lukan use
of the literary and dramatic motif of recognition (ἀναγνώρισις).[24] Just as
the pathos of the Joseph narrative in Genesis is heightened by showing his
brothers speaking about Joseph to the unrecognized Joseph, and Joseph's
weeping response (Gen. 44:18–45:3), so the pathos of the Emmaus story
is heightened by showing the disciples despairingly talking about Jesus to
the unrecognized Jesus (Luke 24:19–24). Though the disciples are
astounded at the incognito Jesus' "ignorance" of events at Jerusalem
(Luke 24:18), they are actually the ignorant ones (24:25).[25] Only with the
recognition scenes do Joseph's brothers and the disciples at Emmaus come

to share the knowledge of the hero's identity that the narrator and audience have all along.

THE IRONY OF SCATTERING AS SPREADING THE WORD

An ironic theme in Acts, which plays a major role in its plot structuring, is that persecuting attempts to suppress God's word lead to the spread of that word.[26] This theme is a major instance of the Lukan motif of reversal—God reverses or overrules human attempts to control history—and is a natural occasion for irony.[27] One of the strongest such ironies in Acts is that the persecution associated with Saul occasions the spread of Christianity, eventually to Antioch, where the converted Paul is summoned (coming full circle) to minister to Christians. Acts structures this theme in three steps: Acts 8:1, 3–5; 11:19–20; and 11:25–26.

First Step: Acts 8:1, 3–5—Scattering of Disciples

The beginning of the scattering of Christians takes place in the persecution related to Stephen's death. The narrator had gone out of his way to mention first the presence, then the consent, of "a young man named Saul" (Acts 7:58b, RNAB) in Stephen's stoning (7:58; 8:1). Thus he prepares to include Saul's persecuting activity (8:3) in the context of the persecution related to Stephen (8:1).

The narrator's selection of events results in an ironic pattern: scattering of disciples leads to spread of the word. First, on the day of Stephen's death a great persecution of the church in Jerusalem broke out, in which all but the apostles were scattered (διεσπάρησαν, 8:1b) through the regions of Judea and Samaria. This pattern has resonances with Jesus' prophecy in Acts 1:8, that "you will be my witnesses in Jerusalem, throughout Judea and Samaria, and to the ends of the earth" (RNAB). But the prophecy is fulfilled in an unexpected way, not through the apostles to whom Jesus spoke in Acts 1:8, but through all those *except the apostles* (8:1b) who were scattered from Jerusalem.[28]

Second, right after mentioning in Acts 8:3 that Saul was ravaging the church in Jerusalem, the narrator makes a summary statement that the resulting refugees evangelized: "Now those [Οἱ μὲν] who had been scattered [διασπαρέντες] went about preaching the word" (8:4, RNAB). In 8:5–13, 26–40 this summary leads directly into scenes showing the evangelizing activity of Philip (Φίλιππος δὲ, correlative to the Οἱ μὲν in 8:4) as one of those scattered. Interspersed in 8:14–25 into the narrative of Philip's activity is the account of the apostles in Jerusalem confirming Philip's work and of the confrontation between Simon Peter and Simon Magus. Finally, the narrator completes his framing of the Philip accounts by the persecutions of Saul. Besides his preface of the Philip material by a summary of Saul's persecution in Acts 8:3, he now returns his attention from Philip to Saul in 9:1: "Now Saul ['Ο δὲ Σαῦλος], still breathing murderous threats against the disciples . . . " (RNAB).

Second Step: Acts 11:19–21—Word to Greeks by the Scattering

The next step in the ironic spread of the church through the Stephen persecution (in which Saul played a role) is the carrying of the word to Antioch in Acts 11:19. A good many events have been recounted since the expansion of the word through Philip in Acts 8. The arch-persecutor Saul has been changed by the risen Lord into a preacher of the word (9:1–30). With the return of peace to the church (9:31), the apostle Peter leaves Jerusalem for the coast, which results in healings and the conversion of the first Gentiles, the household of Cornelius (9:32–11:18).

The narrator calls explicit attention to the fact that he is resuming a progression of events that he had temporarily interrupted, by again referring to the refugees from the Stephen persecution: "Now those who had been scattered [Οἱ μὲν οὖν διασπαρέντες] by the persecution that arose because of Stephen went as far as Phoenicia, Cyprus, and Antioch, preaching the word . . . " (11:19, RNAB). The catchword *scattered* (διασπαρέντες, which is related to the important theological term *diaspora*) returns to punctuate this series of episodes (Acts 8:1, 4; 11:19).[29]

The scattering that began in Acts 8 has brought the word of the Lord the next ironic step, all the way to Syrian Antioch. Although originally those who were scattered preached only to Jews (11:19b), now some come to Antioch preaching to the Greeks as well. The narrator has just finished the theological preparation for this move to the Gentiles with the Peter-Cornelius narratives in 10:1–11:18. Like the first outreach to Samaritans, which was begun by Philip and only confirmed by the original apostles coming from Jerusalem, this outreach to Greeks at Antioch is initiated not by the apostles but by Cypriots and Cyrenians. Only when news of this successful mission to Greeks reaches Jerusalem does the mother church there send a delegate, Barnabas, to confirm the developments in Antioch.[30]

Third Step: Acts 11:25–26—Saul the Scatterer's Full Circle

Thus the stage is set for the final ironic step in the progression. The man whom Barnabas brings to Antioch to minister to the new disciples, who were converted by those scattered in that original persecution, is none other than the arch-persecutor himself turned preacher, Paul! We have witnessed an ironic full circle: from Saul's persecution, to the scattering of disciples, to the word reaching Greek converts in Antioch, to Paul being brought to minister to them. The irony of this divine reversal of misguided human attempts, which is shared among narrator and audience behind the backs of the actors, is exquisite.

ACTS 5:39: GAMALIEL'S IRONY: "LEST WE BE FIGHTING GOD [θεομάχοι]"

Another ironic statement that plays a major role in the plotting of Acts is that by Gamaliel in Acts 5:39. In a major showdown between the Sanhedrin and the apostles, Gamaliel addresses to the Sanhedrin his ironically prophetic advice to wait and let Christianity fail of its own lack of inspiration: "For if this endeavor or this activity is of human origin, it will destroy itself. But if it comes from God, you will not be able to destroy them; you may even find yourselves fighting against God [θεομάχοι]" (5:38–39, RNAB).

The striking irony in this quasi-official statement by a leading Pharisee in the Sanhedrin is reminiscent of a similar irony in the high priest's prophetic statement in John 11:49–53. As the Sanhedrin in Acts worried about trying to stop the preaching, signs, and success of the apostles, so the council in John 11 had similar concerns about Jesus. Caiaphas's ironic prophecy about Jesus dying for the nation has a Christian meaning (which the Johannine narrator makes explicit) that is almost the opposite of his intended meaning. The narrator in Acts also shows Gamaliel ironically speaking the opposite of his intentions, but leaves the irony implicit. The later attempts by Jews to check the work of the apostles and of Paul all prove ultimately fruitless. Since in the narrator's point of view God is clearly behind the apostles' efforts, they ultimately show themselves to be doing that which Gamaliel warned them against: fighting against God [θεομάχοι]. By this irony, the narrator supplies implicit commentary: actions against the apostles are actions against God.[31]

ACTS 19:15 THE NARRATOR'S MOCKING OF THE JEWISH EXORCISTS

Another important kind of implicit commentary through irony in Acts is the narrator's mocking treatment of opponents and competitors of Christianity (e.g., Acts 19:15). When the Jewish exorcists try to make magical use of the name of Jesus for exorcisms, the narrator makes them look foolish by describing the evil spirit stripping and beating them. To this implicit commentary on the folly of magic, the narrator adds an account of how fear caused by this episode prompted many who had practiced magic in Ephesus to burn their magic books (Acts 19:17–20). Without actually preaching directly to his audience about the folly of magic, the narrator could hardly make his point more unmistakable.[32]

Misunderstanding

Misunderstanding by Lukan Narrator in Conflicting Views from Jesus?

In a perceptive but maverick book, James M. Dawsey argues that the voices in the Gospel of Luke for Jesus and the narrator are quite distinct.[33] Through close reading of the Greek text, he demonstrates the different vocabulary and level of Greek between sections attributed to Jesus and those attributed to the narrator.[34] He finds that these linguistic differences correspond to theological differences between Jesus and the narrator.[35] He explains these differences by attributing to the Lukan author the use of what amounts to an "unreliable narrator," whose views do not represent the author's but contradict the views of both Jesus and the implied author, for whom only Jesus in the text speaks. As Stephen D. Moore objects, "To my knowledge, the view of Scholes and Kellogg, that the unreliable narrator is 'quite uncharacteristic of primitive or ancient narrative,' has never been seriously contested. . . . Does Dawsey realize just how revolutionary his casting of the Lukan narrator as unreliable is? He presents us with a narrative technique and a matching audience response almost two millennia out of time."[36] In Dawsey's defense, one can point to a few unreliable narrators in ancient literature, as in some of Lucian's satires and in *The Golden Ass* by Apuleius. But the unreliability of the narrator is evident from the ironic genre in which such works are written. To find such an unreliable narrator in a serious Gospel narrative surely does seem anachronistic and beyond belief.[37]

However, it is not enough merely to rule out Dawsey's thesis a priori. One can also point to internal evidence for which his thesis cannot account. The main deficiency in this thesis is that it fails to explain the Lukan use of the same narrator(s) in Acts as in the Gospel, and the confirmation and continuation by the narrator in Acts of the point of view of the Gospel narrator.[38] Moreover, Acts has no countering voice of Jesus to provide the author's perspective, such as Dawsey finds in the Gospel. The speeches of Peter, Stephen, and Paul do not depart from the narrator's voice, style, and point of view the way the sayings of Jesus in the Gospel do. The undeniable differences Dawsey finds between the voices each of Jesus and of the Gospel narrator can be attributed rather to

both the traditional collection of sayings of Jesus on which his speeches
are based and to the careful *prosopopoeia* used to distinguish the utter-
ances of all the characters in Luke and Acts.[39]

Moreover, the theological worldview of the narrator with its concern
for eschatological periodization is consistently confirmed in Acts, especially through promise-fulfillment links between the Gospel and Acts. It
is no surprise to find a tension between the point of view found in sayings
attributed to the historical Jesus, which reflect his preresurrection perspective, and the postresurrection point of view of the narrator. Yet since
both the narrator and Jesus are undoubtedly treated as reliable in Luke-
Acts, one cannot simply choose between them as Dawsey does, but one
must study the results of their interplay. In effect, the Gospel presents
both the preresurrection views attributed to Jesus and the postresurrection perspective of the narrator and his audience. They mutually interpret
each other, rather than the one cancelling out the other.

Dawsey especially contrasts the periodization of history in the Lukan
narrator with the earthly Jesus' imminent expectation of God's kingdom.[40] A few examples can show rather how foreshadowings and
promises in the speech in Luke 21, which so explicitly features eschatological periodization, are shown by the narrator of Acts to have their
fulfillment in the events it reports. The promise of Jesus in Luke 21:18 for
the period of persecution, that "not a hair on your head will be destroyed" (θρὶξ ἐκ τῆς κεφαλῆς ὑμῶν οὐ μὴ ἀπόληται, RNAB), is echoed by
Paul to others on board during the storm in Acts 27:34: "Not a hair of the
head of anyone of you will be destroyed" (οὐδενὸς γὰρ ὑμῶν θρὶξ ἀπὸ τῆς
κεφαλῆς ἀπολεῖται). Jesus' promise that when the cosmic signs occur at
the end of time "then they will see the Son of Man coming in a cloud with
power and great glory" (Luke 21:27, RNAB), finds resonance with the
narrator's account of Jesus' ascension in Acts: "a cloud took him from
their sight. . . . 'This Jesus . . . will return in the same way as you have
seen him going into heaven.' " (Acts 1:9, 11, RNAB). Jesus' promise in
Luke 21:15 for the period of persecution—"I myself shall give you a
wisdom in speaking that all your adversaries will be powerless to resist or
refute" (RNAB)—is presented by the narrator as partially fulfilled in Stephen's debates in Acts—"they could not withstand the wisdom and the
spirit with which he spoke" (Acts 6:10, RNAB).

Thus, although Dawsey has documented differences in point of view
between Jesus and the narrator in the Lukan Gospel, one does not have to
accept his further thesis that the narrator's point of view represents misunderstanding, because the narrator is unreliable. Rather, the preresurrection perspective found in the remembered and collected sayings of Jesus

incorporated in Luke's Gospel is complemented by the postresurrection perspective of the narrator of both Luke and Acts.

ACTS 3:17–18: IGNORANCE THEME AND MISUNDERSTANDING

A major theme in both Luke and Acts that does indeed illuminate the motif of misunderstanding is that of ignorance (ἄγνοια), programmatically expressed in Acts 3:17–18: "Now I know, brothers, that you acted out of ignorance, just as your leaders did; but God has thus brought to fulfillment what he had announced beforehand through the mouth of all the prophets, that his Messiah would suffer" (RNAB). God used the ignorance of the people and leaders of Jerusalem to fulfill his biblical prophecies. Acts 13:27–33, Paul's inaugural sermon to diaspora Jews at Antioch of Pisidia, develops this ignorance theme further under the form of nonrecognition: "The inhabitants of Jerusalem and their leaders failed to recognize [ἀγνοήσαντες] him, and by condemning him they fulfilled the oracles of the prophets that are read sabbath after sabbath" (13:27, RNAB). Acts 17:30, part of Paul's speech at Athens, extends the ignorance theme beyond the Jews to the Gentiles: "God has overlooked the times of ignorance [χρόνους τῆς ἀγνοίας], but now he demands that all people everywhere repent . . . " (RNAB).[41]

In all three cases, a time of ignorance, in which the Jews sinned by rejecting their Messiah and the Gentiles sinned by their idolatry, is coming to an end in the preaching of Peter and Paul. God wants to forgive actions done in ignorance, but once that ignorance is dissipated by the apostolic preaching of the word of the Lord, judgment awaits those who fail to repent (cf. Acts 17:31 and 3:19, 22–23).

One would not expect such an extensive theme of ignorance to appear in Acts without grounding in Luke's Gospel. With several scholars I argue that the ignorance theme in Acts is in fact introduced in Luke's Gospel by Jesus' word of forgiveness on the cross in Luke 23:34: "Father, forgive them, they know not [οὐ γὰρ οἴδασιν] what they do" (RNAB). This argument requires accepting the authenticity of that disputed verse, despite the strong early manuscript evidence against it.[42]

MISCELLANEOUS EXAMPLES OF MISUNDERSTANDING MOTIF IN LUKE AND ACTS

Besides the structural theme of ignorance, the several individual examples of misunderstanding that are sprinkled throughout Luke and Acts attest to Lukan awareness and use of this motif in ordinary narration. Brief mention of these suffices to validate that Luke-Acts does employ the misunderstanding motif, even though it is more subtle and implicit than the Johannine usage.

In the programmatic Nazareth scene, which grounds Jesus' ministry and death in his identity and prophesied destiny, the narrator contrasts Jesus' explicit claims to be Spirit-anointed Messiah in Luke 4:18–21 with the Nazarenes' misunderstanding of his identity—"Isn't this the son of Joseph?" (4:22, RNAB). The narrator thus implies that the knowledge of the audience about Jesus' true identity is superior to that of even contemporaries from his home town. Not only does the narrator give to the readers inside knowledge of Jesus' true identity (Luke 1:31–35, 3:23, 38), he confirms that knowledge by the testimony of superhuman witnesses immediately after the Nazareth scene. Despite the ignorance of Jesus' identity by his Nazareth neighbors in 4:22, the demon in Capernaum affirms, "I know who you are—the Holy One of God!" (4:34b, RNAB). The demons whom he expels later that day acclaim, "You are the Son of God" (4:41a, RNAB), to which the narrator adds, "But he . . . did not allow them to speak because they knew that he was the Messiah" (4:41b, RNAB). By his own evidence and by angelic and demonic testimony, the narrator identifies Jesus as both Son of God and Messiah and asserts the functional identity of the two titles (4:41).[43]

Not even Jesus' disciples are immune to human misunderstanding about his identity and destiny. Although Luke omits the Markan charge against Peter as the "satan" who thinks the thoughts of humans, not of God (Mark 8:33), he nevertheless reveals the disciples' continual ignorance after Jesus' second passion prediction: "But they did not understand this saying; its meaning was hidden from them so that they should not understand it, and they were afraid to ask him about this saying" (Luke 9:45, RNAB). Not only does he mention their misunderstanding, but he invokes divine causality for it, in addition to their understandable human fear to comprehend it.[44]

Closely related to the motif of misunderstanding is a traditional statement of Jesus appearing in both Matt. 11:25 and Luke 10:21: "I give you praise, Father . . . for although you have hidden these things from the wise and the learned you have revealed them to the childlike" (Luke 10:21, RNAB). Already the tradition of the sayings of Jesus features the motif of hidden revelation and the distinction between one group that understands and another that does not. This suggests that the misunderstanding motif is both quite early and widespread in Christianity and not distinctive to Luke-Acts.[45]

A more specifically Lukan use of this motif, however, appears at the end of Jesus' farewell address in Luke 22:38. The narrator makes it obvious that when Jesus announces a reversal of his earlier instructions to bring not only a money bag but a sword, the disciples misunderstand him by taking him literally (22:36, 38). Since this misunderstanding ends Jesus' farewell address, it is reminiscent of Socratic dialogues like the *Phaedo*, in which Socrates ends his farewell address to his disciples on a note of their misunderstanding.[46] Jesus' rebuke when his disciples shortly afterwards use a sword against those coming to arrest him accentuates their misunderstanding (22:49–51).

The misunderstanding motif is also closely related to the recognition motif discussed previously, as in the Emmaus story at Luke 24:16–26, in which the disciples' eyes are blinded from recognizing Jesus. It also relates to the disciples mistaking the risen Jesus for a ghost in Luke 24:39. In the Lukan resurrection account of chapter 24, the disciples throughout have a hard time grasping the risen reality of Jesus, even if they recognize him. The narrator's focus on this difficulty makes an important point, reminding readers who take the postresurrection viewpoint for granted about the uniqueness and mysteriousness of the resurrection event.[47]

Acts reverts to more commonplace uses of the misunderstanding motif. In Acts 1:6, the disciples ask the risen Jesus whether at this time he would restore the kingdom to Israel. Because of what the narrator has taught the audience during the passion narrative about the nonpolitical nature of God's kingdom, this question allows them the sense of having superior insight to that of Jesus' disciples. He shows Jesus again correcting the desire "to know the times or seasons that the Father has established by his own authority" (Acts 1:7, RNAB). Instead, Jesus directs their attention to the coming of the Holy Spirit and their mission to witness to him throughout the world.

Another misunderstanding of facts obvious to the audience occurs in the Pentecost story in Acts 2:13 and 15, in which Peter rebuts the charge that the apostles are drunk. Because the mistake is so obvious to readers, the narrator's mention of it functions primarily to remind them of the mysteriousness and extraordinary nature of the Pentecost phenomena for those who are exposed to them for the first time. Christians can get so used to talking about the resurrection and manifestations of the Spirit that they can forget how incredible these things appear to outsiders who do not share their faith.

A final example of misunderstanding in Acts occurs not in the main narrative but in Stephen's story within a story in Acts 7:25. As Stephen recounts the life of Moses, he portrays the people's misunderstanding of Moses in ways that clearly parallel their misunderstanding of Jesus, which does pertain to the principal narrative of Acts. Stephen relates of Moses: "He assumed [his] kinsfolk would understand that God was offering them deliverance through him, but they did not understand" (7:25,

RNAB). He later recalls the incident, underlining its importance as an instance of the people of God rejecting their savior: "This Moses, whom they had rejected with the words, 'Who appointed you ruler and judge?' God sent as [both] ruler and deliverer . . . " (7:35, RNAB). This motif applied to Moses' career functions as a figure for similar misunderstanding of Jesus, especially through the link between Moses and Jesus made by the quotation of Deut. 18:15 later in Stephen's speech in Acts 7:37.[48]

ACTS' MOCKERY AND POLEMIC AGAINST MAGIC AND PAGAN MISUNDERSTANDING

Another major application of the misunderstanding motif appears in Acts, where the narrator engages in a major polemic against all forms of magic and against pagan misunderstanding of Christian phenomena.[49] One set of scenes mocks magicians and barbarians who utterly misunderstand Christian signs and wonders. Another extends the polemic even to cultured Greek philosophers and Roman rulers, but without the satire used against magicians and the superstitious.

The first of the mockery scenes, in Acts 8:18–24, ridicules the attempt by Simon the magician to buy the apostolic power to confer the Holy Spirit. Peter excoriates him "because you thought that you could buy the gift of God with money" (8:20, RNAB). After Simon begs them to intercede for him that he be spared the threatened punishment, the narrator has made his point against magic and does not even bother to report whether Simon is punished or spared.

The second scene in which the narrator mocks misunderstanding of Christian signs and wonders occurs in Acts 14:11–18, where, after Paul heals a lame man, the barbarian Lycaonians ignorantly proclaim Barnabas and Paul to be the gods Zeus and Hermes, respectively. He pictures the ridiculous scene of the priest of Zeus bringing oxen and garlands to offer sacrifice to them. In response to this nonsense, he portrays Barnabas and Paul tearing their garments and preaching that the one true God will no longer permit the Gentiles' idolatrous ways: "Even with these words, they scarcely restrained the crowds from offering sacrifice to them" (14:18, RNAB). Yet in the very next verse, the narrator portrays the incredible fickleness of the crowd. Because of the instigation of Jews from Antioch and Iconium, after almost worshipping him the crowd "stoned Paul and dragged him out of the city" (14:19, RNAB).[50] The narrator plays on the added irony that they do to Paul what Paul himself had approved doing to Stephen in Acts 7:58 and 8:1.

A third major mockery of barbarian ignorance occurs in Acts 28:4–6, where the barbarians on the island of Malta misunderstand Paul's fate. The narrator portrays the natives' reaction to seeing the snake dangling from Paul's hand: "This man must certainly be a murderer; though he escaped the sea, Justice has not let him remain alive" (28:4, RNAB). Then, after humorously picturing them waiting in vain for Paul to swell up and fall dead, he recounts their astonishing reversal of opinion: "they changed their minds and began to say that he was a god" (28:6, RNAB). In these two scenes of natives' reactions to Paul's signs, the narrator uses caustic satire against barbarian superstition, which sharply contrasts with his usual reverence for Jewish religious sensitivities, practices, and beliefs.[51]

The Lukan polemic, however, extends beyond magicians and barbarians to include even cultured Greeks and Romans, such as the philosophers at Athens and the Roman procurator Festus. In Acts 17:18, the narrator shows even the Epicurean and Stoic philosophers misunderstanding Paul's message, thinking that he was preaching foreign deities named "Jesus" and "Anastasis" (Resurrection). He has already hinted that his estimation of them is not especially high by his comment when introducing this episode: "While Paul was waiting for them in Athens, he grew exasperated at the sight of the city full of idols" (17:16, RNAB). In the narrator's ideological point of view, idolaters do not get high marks for understanding, even when they are philosophers. Their "Anastasis" blunder is a case in point and allows the Lukan audience to feel superior in knowledge even to Greek philosophers.[52]

Despite the frequent scholarly assertion that Acts apologetically portrays Roman officials in the best possible light, the Lukan narrator does not spare even a Roman official as exalted as Festus from his polemic use of the misunderstanding motif. That motif enables him to allow his intended Christian audience to bask in their comprehension, which is seen as superior to that of the procurator Festus. Even more injurious to the apologetic interpretation of Acts is that the narrator represents the knowledge of Festus as decidedly inferior even to that of the Herodian Agrippa. He shows that Paul's whole christological apology is addressed to Agrippa, and when Festus interrupts with his exclamation, "You are mad, Paul; much learning is driving you mad" (26:24, RNAB), Paul retorts: "The king knows about these matters . . . " (26:26, RNAB).[53] Of course his audience is meant to see this as even more true of themselves.[54]

CLIMAX OF MOTIF OF MISUNDERSTANDING: ISA. 6:9–10 IN ACTS 28:26–28

At the end and climax of Acts (28:26–28), the narrator turns a final time to the motif of misunderstanding, taken now to the ultimate extreme of blindness. The form that the motif takes in this passage is solidly grounded in the Gospel traditions, appearing in John 12:40 and in all the Synoptics (between the parable of the sower and its explanation in Luke 8:10 and parallels, and in Luke 19:42, where Jesus weeps over Jerusalem because salvation "has been hidden from your eyes"). In all these Gospel passages, the motif is usually expressed by citing or alluding to Isa. 6:9–10, thus grounding it in God's saving plan and word. A related point is made by Acts 13:40–41, a passage based on a similar text in Hab. 1:5 LXX.

In Acts 28:26–28, with little advance warning, the narrator shows Paul solemnly quoting to the leaders of the Roman Jews the entire passage from Isa. 6:9–10:

> Go to this people and say:
> You shall indeed hear but not understand.
> You shall indeed look but never see.
> Gross is the heart of this people;
> they will not hear with their ears;
> they have closed their eyes,
> so they may not see with their eyes
> and hear with their ears
> and understand with their heart and be converted,
> and I heal them.
>
> (Acts 28:26–27, RNAB)

Before this the narrator shows Paul witnessing to the Jews during his house arrest and trying to persuade them about Jesus from the Law and the Prophets. He shows a mixed Jewish reaction: some were persuaded, others disbelieved. Paul gives his final statement from Isa. 6:9–10 as the leaders begin to leave without reaching agreement about his message. Real readers like contemporary commentators have often struggled with the apparent disproportion between the mixed reception of Roman Jews and Paul's apparent Isaianic rejection of the Jews in favor of the more receptive Gentiles (28:28)[55] This extensive quotation from such a damning Old Testament text seems to close Luke-Acts with a clear rejection of Jews for their blindness.[56] Tannehill interprets it as indicating Paul's assumption of the role of Isaiah, to deliver Isaiah's ironic and tragic message to his people.[57]

Whether or not this rejection of the Jews and adoption of the Gentiles should be considered the definitive position of the author of Luke-Acts, it clearly marks an emphatic application of a biblical form of the misunderstanding motif to the Lukan plot. It grounds that motif in God's prophetic warning not to close one's eyes, ears, and heart to God's word. It also provides an explanation for the disturbing failure of Christianity among so many of the Jewish people of God to whom this salvation was originally promised. Christian mining of Isa. 6:9–10 to explain Jewish rejection of Jesus goes back to the earliest tradition of Christian use of the Old Testament.[58] By quoting the passage in full at the end of his two-volume work, the narrator of Luke-Acts emphatically endorses that tradition and makes it his own.

The last six chapters have applied narrative-critical approaches especially to how Luke and Acts are narrated, including the narrator's use of implicit commentary through irony and the motif of misunderstanding. The focus has been on how Luke-Acts works as a narrative. The concluding Part 4 will first address how the narrative approaches are affected when Luke-Acts is read as a specific kind of narrative, *biblical* narrative. What special emphases and limits does a canonical treatment of Luke and Acts bring to treating them as narrative? What effect does their status as part of Christian scripture have on how Christians read the narrative they contain?

4

Conclusions:
Luke-Acts
as Scripture

10 Luke and Acts as Canonical

Our treatment of Luke-Acts as narrative has differed significantly from "Bible as Literature" approaches found in some state and secular universities and high schools. As Powell remarks, "The emphasis in courses taught at secular institutions is normally on studying the Bible as literature *instead of* as Scripture. . . . [By contrast, here] The intention is to read the Bible as Scripture in story form."[1] Reading the Bible as *biblical* narrative entails a dimension beyond that of a purely literary approach, as has been implied throughout our treatment and those of most narrative critics of scripture. It is time to make explicit some of the implications of that biblical dimension.

The following factors especially seem to necessitate modifications of purely literary approaches to the Lukan two-volume narrative when it is read as part of the Christian Bible. (1) Since interpretation is always context dependent, the absorption of Luke and Acts into a wider context and into the new and different canonical structure of the New Testament, namely Fourfold Gospel and Apostles, affects their interpretation. (2) As part of the (later) Christian Bible, Luke and Acts have expanded implied readership and a different setting than when originally written. (3) As part of a larger biblical totality, Luke and Acts are read within the full biblical historiographical sweep from Genesis to Revelation, as part of the Holy Book, and in light of the tradition and life of the church. (4) Assessing Luke and Acts as part of the Christian Bible has an unavoidably harmonizing effect, as it is interpreted alongside other canonical perspectives. (5) Read as parts of the whole New Testament revelation, Luke and Acts cannot be simply treated in distinction and tension (or even contradiction) to other parts, such as the Pauline letters or other Gospels. The unavoidable unifying and harmonizing effects of canon lead to concentrating more on complementarity than on contradiction in relating Luke and Acts to other books of the New Testament. (6) Christian readers of Luke and Acts from later times and different places often have to read particular issues or incidents as examples or types for the analogous situations of this expanded readership. These factors will provide the framework of our treatment of Luke-Acts as a biblical work.

LUKE AND ACTS IN BIBLICAL AND CHRISTIAN CONTEXT

The reception of Luke and Acts into the Christian canon broadens the context in which they are interpreted beyond their limited, original first-century context. Since interpretation is heavily context dependent, the expanded context from canonical inclusion affects and changes the interpretive questions brought to bear on Luke and Acts.[2]

As Luke-Acts is subsumed into the later canonical context of the Christian Bible, the two-volume totality that is Luke-Acts becomes separated into Luke and Acts, which are respectively subsumed into different sections of the larger canonical whole of the New Testament: Luke into the four Gospels section, Acts into the Apostles section (with the Gospel of John intervening between them). Therefore, the intrinsic concerns and evidence of Luke and Acts are no longer viewed primarily in relation to each other, but within a different canonical structure (Part 1, Gospels: Matthew, Mark, Luke, John; Part 2, Apostles: Acts, letters, Revelation), and in a context of far wider concerns, and using the evidence of many other documents.

BEYOND ORIGINAL IMPLIED READERS AND HISTORICAL SITUATION

The presence of Luke and Acts within the canon of the Christian Bible therefore relativizes the importance of the original implied readers. The original implied readers are deduced from the text read in its first-century context, which historical criticism helps to understand. Since canonization of Luke and Acts broadens the context in which they are read, this cannot fail to affect the role, importance, and range of their implied readers. As components of the New Testament, which is translated into most languages of any age, Luke and Acts are now meant to be read by Christians of virtually all ages and cultures, not just by first-century Christians proficient in Greek. As parts of the canonical book of the church, Luke and Acts become texts for Christian worship, prayer, belief, theology, and practice. Such uses would seem to far surpass any original expectations the writer may have had for them, although Luke-Acts actually does contain indications that its intent is to extend the biblical history up to the events concerning Jesus and the incipient church.[3] If that is true, it is not a huge further step for Luke and Acts to become part of the Bible itself.

Similar points can be made about how canonizing Luke and Acts relativizes the importance of the original situation for which they are destined. If at first Luke and Acts were intended primarily to be used in the same contexts as the books of Samuel, Kings, Chronicles, and Maccabees (earlier biblical histories), their life setting would seem to be the life of the early church, especially its worship and catechesis. Once Luke and Acts are part of the New Testament of the Christian Bible, their life setting reaches beyond the original one to include all the contemporary Christian uses of scripture.

PART OF A LARGER TOTALITY, NOT COMPLETE BY ITSELF

Reading the account of Luke-Acts as biblical adds a further perspective beyond a study devoted solely to its narrative features. Despite the lack of closure that many find in the ending of Acts, and the search by some for a third volume beyond Acts, Luke-Acts can be investigated as a completed narrative unity, without reference to the rest of the New Testament except perhaps those documents that provide evidence for Lukan sources or insight into the history it narrates.[4]

Reading Luke-Acts as biblical, however, implies reading it as part of the historiographical sweep of the Bible from its Genesis foundations to the eschatological expectations of Luke 21 and Revelation. It implies reading it in dialogue with the other three Gospels for what it tells us about the life, death, resurrection, and identity of Jesus. It implies reading it with awareness of the tradition of Pauline letters and their insights into the protagonist of the second part of Acts.

Seen as part of the Christian Bible, Luke and Acts become part of the larger context, not only of the Holy Book, but of Christian tradition and the life and history of the church. They appear in pericope form in the church's lectionary for worship. They undergird church sacramental practice, as in the Eucharist and baptism and confirmation and orders. They nourish the personal prayer life of believers of all centuries and nationalities and cultures.

HARMONIZATION OF LUKAN
AND OTHER CANONICAL PERSPECTIVES

The relativizing and harmonizing effect of reading Luke-Acts as part of a larger canonical whole is inevitable. For the peculiar emphases of Luke-Acts are no longer probed in isolation from those of the other three Gospels and of the Pauline and other New Testament letters. Those who read Luke and Acts as part of their Bible are concerned not just with Lukan ideas and approaches but with the actualities to which Luke-Acts refers (hence the approach called *Sachkritik*), some of which they may have personally experienced.[5] Since Luke and Acts are not the only writings to focus on the realities of Jesus, church origins, and salvation both as individuals and as the people of God, Christian readers naturally turn to other biblical writings that give additional insight into these faith realities.[6] They naturally compare what Luke-Acts says about Jesus and faith with what they learn both from other biblical books and from their own experience, and they tend to harmonize all this knowledge in a personal synthesis.

The harmonizing and relativizing effects of canon on an individual document are most evidently illustrated by what happens to a single letter of Paul when it is subsumed into a collection of letters and read by readers other than those originally envisaged. The particularity of the Pauline document, instead of being the focus, as it is in both historical and literary criticism, becomes "the scandal of particularity" when read canonically.[7] Christians from different regions, cultures, and centuries simply do not care, for example, about some of the peculiarly Corinthian issues that Paul addressed in those letters. Some of the original controversies, such as what males and females were to wear on their heads at worship (1 Corinthians 11), are no longer completely recoverable by, let alone relevant to, later readers. And for the deeper and perennial issues of male and female social and religious roles, later generations will consult more than an isolated Pauline letter, including relevant texts by other New Testament writers.[8] Thus the pertinent passage in this letter will usually be consulted in context with other New Testament passages that throw light on male and female roles.

COMPLEMENTARITY RATHER THAN COMPETITION
WITHIN THE CANON

The tendency to harmonize canonical materials can be and often has been excessive, to the point where the specific contributions of individual documents and writers are submerged in an amorphous "biblical" blend, which more closely replicates the current theology or ideology of the readers than the meaning of those documents. Paradoxically, ideology can also overwhelm the text's meaning in a process that is antithetical to this one, namely, when the different voices within the canon are played off against each other as irreconcilable contradictions. The usual effect of the latter practice is to allow the readers to pick and choose what they want to hear among such conflicting messages and to ignore or explain away what they find less congenial. Thus a bland Sunday-school fundamentalist harmonization can ironically have a result similar to a hypercritical reading or a hermeneutics of suspicion or an extreme "canon within a canon" approach: the specifics of the text are not allowed their full authority but are subordinated to the readers' ideology, whether of the right or of the left.[9]

The canonical approach advocated here tries to find a middle way between harmonizing and dichotomizing the biblical differences. Based as it is on literary criticism, which in turn respects the assured findings of historical criticism, this approach to Luke-Acts primarily seeks the characteristic contributions of that narrative to the canonical whole of which it is a part. While recognizing the distinctiveness of the Lukan vis-à-vis the Pauline or Markan perspectives, it views the distinct contributions as complementary, not as contradictory, which is in fact the way most churches have treated the diverse books of the scripture.[10]

Treating Luke and Acts as a distinctive but complementary presentation of the Christian story and message responds to a major current malaise in historical-critical studies. The search for more holistic approaches has fed the recent turn to literary treatments of biblical narratives. The chorus of discontent with historical criticism has included the most radically diverse voices, from fundamentalists to charismatics to systematic theologians to liberation and feminist theologians.[11] While the reasons for discontent can often be mutually contradictory, the criticisms nevertheless share a sense that some historical critics' atomizing and historicism are alienating the Bible from contemporary concerns. Some of the atomizing tendencies of excessive source-critical approaches are being overcome by studies of whole narratives, like the present study of Luke-Acts. One of the acknowledged concerns of this book is to "put Humpty Dumpty back together again" from the many sources into which Gospel texts have been atomized.[12] Another is to return to the Bible with a "second naiveté," rescue it from the past into which historicism has often fixed it, and let it speak again to believers as scripture today.

This book therefore attempts to read Luke-Acts as biblical narrative, which has a composite unity formed from disparate sources, as contributing to the Christian Bible viewed as fountainhead of Christian life and theology. Focus on narrative and on Lukan narrators highlights the Lukan point of view on the events recounted, both as subsuming traditional materials and sources and as adding a distinctive voice to the harmony of the New Testament. As acknowledged from the introduction, not all current methods of literary criticism seem appropriate for the kind of traditional community narrative that Luke-Acts is. Some of the deconstructionist approaches especially have dichotomizing effects similar to the source methods whose exclusive or excessive uses have proven unsatisfactory for the scripture as scripture. Nor do some alienating and agnostic contemporary literary trends seem appropriate for approaching a document of a community's faith. Therefore this book has deliberately been limited to applying only those methods that seem appropriate and helpful for the special kind of traditional religious literature that Luke and Acts are.[13]

FROM PARTICULAR TO EXAMPLE AND TYPE

Because of the relativizing and harmonizing effects of canonizing, Christians of different centuries and cultures will inevitably tend to read an individual letter with its ancient concerns typologically, as examples for which contemporary analogies and applications are sought. Recovering the original historical issue, which sometimes seems no longer possible, is in any case not the final word for exegesis, since it is being used as an example or model of some more fundamental issue or virtue or of a more current concern.[14] Despite the many disputes over Paul's treatment of women's head wear in 1 Corinthians 11, for example, few of the disputants from any part of the ideological spectrum would focus exclusively on head wear or hair styles. Virtually all contemporary readers would subsume those questions into instances of male-female roles.

An analogous point can be made about the relativizing and harmonizing effect of canonizing the narrative(s) of Luke-Acts. Although the story deals with its own first-century occurrences and concerns, readers from distant times and cultures tend to read them as examples or analogies to their contemporary issues. Nor do canonical readers of Luke and Acts tend to keep them as distinct from other narratives and New Testament documents as historical-critical and literary readers have to do. People who consult or read Luke or Acts because they are part of Christian scripture tend to interpret and apply the Gospel of Luke in context not only of the other Synoptic Gospels but of John, and Acts in the context of the Pauline and Petrine letters. In this broader canonical context, the narratives of Luke and Acts become mines for types and examples that illustrate Christian life in general, or are applied to contemporary situations by analogy.

Grounding and warrant for such applications of Lukan stories to later concerns is already present in Luke-Acts itself, in the way the narrator (speaking for the implied author) already adapts stories of earlier events to the situations of his implied readers. For example, in the farewell address of Acts 20, he treats Paul's behavior in Ephesus as a model for later overseers of Christian communities. Thus, expanding the original concerns for a broader canonical context, and applying them by typology and analogy to later generations, are not foreign to the original intent of the documents.[15]

The sense of reading Luke and Acts as part of the Christian Bible for contemporary concerns advances the treatment of Luke and Acts far beyond questions about the original narrative concerns and life settings. For ordinary Christian believers, they help to reclaim from purely academic historical and literary concerns some of the scriptural uses Christians most often make of Luke and Acts.

Reading Luke and Acts as canonical or biblical adds to historical and narrative criticism the important dimension of direct relationship with human life and with the events to which Luke and Acts refer. Contemporary Christians read them within the interpretive community of the church (by whom the canonical list was articulated), in the light of the traditions of interpretation and the doctrines of their denomination. Such an ecclesial and canonical reading cannot avoid relativizing and harmonizing Lukan peculiarities, because their context of interpretation has been broadened and their meaning resignified for new situations.[16]

Reading Luke and Acts as canonical scripture also regards them as documents written from faith and addressed to the potential or actual faith of the intended readers. As scripture, therefore, Luke and Acts have implied readers who are (actually or potentially) Christian.[17] Reading Luke and Acts as biblical infers treating them as authoritative guidance for one's values and living and finding in them examples for behavior in contemporary situations.[18] Luke and Acts become more than interesting historical documents and literary achievements from the past. They become sources of inspiration and prayer and guidance for the present. They become focal points of unity within each church and of ecumenical progress among differing ecclesial communions.[19] For example, Acts 10–11 and 15 have been read as models for the settling of ecclesial disputes and of issues about how to adapt evangelization to new cultures and peoples.[20]

Read canonically, Luke and Acts have also inspired joint efforts toward justice and peace by members of disparate denominations and are favorite sources for many Christians who strive for liberation of the oppressed or inculturation of the Christian message for diverse peoples.[21]

At this point in the development of scholarship, canonical criticism is not a single method applied to Luke-Acts but more a stance toward those books that reaches beyond the results of historical and narrative-critical approaches.[22] As this concern for biblical meaning grows, hopefully scholars will develop and perfect more universally applicable methods and approaches for reading Luke and Acts as the special kind of narrative that is *biblical*.

11 Epilogue: Literary Criticism, Canon, and Orality

Positive Results of Literary Reading of Luke-Acts as Narrative

We have seen narrative analysis provide insight in several areas that have persistently eluded consensus among Lukan interpreters, primarily through its focus on the primary evidence in the text without reliance on extratextual conjectures. Instead of inconclusive debates about the identity of the author of Luke and Acts and the community for which it was written, narrative study disclosed the narrators evident in the narrative itself, ranging from the prologue's *histor*, the omniscient narrator for most of Luke-Acts, the "we" character narrator, to character narrators of stories within stories (like Paul in Acts 22 and 26). These narrators in turn project corresponding personae for the author implied by the text, including a historian sifting and arranging traditions in the prologue, an occasional Pauline travel companion in "we" passages, and in general a Christian apologist continuing the biblical history up to Paul's preaching in Rome. Explicit textual indicators also imply the kinds of knowledge readers needed to fill the narrative's gaps, namely, Christian catechesis, experience, and knowledge of the Greek Old Testament, and therefore that the intended audience was Christian.

Focus on narrative aspects of the text threw new light on several problematic passages in Luke-Acts. The prologue accurately characterizes the narrative as a traditional, not original, tale, in which disparate episodes are plotted into a narrative ordered according to previous plots (e.g., Mark's), kerygmatic summaries, and journey motifs. We observed that the problematic "we" companions of Paul were present with Paul on his journeys to Jerusalem and Rome but not at his trials, just as the Twelve were companions with Jesus on his journey to Jerusalem but not at his trials. Some scholars have found these narrative claims of occasional eyewitness grounding of a few accounts by this "we" narrator not totally lacking in historical plausibility.[1]

The inconsistencies about Paul's conversion in Acts 9, 22, and 26 were seen to be more than redactional carelessness: they relate to differing points of view and access to knowledge between the omniscient narrator and the character narrator Paul, with the omniscient narrator's version as authoritative. Also, literary treatment of irony in Luke-Acts sheds light on Lukan theology. God's plan (known to implied readers) works through the blindness of characters, as when Jewish nonrecognition of their scriptural promises leads to their ironic fulfillment in Jesus' passion, or when resistance to the word in Acts scatters preachers who spread the word.

POSITIVE RESULTS OF CANONICAL READING OF LUKE-ACTS AS BIBLICAL

The previous chapter has suggested ways that the narrative-literary approaches to Luke and Acts have to be modified when they are treated not just in isolation as a literary two-part narrative, but also in their biblical context of the Christian New Testament. These include the expansion of their literary context as part of the Christian canon, with the consequent expansion of the audience intended by Luke and Acts as *biblical* documents, the harmonizing effects of canonical reading, and the typological and analogous uses to which they are put in later settings. Such canonical uses relativize both historical and literary approaches to Luke and Acts and render some of them less appropriate and fruitful for the new task at hand. Canonical treatment of Luke and Acts as biblical accentuates their religious meaning for the contemporary interpretive community of believing Christians in the church.

LITERARY NARRATIVE METHODS IN CONTEXT OF OTHER APPROACHES

As practiced in this book, literary-critical reading of Luke and Acts as narrative builds on the foundations of historical-critical exegesis to which it is closely related, especially to redaction and composition criticism that focus especially on the Lukan contributions and arrangement into the current coherent whole of whatever traditional and original materials have contributed to Luke and Acts. But redaction and composition criticism still function primarily in relationship to the earlier form, source, and historical criticisms, all of which maintain a special focus on the historical past, that is, on the original occasion of the writing. Moreover historically, redaction criticism has tended to focus more on the theologies of the redactors or on reconstructing the situations of the audiences than on the stories specifically as narratives.

But Luke and Acts are neither theological treatises nor merely occasions for historical conjectures about communities they address; they are narratives. The narrative approaches enable critics to appreciate the narrative genres and forms in which any such theologies have been embodied, prior to further historical hypotheses about original readers. In some senses, this limits former theological emphases, which are now seen to be contained in story form which may not be as universally applicable as a treatise or essay.

But in other ways, the very story form gives to a baldly stated theological "essence" a richness, form, and context in narrative that has far more imaginative power than any theological distillation. Thus, the vivid narratives of Genesis 1–3 seem endlessly open to rereadings and inexhaustibly evocative of further theological, humanistic, and psychological insight, whereas some of the theological distillations of those chapters can seem quite bland.

But the narrative approaches in this book not only are grounded on the previously normal practices of historical-critical exegeses; they also go beyond purely literary concerns and practices to read Luke and Acts precisely as biblical, as part of the wider context of the Christian scriptural canon that is treated as authoritative font of belief, life, and practice in the Christian churches. The questions asked and the way gaps in the narrative are filled are not only those of disinterested academic investigations but are also those pertinent to Christian believers and communities. Because of these religious concerns and the special nature of the narratives studied, certain cautions and limits to the kinds of literary criticism that are appropriate for this material have seemed in order.

LITERARY CRITICISM AND THE BIBLE: CAUTIONS

DIFFERENCES BETWEEN CONTEMPORARY AND ANCIENT LITERATURE

Although many of today's literary techniques can be applied to ancient folk writings like the Bible, they were developed to analyze a different kind of contemporary Western writing.[2] Some devices that are commonplace today, like unreliable narrators whose perspective on narrated events differs from the real author's, played minor roles in ancient writings.[3] Therefore caution should precede application of contemporary literary theories to the Gospel of Luke and Acts of the Apostles because of the major differences between Luke-Acts and contemporary fiction.

Robert Weimann has delineated sharp dissimilarities between the modern novel and traditional narratives like epics.[4] Some of these differences are related to the originally oral character of traditional epics, and some are due to the contrast between the epic author's identification with a traditional worldview and a contemporary novelist's individualism. Luke stands somewhere between the epic and contemporary author. Already grounded in a primarily written, rather than exclusively oral, narrative tradition, Luke exhibits both a greater identification with his tradition than the contemporary novelist and a stronger self-awareness as a distinct individual within this tradition than the epic author.

Primary reasons for Luke's differences from contemporary authors are the divergent worldviews that separate traditional writers from individualistic authors today. Traditional authors, like epic narrative poets, worked within a traditional framework and spoke for the tradition to which they belonged, whereas modern novelists have to take a personal stance in their writings: "the epic poet employed a frame of reference that was taken for granted by an audience with which he shared 'some unity of sentiment, some common standard of appreciation.' "[5] Traditional authors did not radically dissent from the point of view of the society to which they belonged.[6] Use of "we" and "us" linked audience and author "in their common attitudes toward both the actual world of experience and the imaginary world of the epic."[7] Traditional authors saw themselves as mediating stories from their tradition to their community more than as inventing new ones. This is generally true of biblical authors, including Luke, who saw Luke-Acts as "a continuation of the biblical history" up to Paul's witness in Rome.[8] Luke certainly is writing from within the worldview of the biblical writings as he shows how "the events that have been fulfilled among us" (Luke 1:1) fulfill God's plan, promises, and prophecies which they contain.[9]

Luke's prologue and the narratives themselves give evidence that he considered himself a spokesperson for the traditional stories, not the creator of new ones. Both his use of sources (probably Mark) and the claims of his prologue indicate that Luke organizes traditional materials into a new narrative. The prologue claims that accounts of the events Luke describes were handed down to him by "eyewitnesses and ministers of the word" (αὐτόπται καὶ ὑπηρέται . . . τοῦ λόγου, Luke 1:2) and that these events took place "among us" (ἐν ἡμῖν, 1:1), the Christian community or communities with which Luke identified himself. His stated purpose of providing Theophilus written assurance of the things about which he had been informed (presumably orally) precludes any claim to originality in creating the stories themselves, since most of them were already known to Theophilus (1:4). But like the modern novelist, Luke is conscious of an individual approach to the material, however traditional the latter may be. The originality that Luke does claim is in the plotting of these commonly known events (1:1,3). He has personally determined how the narrative would begin (e.g., differently from Mark), how its middle would be ordered (ἀνατάξασθαι διήγησιν . . . καθεξῆς σοι γράψαι), and how it would end (in contrast to Mark). He has taken the unprecedented step of adding to his Gospel narrative a sequel with its own beginning, ordered middle, and end.[10]

Other major differences between Luke-Acts and contemporary writings, many of which follow from these foundational differences, can be mentioned briefly. Recent literature often makes dramatic use of multiple narrators with quite varied points of view, including unreliable narrators. Biblical narrators tend to be reliable and to project the community's worldview. Their point of view truly corresponds to that of the book's writer.

Contemporary literary plots often strive for uniqueness and complexity and avoid predictable happy endings or narrative closure, often mirroring the nihilistic relativism of current culture. By contrast, biblical plots were normally common knowledge—well-known stories about people and events familiar to the Hebrew and Christian communities for whom they are written.[11] One can often spoil a contemporary novel for readers by revealing the end ahead of time, but the end of most biblical narratives were known beforehand (e.g., Jesus' resurrection), so that plot interest pertains more to how the story is told than to suspense.

Today's characters are seldom heroic; often they are anti-heroes. Biblical characters are typically heroic models for community behavior who incarnate community values or anti-values.

DIFFERENCES BETWEEN PROFANE AND SACRED LITERATURE

Contemporary novels and the Bible belong to two quite different kinds of writings: secular and sacred. Current literature is primarily for entertainment. When it has an ideological thrust, that ideology is usually not religious but social or political. Even if it is religious, contemporary authors generally promote their own views self-consciously rather than speak anonymously for a sacred tradition to which they belong.

For those who believe that it is sacred literature, the Bible communicates revelation from God, the religious community's traditions of origins, and accounts of great prophets, holy people, and the Son of

God.[12] Most of the biblical traditions were familiar to readers from religious worship, instruction, and preaching before they were written in the Bible.[13] Authors of sacred literature, among whom the writer of Luke and Acts classifies his implied author, found their plot choices severely circumscribed by communal religious traditions. Most of their creativity focused on how to embody the traditional story of Jesus and the apostles, not on creating a new story. Thus the plot of the Lukan Gospel is a variant of Mark's basic synoptic plot line. The Jesus of Luke's narrative had to correspond to the Jesus who was already known, followed, and even worshipped by the Christian community. The Lukan portrait of Jesus could not diverge as sharply from Christian tradition as, for example, that in the apocryphal childhood narrative of the boy Jesus angrily striking another child dead with a word.[14] The attitudes and points of view of Jesus and the main characters and the narrator had to correspond to and express the Christian revelation about God, humans, Christ, the world, and their interrelationship. They could not be idiosyncratic to the Lukan author.

NEED FOR DISCERNMENT IN SELECTION OF METHODS

Dissimilarities between contemporary and ancient, and between profane and sacred writings, require discerning application from among contemporary literary methods. Not all are appropriate for the Bible as an ancient sacred text. Caution needs to be exercised in using the kind of analysis called deconstruction, for example. Many principles of deconstruction presuppose a worldview that cannot easily be reconciled with that of biblical verbal revelation. Some deconstructionist theories of knowledge are idealistic, precluding any reference beyond perceptions or ideas to extramental realities. Some are reductionistic, finding cultural or other bias in the very perception of reality and its consequent expression in texts, which renders them oppressive to the marginalized and in need of complete deconstruction and reformulation in terms of the latter's experience. Other deconstructionist theories of knowledge are nominalistic, or even nihilistic or totally relativistic, where words simply interrelate to each other in a kind of linguistic set or word game with no reference to external reality or even to ideas.[15] Such theories of knowledge cannot without distortion support a biblical worldview of God revealing particular truths to historical human beings and interacting with them through commands and promises, rewards and punishments. Nor are they easy to reconcile with any realistic kind of biblical authority over the lives of believers.

COMMUNICATION CONTEXT OF NARRATIVES

Authorial Intention to Communicate with Readers Through Text

Critics who apply speech-act theories to written narratives remind us that narrative writing normally takes place in a context of communication.[16] The writer of Luke and Acts was not merely amusing himself by doodling on papyrus or parchment but was attempting to communicate with intended readers through his written text. The key participants and factors of this act of communication are objective (extramental) realities, not figments of readers' imaginations, as some might deduce from certain forms of literary criticism. Thus the writer of Luke existed as a historical individual, whether or not we can identify him today. If there had been no writer, there would be no text.

The writer intended the Gospel for certain types of readers, which can be characterized by clues in the text. Though the readers are envisaged in the writer's imagination, those imagined readers are meant to have some relationship to readers who exist independently of the writer's imagination. The writer who went to so much effort would surely want actual readers to read what he wrote.

Finally, the text of the Gospel itself is an extramental reality, available for public scrutiny. In the written text of the Gospel, the actual writer has placed linguistic code through which to communicate with potential audiences. The act of reading the written text actualizes this communication between writer and readers.[17]

LIMITATIONS ON READER RESPONSES WITHIN CHRISTIAN FAITH CONTEXTS

Applying some contemporary literary approaches to scripture can amount to resistance to, if not outright rejection of, the biblical text as sacred and authoritative. Thus it is not always apparent how some forms of the "hermeneutics of suspicion" are compatible with the trust involved in believing scripture as God's word. Nor is it clear how they can avoid undermining the authority of the sacred biblical text over suspicious readers' lives and beliefs. If one suspects economic or patriarchal oppression behind even the sacred texts, what happens to one's belief in their sacredness or inspiration or authority? If even Jesus' Gospel statements and actions that challenge current outlooks are mistrusted as culturally conditioned, what happens to the authority of someone like Paul or a deutero-Pauline writer? If the Bible is God's revelation to humans, as both Jews and Christians have consistently claimed, it has to be expected that sometimes it will challenge contemporary human or cultural or ideological mind sets. It will not always be "politically correct."[18] The scriptures themselves express such a challenge: "For my thoughts are not your thoughts, nor are your ways my ways, says the LORD"(Isa. 55:8, RNAB).

Limitations on Hermeneutics of Suspicion

Most contemporary approaches promise to bear some fruit if used with discretion. One can sift out the wheat from chaff in applying them to Luke-Acts. Thus deconstruction of some contemporary prejudgments about the meaning of biblical narratives or commands can be useful. Hermeneutics of suspicion can sometimes prevent reading current prejudices back into texts that originally meant something quite other. Yet most current approaches have to be used with restrictions. Unlimited use of methods like deconstruction can substitute a new set of reading rules quite alien to reading the Bible as sacred scripture and God's word. It can amount to refusing to play by the rules for reading according to which the original biblical writing was produced and canonized.

Reader Response as Mediating Historical and Canonical Readings

A discerning use of reader-response methods promises some redress from the failure of historical criticism to approach the text as canonical and as biblical authority for the later Christian church. As Walter Wink has observed, historical criticism provides an important distancing in reading scripture, by which the Bible is rescued from contemporary prejudices about its meaning to recover what it meant historically at the time of its production. But once the Bible is thus detached from present preconceptions, it remains locked in the past unless one has ways other than historical criticism by which to dialogue and find some communion with the text.[19]

Reader response offers one such way for contemporary dialogue and communion with the ancient text. Among the varieties of reader-response approaches is usually a common concern for not just how original readers would have responded to the text but for how any reader, including the current one, can respond to it.[20] When applied to contemporary literature, reader response often focuses on the reader's entertainment in reading or on questions of how the reader is affected by it (sometimes ideologically, as in feminist readings).

These foci apply also to readers of the Bible, but scripture's canonical status adds another important dimension. When believers approach scripture, they generally seek guidance or revelation. They want the scripture to speak to their present lives, not just be a document from the past. Reader-response approaches, which elucidate what happens every time a reader brings the text alive in her or his consciousness, can help articulate a way for believers to employ their Bible as God's word to them today.

However, reader-response approaches must likewise be exercised within limits if they are to remain appropriate to the Bible as scripture. The codes inscribed in the text demarcate the free play of readers' imaginations.[21] Further, insofar as reader response overlaps with deconstruction and hermeneutics of suspicion, it needs the same cautions and discernment as they in its application to scripture.

Some of the uses biblical scholars make of literary approaches seem philosophically naive. Disparities between contemporary perspectives and the traditional philosophical worldviews of many believing Christians render some current methods problematic. Such methods were developed within a secularistic and relativistic worldview for sophisticated recent literature. Without a strong philosophical training, which is not a standard component of biblical studies programs, scripture scholars can be unaware of the epistemological incompatibilities of some forms of deconstruction with Christian faith in revelation.[22] Unawareness of the philosophical limitations of some current perspectives can lead biblical scholars to a contemporary arrogance vis-à-vis previous and alternate worldviews, including those in scripture. Contemporary relativism and some current epistemologies are problematic for faith in revelation and for revealed religion. Nor have they proven their value in dealing with human existence over a long period of time. We cannot simply presume a priori that the contemporary worldview is better or more adequate to dealing with life and reality than that given in biblical texts.

Thus, complaints that biblical scholars are like dilettantes only touching the surface of literary studies can in some cases be countered by pointing to the inappropriateness of certain of these current methods for biblical study.[23] This book has employed a deliberately eclectic literary approach, using current methods only to the extent that they seem suitable for the biblical literature and Christian worldview, which differ so profoundly from the individualistic narratives for which and worldviews within which so many of those methods arose.

A corollary to this is that Christians need not be apologetic or defensive about our faith reading of the Christian Bible, even though it is strongly counter-cultural and may even be deemed offensive to current religious relativism, to some Jewish readings of Hebrew Scriptures, or to some hermeneutics of suspicion. Christian exclusive claims for the Bible as giving God's final revelation of his Son Jesus Christ fly in the face of religious relativism, which denies all absolute religious claims. American relativism is especially intolerant of any religious "intolerance" deemed inherent in exclusive claims.[24] Derisive media treatment of Protestant fundamentalists and traditional Catholics as irrational extremists has a common basis in rejection of all absolute claims that go beyond personal or group preferences in ways that might affect others.

Thus Christian claims for Jesus as Son of God and Messiah cannot be reconciled to Jewish denials of these claims. While Christians can be expected to avoid anti-Semitism and triumphalism, they cannot as Christians be expected to refrain from expressing their belief in Jesus and his claims. Interfaith dialogue has to be grounded on the basis of both partners speaking from their respective beliefs, even when these are mutually incompatible or contradictory.

The question of sensibilities also applies to various hermeneutics of suspicion. Some particularly alienated feminist treatments of God or religious language are profoundly offensive to Christian sensitivities, including those of many Christian women. For the views and feelings of believing Christian women to be summarily and systematically dismissed, because such women are prejudged to be too ignorant or indoctrinated to realize their oppression, is one of the most condescending kinds of sexism being practiced today.

ORAL TRADITION AND ORAL READING OF BIBLICAL NARRATIVE

READING AND LISTENING: ORAL CONTEXT FOR THE GOSPELS

Perhaps one of the most demanding adjustments contemporary readers and critics must make in applying current literary methods to the scriptures is to recall both the oral origins of many biblical traditions and their normally oral delivery to everyday Christians. Centuries of written and print culture can blind us to how pervasive orality was, not only for much of the Hebrew Scriptures but for traditions about Jesus and church origins. The ancient scarcity of private copies of Luke's Gospel and Acts presupposes that the Lukan audience was normally expected to hear Luke and Acts read aloud rather than to read them privately. Furthermore, even private reading tended to be done out loud.[25]

The distinctions in Luke's prologue between oral reports and written narratives call to mind some important distinctions between these two forms of communication. Using the work of Walter Ong on the differences between oral and written communication, Werner Kelber argues that the transition from oral to written Gospel entails a major change in direction, not just a natural evolution.[26] It is common knowledge that oral consciousness and storytelling is quite different from writing, which restructures consciousness by providing both distance, precision, and stable aids to memory.[27]

Speech of any sort (oration, narrative, command, question) is normally interpersonal communication: one person speaks to others who are present (at least through technology like the telephone) and listening to what the speaker is saying. In oral narrative, the listeners are aware of the narrator who is "telling the story," though their attention is primarily on the narrative.

However, with written narration "a writer's audience is always a fiction."[28] Whereas oral storytellers can adjust their tales to the reactions of the listeners and shift direction as they speak, emphasizing or leaving out details according to their response, writers of narratives have to imagine their absent readers and adjust to what they project their intended readers' responses will be. Neither oral nor textual storytellers can recall their words once spoken or committed to writing and released to others, but *"verba volant; scripta manent"*: spoken words are fleeting (unless "captured" on electronic media) whereas written words remain.[29] The oral context is one of mutual communication and give and take. Even if the narrator does all the talking, the listeners respond with attention or inattention and with bodily and sometimes vocal responses, to which the narrator responds in turn by abbreviating, elaborating, emphasizing, or sliding over unpopular sections. In response to their listeners, oral storytellers can also modify what they have said (as when children correct a storyteller who has confused or forgotten an important detail in a standard fairy tale).

Writing, however, produces "autonomous discourse," freed from the immediate temporal and spatial context of oral exchange. Ricoeur notes that writing explodes the face-to-face (or voice-to-ear) dialogical situation. The reference to the speaker in spoken discourse is immediate so that the speaker's intention and discourse's meaning overlap.

> With written discourse, however, the author's intention and the meaning of the text cease to coincide. . . . Inscription becomes synonymous with the semantic autonomy of the text, which results from the disconnection of the mental intention of the author from the verbal meaning of the text, of what the

> author meant and what the text means. . . . What the text
> means now matters more than what the author meant when
> he wrote it.[30]

In oral storytelling, the author creates the narrative as she or he speaks, either based on a previously known story line or by inventing it on the spot. Writers create their narratives before the readers read them (at different times and usually in different places), nor can authors normally control, the way speakers can, who shall read what they write by directing their comments to only one person or group. Writers even of personal letters cannot guarantee that their intimate or confidential writings will not be read by unforeseen readers, which often leads to less frankness in written compared to private oral communication. But the advantages of writing outweigh its disadvantages. Ricoeur notes that because of the material fixation of writing, political rule can be exercised at a distance, and economics, history, juridical codes, etc., are born. The communicative function of discourse is deeply affected by writing.[31]

However, in written biblical narratives, several oral components retain their importance. The oral traditions behind many biblical narratives, including those of the Gospels and Acts, influence the style of those narratives and carry over the nature of those oral traditions as interpersonal communication between narrator and narratees. Furthermore, the writer of Luke-Acts was writing primarily for oral delivery of his text to assembled congregations. The expected reading dynamics differ greatly from what contemporary authors anticipate for their writings. The rhetoric used in a text intended for oral delivery also differs greatly from that created for silent reading. Oral delivery retains a close link to interpersonal communication and requires oral rhetorical methods of emphasis like repetitions.[32]

The oral traditions incorporated in Luke and Acts demand greater attention than does contemporary literature to the oral dimensions of their context, style, and structure. Thus the sharp contrast in style between the flowing classicist initial sentence of the prologue in Luke 1:1–4 and the "contaminated" biblicist Semitic style beginning with Luke 1:5 would stand out in an oral reading. Repetitions like "It happened in the days of Herod" (Ἐγένετο ἐν ταῖς ἡμέραις Ἡρῴδου, Luke 1:5) and "And it happened in his priestly serving" (Ἐγένετο δὲ ἐν τῷ ἱερατεύειν, 1:8) create audible indications of a new "paragraph" or topic.

The intended oral delivery of Luke and Acts also makes it advisable for readers today to read aloud the sections of Luke-Acts treated in this book.

Not only in Greek, but even in translation, oral reading can generate greater awareness of some of the Lukan oral rhetoric.

"DISTANCIATION" AND "ALIENATION" IN ALL WRITING

Of its very nature, writing produces distance compared to the intimacy of speaking. Ricoeur can therefore refer to "the hermeneutical function of distanciation."[33] Others commonly refer to the "alienation" in all writing. Even physically, writers have to withdraw from other forms of communication (often into physical or at least psychological isolation) in order to write. They are usually not actually in the presence of their readers. Therefore, writing can be a lonely experience. On the positive side, its alienation enables a separation from group psychology and pressure, recollection of consciousness and the ability to think through very carefully what one wishes to express in writing, and to test and change it before showing it to anyone else. By intensifying the sense of self, writing aids conscious interaction between persons and is "consciousness-raising."[34]

Another distancing or privatizing effect of writing rather than telling a narrative concerns its reception either as a private act or as a group experience. Listening to an oral narrative is a group experience. The listeners are affected by the reactions of those around them, which can either heighten or distract from their experience of the narrative. Silently reading a story, even if a whole roomful of people are reading the same story, is essentially a private affair.[35] However, oral reading of a written story to an individual and especially to a group has an effect closer to oral storytelling than to private reading. Oral readers of stories need to stick closer to the script than oral storytellers, but they tend to make modifications at least in their voice and emphasis in response to their listeners, which the original writer of the narrative cannot do. Most ancient narratives were meant to be read aloud, sometimes by an individual to herself or himself, more often by a reader to a group of listeners. The Gospels, including Luke despite the dedication to his patron Theophilus, were usually read aloud to communities at worship.

Because oral reading presupposes and builds community, liturgical reading of narratives even today is oral. One does not simply announce the reading and then have the members of the congregation silently read their own copies of the scripture. The variance between the dynamics of silent reading and listening also explains the tension liturgical lectors often feel if people read their own biblical texts or missalettes instead of paying undivided attention to the person reading. The silent reading of the text, even during an oral reading of it, usually has an alienating effect between the lector and those reading along in their own texts, and among members of the congregation reading their own texts. It is usually because of problems of acoustics or hearing that some congregations reluctantly provide individual texts during liturgical readings.

This oral dimension of reading Luke and Acts to a gathered community is an important distinction from contemporary narratives.[36] The oral dimension is another reason why textualist approaches like deconstruction, which were developed for more privatized narratives, are less appropriate for biblical narratives like Luke and Acts.[37]

WRITING'S TRANSCENDENCE OF ORIGINAL OCCASION, RECIPIENTS, AND INTENTIONS

Ricoeur treats these three effects of writing's distanciation as a positive contribution of writing.[38] Against Hans-Georg Gadamer's disjunction between alienating distanciation and participation by belonging, Ricoeur sees the written text communicating by means of distance. By transcending its sociological conditions of production, writing is open to readings in different sociological contexts. Reading recontextualizes texts in new contexts.[39] Thus the reading by Luke's original addressees has a different context from readings by later Christians of Luke's now canonical Gospel. Writing by its very nature is not limited to the original situation but is applicable to multiple occasions and recipients. The ability of all writing to transcend its original source, occasion, and destination grounds the assumption of texts into canon and their consequent canonical interpretation. When any New Testament writing like Luke or Acts is received into the canon of Christian scripture, it transcends the limits of its original context and is applied to a much broader group of readers than those originally envisaged by Luke. What was initially intended for one audience is given a kind of typical value for later readers, who are to apply it analogously to their new contexts.[40] This also grounds the paradigmatic use of biblical narratives like Luke and Acts for later Christian living and the patristic and medieval topological reading or "moral sense" of scripture.[41]

ORAL TRADITIONS AND WRITING

"FREEZING" OF ORAL TRADITIONS BY WRITINGS

The limits of memory restrict transmission of oral narrative traditions to individual episodes, collections of episodes linked by topic or mnemonic devices, or summary plots. Lengthier narratives depend on mnemonic devices and a cultural fund of formulaic expressions, and they never come out exactly the same in any two tellings. Writing enables a longer narrative to be planned and recorded for indefinite numbers of identical readings, thus providing a permanent form for its narrative.[42]

The Lukan preface seems to allude to this contrast between the permanency of written and the flux of oral narratives about "the events that have been fulfilled among us" (Luke 1:1) as one aspect of the "assurance" or "security" it was promising "concerning the things of which you have been informed" (1:4). Other writers had already tried to "compile" or "put in order" a narrative about the events that had taken place "among us" (1:1) from what had been "handed down [orally] to us" by "eyewitnesses and ministers of the word" (1:2). Luke distances himself from these earlier narrative efforts: "it seemed good to me also" carefully to investigate everything anew (or "from the beginning") and carefully to write the results "in order" (1:3). The "order" or plot is what the written account claims to add to the oral traditions, and this plotting provides at least some of the promised assurance for information received orally.

In other words, the written narrative fixes the free-floating oral narrative episodes in the orderly sequence of its plot. The fact that Luke claims to be redoing what others had already done infers the possibility of providing more than one plot order for such episodes, and that all such plots are to some extent a matter of the writer's art and practical judgment. This in turn implies a necessarily fictional element to all plotting of multiple independently transmitted episodes. Beginning from many unrelated episodes, writers would have no way of knowing the actual chronological sequence in which they occurred without the help of some temporal or geographical clues in the accounts. Differences in plot order between the probably independent Gospels of Luke and John are inevitable, given the earliest transmission of most of the episodes as independent oral units. Even where some interdependence is probable, as in the synoptic accounts, the nature of the initially oral transmission of most of the episodes provided a warrant for individual writers like Luke, Matthew, and Mark to make at least some changes in the plot order of whatever written sources each may have had. This is precisely what Luke in his prologue claims to have done regarding the plotting in previous written narratives (1:1, 3).

How a plot order that is at least partially arbitrary contributes "assurance" or "security" to orally transmitted information is not self-evident in the prologue. The use of the word "fulfilled" or "accomplished" (πεπληροφορημένων) for events that took place "among us" suggests

Luke's intent to use his narrative to show fulfillment of biblical promises, prophecies, and God's plan of saving history.[43] This is confirmed by the frequent efforts in the narrative to demonstrate biblical warrants for events (e.g., Joel 3:1–5 LXX for the Pentecost outpouring of the Spirit). Luke's plotting grounds the stories he has received on the foundation of God's saving plan found in scripture. For an extended narrative, this too is much easier to do in written than in oral form.

RELATIVIZATION OF ALL METHODS
BY CANONICAL CONTEXT

We have already seen that canonization of a text drastically changes its interpretive context. This is easiest to illustrate for occasional documents like Pauline letters. Historical criticism aims to uncover the original audience and historical situation so as to place the letters' advice in their original context. Once these letters are gathered into a corpus and read by the church at large, however, their original circumstances and concerns become simply illustrative for how Paul would handle concerns of other and later churches.[44] Most Christian readers are less concerned than historical critics about what original situation Paul was addressing in Galatia or Philippi. They read Galatians or Philippians for what God may be saying for their own situations.

The gathering of the particular letters into a general corpus for the church at large also relativizes the message of each letter by balancing it against those in others. Canonizing has an automatically harmonizing effect.[45] The angry outbursts in Galatians are tempered by the milder treatments of the same topics in Romans. Romans in turn is balanced by James in some church usage. The theology and practice of the universal church is more inclusive than that found in any one letter or even letter writer.

In an analogous but less obvious way for narratives, the canonical status of Luke and Acts relativizes results from the normal methods of exegesis and literary criticism. Even from the outset, narratives have less reference than letters to the setting of the intended audience. Their plot lines have more internal cohesion and independence from settings of origin. They refer more directly to the historical or fictional events that they recount. Still, historical critics have demonstrated some effects on Luke-Acts of the situation of the original addressees. But as soon as the Lukan narratives were accepted by the larger church, their interpretive context went beyond the first setting for which historical criticism searches. Also, because the Lukan volumes have become a frequently read and well-known part of the church's scripture, tracing a reader's initial responses to the text has diminished critical relevance to the rereadings that are their normal usage. Further, the sacred nature of biblical texts for believers limits use of some of the more relativistic literary approaches toward Luke and Acts.

When individual narratives are canonized, the historical instance often takes on an additional paradigmatic significance. Thus the sayings of Jesus find application in later church life beyond both their original circumstances and their contexts within the Gospel narrative. The activities of the Twelve or Paul can become models for evangelizing actions of later Christian missionaries. Readers tend to place themselves imaginatively within the narrative and to listen to Jesus' words as addressed to themselves. Christians of all centuries and both sexes have identified with the prodigal son. Or they participate in the actions of the characters, as in Martha's complaint about Mary in Luke 10 or the repentant criminal's petition to the crucified Jesus in Luke 23. This is not a misreading of the text, as historical critics can sometimes imply, thus disparaging a popular Christian use of biblical narratives for preaching, personal living, and prayer. This approach was commonly used by later readers of earlier stages of the Hebrew Bible, including Jesus and the earliest Christians. The Gospel of Luke and Acts of the Apostles also evidence this kind of application of the Greek Old Testament and therefore were probably expected to be used in similar ways by later readers.[46]

Awareness of the limitations of a purely historical exegesis of scripture for Christian life has led to a widespread application of other methods, especially literary and canonical approaches. These approaches have demonstrated their value for deeper understanding and appreciation of the Lukan volumes. Since all of them also have their own respective limits, the Christian reader can benefit from a judicious use of multiple approaches as complementary ways to read and reread the Lukan narratives. New questions to the text yield new insights. As we presume and build on historical-critical exegesis, we also hope to appreciate how Luke-Acts works as a narrative with its sequel, and as a canonical text consulted by Christian churches and individuals for instruction and guidance.

Notes

Full publishing information not given here may be found in the bibliography.

1. Introduction: Reading Luke-Acts as Biblical Narrative

1. Moore, *Literary Criticism and the Gospels*, passim.

2. Cf. Weimann, *Structure and Society in Literary History*, esp. 234–266; Ong, *Orality and Literacy*, 165–170; Kurz, "Narrative Approaches to Luke-Acts," 197–200.

3. Culpepper, *Anatomy of the Fourth Gospel*, 149–202.

4. Cf. the interrelationship among historiography and other Greek genres in Fornara, *The Nature of History in Ancient Greece and Rome*, 169–193.

5. For readable introductions to narrative criticism and scripture, see Powell, *What Is Narrative Criticism?*; Kurz, "Narrative Approaches," with bibliog.; Rhoads and Michie, *Mark as Story*; Culpepper, *Anatomy*; Petersen, "Literary Criticism in Biblical Studies," 25–50 and his *Literary Criticism for New Testament Critics*; Fowler, *Loaves and Fishes*; and Sternberg, *The Poetics of Biblical Narrative*.

6. See Fitzmyer, "Historical Criticism: Its Role in Biblical Interpretation and Church Life," 244–259; on 244–245 he sketches attacks from many quarters, then explains and defends the basic methods. Cf. Petersen, *Literary Criticism*, 9–23; Krentz, *The Historical-Critical Method*, 55–88; Güttgemanns, *Candid Questions Concerning Gospel Form Criticism*.

7. Petersen, *Literary Criticism*, 9–10; Crossan, " 'Ruth Amid the Alien Corn' ": Perspectives and Methods in Contemporary Biblical Criticism," in Polzin and Rothman, eds., *The Biblical Mosaic*, 199–210; cf. Kurz, "Narrative Approaches," 195; Donahue, "The Changing Shape of New Testament Theology," 314–335, esp. 327–335. Donahue gave a panel discussion report on these changes of paradigm at the August 1990 Catholic Biblical Association meeting at Notre Dame.

8. E.g., see J. P. Martin, "Toward a Post-Critical Paradigm," 370–385; the special issue on biblical studies in *Theological Studies* 50, no. 2 (June 1989) with critical overviews of historical criticism (Fitzmyer), social sciences (Osiek), feminist hermeneutics (Trible), narrative studies (Perkins), NT theology (Donahue), etc.; and Moore, *Literary Criticism.*

9. See Stuhlmacher, *Historical Criticism and Theological Interpretation of Scripture* and his *Vom Verstehen des Neuen Testament;* Stendahl, "Contemporary Biblical Theology," 418–432. Cf. the following surveys: Donahue, "Changing Shape of NT Theology"; Osiek, "The New Handmaid: The Bible and the Social Sciences," 260–278; McKnight, *Post-Modern Use of the Bible,* 44–65, esp. 67–114.

10. J. A. Sanders, *From Sacred Story to Sacred Text,* with bibliog., 195–200; cf. his *Canon and Community.*

11. Childs, *Introduction to the Old Testament as Scripture* and his *The New Testament as Canon* with bibliog.

12. See Thiselton, *The Two Horizons;* Jeanrond, *Text and Interpretation as Categories of Theological Thinking;* J. A. Sanders, "Hermeneutics," 402–407; plus an overview of recent developments in McKnight, *Post-Modern Use,* 92–102; cf. Keegan, *Interpreting the Bible.*

13. McKnight, *Post-Modern Use,* 93–96; Betz, ed., *The Bible as Document of the University.*

14. McKnight, *Post-Modern Use,* 96–102.

15. See Beardslee, *Literary Criticism of the New Testament.* Cf. also rhetorical criticism that applies ancient rules of rhetoric to NT texts: Kennedy, *New Testament Interpretation through Rhetorical Criticism;* Mack, *Rhetoric and the New Testament.*

16. E.g., Petersen, *Literary Criticism;* cf. the recent survey, critique, and bibliog. in Moore, *Literary Criticism.*

17. Cf. Moore, *Literary Criticism,* xiii–xvi, 3–13; Petersen, *Literary Criticism,* 9–23; Kurz, "Narrative Approaches," 195.

18. Cf. Aune, *The New Testament in Its Literary Environment,* 79–80, 83–84, 94–95; Fornara, *Nature of History,* 120–137 on pleasure and amplification in history.

19. For the historiographical notion of "amplification," see Fornara, *Nature of History,* 134–137.

20. Some dispute this unified treatment and object to the hyphen in "Luke-Acts," e.g., Dawsey, "The Literary Unity of Luke-Acts: Questions of Style—A Task for Literary Critics," 48–66; M. C. Parsons, "The Making of 'Luke-Acts': The Unity of the Lucan Writings Reconsidered" (Paper at SBL Southwest Regional Meeting, Dallas, March 1988) (cited in Moore, *Literary Criticism,* 34 n. 9).

21. Johnson, *The Writings of the New Testament,* 204.

2. Implied Authors and Readers

1. See Booth, *The Rhetoric of Fiction*, 70–76, 151; Iser, *The Implied Reader*, 284, 232, and his *The Act of Reading*, 27–38; Chatman, *Story and Discourse*, 151; Moore, *Literary Criticism and the Gospels*, 46, 36 n. 12; 101.

2. The classic is Cadbury, *The Making of Luke-Acts*. Dawsey, "The Literary Unity of Luke-Acts: Questions of Style—A Task for Literary Critics," 48–66; M. C. Parsons, "The Making of 'Luke-Acts': The Unity of the Lucan Writings Reconsidered" (Paper at SBL Southwest Regional Meeting, Dallas, March 1988) (cited in Moore, *Literary Criticism*, 34 n. 9) are dissenting views. Schuler, "Questions of an Holistic Approach to Luke-Acts," 43–47, claims Tyson needs more argument than he gives to justify his holistic analysis of Luke-Acts (in *Death of Jesus in Luke-Acts*), some of which Schuler himself provides, esp. 44–46.

3. See Fitzmyer, *The Gospel According to Luke (I–IX)*, 1.35–57, and his *Luke the Theologian*, 1–26.

4. See Johnson, "On Finding the Lukan Community: A Cautious Cautionary Essay," *SBLSP* (1979) 1.87–100; Fitzmyer, *Luke I–IX*, 1.57–59.

5. For a lucid introduction into these kinds of authors and readers see Keegan, *Interpreting the Bible*, 73–109. Cf. a revised discussion of "implied author" in dialogue with Wayne Booth by Chatman, *Coming to Terms*, 80–87.

6. See J. A. Sanders, *From Sacred Story to Sacred Text*, and his *Canon and Community*; Gamble, *The New Testament Canon*; Childs, *Introduction to the Old Testament as Scripture*, 27–106, and his *The New Testament as Canon*, 3–53. For essays on Catholic, Evangelical, and Lutheran interpretations of scripture, see Hagen, Harrington, Osborne, and Burgess, *The Bible in the Churches*. For a Catholic perspective, see the special issue, "On the Reading of Scripture," of *Communio International Catholic Review* 13/4 (Winter 1986): 280–377.

7. See Sternberg, *The Poetics of Biblical Narrative*, 69–83; Booth, *Rhetoric of Fiction*, 71–76; Fowler, *Loaves and Fishes*, 149–153, 228 n. 12; Kurz, "Narrative Approaches to Luke-Acts," 206–208.

8. On *histor* narrators, see Scholes and Kellogg, *The Nature of Narrative*, 242–243.

9. See Alexander, "Luke's Preface in the Context of Greek Preface-Writing," 48–74. See the excellent recent treatment of Luke's preface in dialogue with previous scholarship (with bibliog.) in Bovon, *Das Evangelium nach Lukas*, 1.29–30. A classic and still valuable starting point has been Cadbury, "Commentary on the Preface of Luke," in Foakes Jackson and Lake, eds., *The Beginnings of Christianity*, 2.489–510. Compare Josephus's longer double prologue in *Ag. Ap.* 1.1 § 1–3, 2.1 § 1.2, and Fitzmyer, *Luke I–IX*, esp. 288.

10. Bovon, *Lukas*, 1.42; Fitzmyer, *Luke I–IX*, 1.293–294; Nolland, *Luke 1–9:20*, 1.7.

11. See the debate among Cadbury, Fitzmyer, et al. over the meaning "fulfilled" of πεπληροφορημένων as summarized in Fitzmyer, *Luke I–IX*, 1.292–293 and Nolland, *Luke 1–9:20*, 1.6–7; cf. Bovon, *Lukas*, 1.35. On professional prefaces see Alexander, "Luke's Preface."

12. See the discussion in Fitzmyer, *Luke I–IX*, 1.300–301; Tannehill, *The Narrative Unity of Luke-Acts*, 1.12; and esp. Bovon, *Lukas*, 1.40–41.

13. For a classic emphasis on the Jewish concerns of Luke-Acts, see Jervell, *Luke and the People of God*. For a subsequent debate on the Jewish apologetic and relationship to Judaism of Luke-Acts, see Tyson, ed., *Luke-Acts and the Jewish People* and bibliog. cited in the notes.

14. See Malherbe, " 'Not in a Corner': Early Christian Apologetic in Acts 26:26," 193–210, esp. 193–194 and bibliog. in n. 4.

15. See Kurz, "Narrative Approaches," 206–208, and the description of the Gospels by some Christian fathers as unfinished drafts or *hypomnēmata* (or the sometimes roughly synonymous *apomnēmoneumata*) as cited in Aune, *The New Testament in Its Literary Environment*, 66–67, cf. 82, 128.

16. See Praeder, "The Problem of First Person Narration in Acts," 193–218, esp. 214.

17. Tannehill, *The Narrative Unity of Luke-Acts*, 2.246–247.

18. Hans Conzelmann's works (*The Theology of Luke* and *Acts of the Apostles*) articulate a classic case for a Gentile Christian community; Jacob Jervell's (*Luke and the People of God* and *The Unknown Paul*) for a Jewish Christian community. Cf. Gasque, *A History of the Interpretation of the Acts of the Apostles*, 357–358.

19. See Malherbe, " 'Not in a Corner,' " and Tyson, *Luke-Acts and the Jewish People*.

20. Fitzmyer, *Luke I–IX*, 1.44–47 speculates whether the author of Luke and Acts could have come from Syrian Antioch; but elsewhere he admits, "As for the place of composition of the Lucan Gospel, it is really anyone's guess" (p. 1.57).

21. Bovon, *Lukas*, 1.23 sees Theophilus as a rich patron through whom the author hoped to reach a wide public, which seems reasonable. His mention of three target groups (educated pagans, Hellenistic Jews, and Christians disturbed by rumors) appears too much like mirror-reading to me. Cf. Johnson, "Finding the Lukan Community."

22. Fitzmyer, *Luke I–IX*, 1.57–59, in dialogue esp. with Jervell, *Luke and the People of God*.

23. See Kurz, *Farewell Addresses in the New Testament*, 44–51, 61–70 on Christian concerns in the farewell addresses of Acts 20 and Luke 22. Cf. Nolland, *Luke 1–9:20*, 1.xxxii–xxxiii for God-fearer theories.

24. This is confirmed by a similar denial that she as a non-Christian can be the implied reader of the Gospel of Mark by Berg, "Reading In/to Mark," 187–206,

esp. her abstract (p. 187), and 190–191, 196–197. She also notes the corollary that the Christians writing in *Semeia* 48: *Reader Perspectives on the New Testament* find it hard fully to apply post-structuralist or deconstructive approaches to the New Testament, which presumes faith in Christ's divinity (esp. 190–192). Stanley Porter also asks, "Why Hasn't Reader-Response Criticism Caught on in New Testament Studies?" But his answer focuses less on religious causes than on the resulting overriding preference in NT research to reconstruct original meanings rather than accentuate contemporary readings.

25. On the importance and role of faith in understanding scripture, see Laurentin, *Comment réconcilier l'exégèse et la foi*, 134–135, 184–194. An example of a responsible exegetical and historical book that is heavily influenced and even inspired by charismatic experience is McDonnell and Montague, *Christian Initiation and Baptism in the Holy Spirit*.

3. Plotting and Gaps

1. The classic definition of a plot (μῦθος) is in Aristotle, *Poetics* 7.1–7, 1450b; cf. 6.7–8, 12–20, 1450a on plotted arrangement of incidents (σύνθεσις τῶν πραγμάτων); 8.1–4, 1451a on the unity of plot action; 9.11–13, 1451b, valuing linked over episodic plot action; 10–11, 1452a–52b on plot reversals (περιπέτεια) and discoveries (ἀναγνώρισις); 16, 1454b–55a on kinds of discoveries; 17, 1455a–55b on how to construct plots; 18.1–3, 1455b on plot complication and denouement (δέσις, λύσις); 23–24, 1459a–60b on narrative representation (epic). See the thoughtful treatment of Aristotle's *Poetics* in Ricoeur, *Time and Narrative*, 1.31–51, esp. 38–51 on plot.

2. See the fine introduction to plot by Matera, "The Plot of Matthew's Gospel," 233–253, esp. 233–240; Scholes and Kellogg, *The Nature of Narrative*, 207–239; Chatman, *Story and Discourse*, 43–95; Rimmon-Kenan, *Narrative Fiction*, 46–58 on ordering and time; Abrams, *A Glossary of Literary Terms*, 139–142.

3. Sternberg, *The Poetics of Biblical Narrative*, 235–237; he refers to the "need to separate omissions or lacunae into relevancies ('gaps') and irrelevancies ('blanks')" (p. 236), admitting, however, that "one reader's gap may prove another's blank." For a view of blanks that is closer to gaps see Iser, "Interactions between Text and Reader," in *The Reader in the Text*, 106–119.

4. Iser, "The Reading Process: A Phenomenological Approach," 279–299, esp. 280–281.

5. Kurz, "Luke 3:23–38 and Greco-Roman and Biblical Genealogies," in Talbert, *Luke-Acts*, 169–187.

6. See Fitzmyer, *The Gospel According to Luke (I–IX)*, 1.91–106 on Lukan literary composition with bibliog. Cf. Papias' claim "that Mark is 'not in order,' a rhetorical term meaning 'not artistically arranged' " as cited in Aune, *The New*

Testament in Its Literary Environment, 67; cf. his discussion of order in historiographical theory on pp. 82–83, 128–130.

7. Authors differ on whether Luke's preface refers to both Luke and Acts. See Nolland, *Luke 1–9:20,* 1.5, who names Haenchen and Schürmann as considering it as referring only to the Gospel, Klein and Fitzmyer as applying also to Acts. He views it as restricted primarily to the Gospel (p. 11). Talbert, *Reading Luke,* 11 treats Luke 1:1–4 as overall preface and Acts 1:1–2 as secondary preface.

8. Most scholars include Mark 1:14–15 in the prologue, as does Guelich, *Mark 1–8:26,* 1.xxxvi, 3–5; but Frank Matera argues that it functions rather as the beginning of the public events in the body of the Gospel after the prologue (Mark 1:1–13) gives inside information to the reader: Matera, "The Prologue as the Interpretive Key to Mark's Gospel," unpublished paper read at the Narrative Task Force of the Catholic Biblical Association Annual Meeting, Santa Clara, 1988, 2–6.

9. The Hebrew has no mention of "the salvation of God," but only of "the glory of the Lord." In Luke and Acts the phrase "the salvation of God" keys the reader in on the interrelationship between Symeon's prophecy in Luke 2:30, this quotation from Greek Isaiah 40, and Paul's final statement to the Jews in Acts 28:28 that "this salvation of God has been sent to the Gentiles; they will listen."

10. BAGD, 394b. Fitzmyer, *Luke I–IX,* 1.518 cautions against reading too much eschatological sense of a critical time into this anarthrous phrase. The statement that the devil departed until (another) time does not connote a Satan-free epoch but is a *plot* device to foreshadow future events.

11. Nolland, *Luke 1–9:20,* 1.195; Talbert, *Reading Luke,* 54–57; Fitzmyer, *Luke I–IX,* 1.529; Marshall, *The Gospel of Luke,* 177–178.

12. In Mark he also shares a home with Simon (1:29) and hears Jesus' eschatological speech at the Temple with Peter, James, and John (13:3).

13. Unlike Mark and Matthew, Luke does not single out these three on the Mount of Olives, but has all eleven disciples near Jesus in his prayer before his Passion.

14. See Aletti, *L'art de raconter Jésus Christ,* 182–184; Tannehill, *The Narrative Unity of Luke-Acts,* 1.295–297.

15. See Parsons, *The Departure of Jesus in Luke-Acts,* 87–88; Aletti, *L'art de raconter,* 182–184; Tannehill, *Narrative Unity,* 1.298–301.

16. See Parsons, *Departure of Jesus,* 189–199.

17. See ibid., 72–91, 111–113; Tannehill, *Narrative Unity,* 1.298–301; and Aletti, *L'art de raconter,* 182–184, all of which deal with closure (and openness) at the end of Luke.

18. An example of modifications made in the Gospel story to coincide with Acts is Luke's unique mention of Herod in Jesus' Passion, to which he will then allude by his use of Psalm 2 in Acts 4:25–28. See the evidence in Pesch, *Die Apostelgeschichte,* 1.24–25.

19. Pesch, *Apostelgeschichte*, 1.24–25 argues from changes in Luke from Mark because of Acts that Luke and Acts were conceived and at least partially written together. See p. 28; Schneider, *Die Apostelgeschichte*, 1.118–121, esp. 120 and 69 n. 25 (style differences suggest a time gap between Luke and Acts); Conzelmann, *Acts of the Apostles*, xxxiii.

20. Compare Tannehill, *Narrative Unity*, 2.9–12; Conzelmann, *Acts*, 3–4 on proems and Acts 1:1–2, esp. 6 on transition to direct address and other Greek writings; Schneider, *Apostelgeschichte*, 1.188–199.

21. See Tannehill, *Narrative Unity*, 2.10–18. He prefers to call Acts 1:8 a summary of the mission, and only in part a summary of Acts (pp. 17–18). Cf. Schneider, *Apostelgeschichte*, 1.199–204; Pesch, *Apostelgeschichte*, 1.64–71.

22. See Johnson, *The Writings of the New Testament*, 222.

23. Sternberg, *Poetics*, 13–23.

24. See also Alter, *The Art of Biblical Narrative*, chap. 7, "Composite Artistry," 131–154.

25. In standard fashion, I will interpret similarities between Luke and Mark as Luke's reliance on his source (hypothetically Mark), and differences as probably his using another source, adding material that has no written source (such as transitions), or making changes in the source material that is attested in both Mark and Luke. Similarly, I will treat similarities and differences between only Luke and Matthew as use of a second hypothetical source Q, or addition to or variation from Q. This process has hypothetical plausibility even if our current Mark was not a source for Luke. Those who do not subscribe to these theories can follow the approach of Talbert, *Reading Luke*, 1–2, which focuses on Lukan features without assuming any source theory. Fitzmyer, *Luke I–IX*, 1.63–106 has a thorough treatment and bibliog. of the debate and dominant two-source theory; Tyson, "Source Criticism of the Gospel of Luke," in Talbert, ed., *Perspectives on Luke-Acts*, 24–39, cites objections of the significant minority, for which the classic treatment is Farmer, *The Synoptic Problem*. Nolland, *Luke 1–9:20*, 1.xxviii–xxxi, mentions the Farmer objections but takes a similar stance to mine.

26. Bovon, *Das Evangelium nach Lukas*, 1.169 also remarks how this synchronism raised the folk traditions about the Baptist to the level of literature, as well as following dating of prophetic books.

27. See Bovon, *Lukas*, 1.165, 169.

28. Luke prepares for the Baptist's question in 7:20 (=Q) by inserting two episodes that are probably not from Q, the healing of the centurion's sick servant and the raising of the widow's son at Nain from the dead. These exemplify the healing and raising of the dead that Jesus cites to John in 7:22 as signs of his identity. The crowd's responses to the Nain raising, "A great prophet has been raised up among us" and "God has visited his people" (7:16), directly introduce the pericope containing the Baptist's question about Jesus' identity, as well as

alluding to the prophetic hymn by John's father in Luke 1:78, "when the dawn from heaven [literally, "the rising from on high"] will visit us."

Luke apparently has a greater redundancy than his Q source, namely the full repetition of John's question, "Are you he who is to come, or are we to await another?" which is lacking in Matthew's version (Luke 7:20/Matt. 11:3), unless Matthew dropped it from Q. The redundancy both deepens the biblical flavor of the account and emphasizes the question. Luke also motivates Jesus' answer, "tell John *what you have seen and heard*" (7:22), by inserting mention of Jesus' healings (v. 21) between the question from the Baptist's disciples and Jesus' answer (vv. 22–23).

29. Kurz, "Luke 3:23–38," 169–172. Compare Tobit 1:1, in form the closest genealogy to Luke's. The Greek form of the genealogy is: υἱός, ὡς ἐνομίζετο, Ἰωσὴφ τοῦ Ἠλί . . . τοῦ Ἀδὰμ τοῦ θεοῦ.

30. Kurz, "Luke 3:23–38," 172–175.

31. E.g., see Bovon, *Lukas*, 1.19–22; Fitzmyer, *Luke I–IX*, 1.91–97, 105–106.

32. See Fitzmyer, *Luke I–IX*, 1.313–315; Brown, *The Birth of the Messiah*, 250–255 with bibliog., esp. Laurentin, *Structure et Théologie de Luc I–II*.

33. See Nolland, *Luke 1–9:20*, 1.155–157, and his citation of S. Giet, "Un procédé littéraire d'exposition: l'anticipation chronologique," *Revue des études augustiniennes* 2 (1956): 243–249, on anticipation as a common literary procedure in antiquity.

34. Sternberg, *Poetics*, chap. 11, "The Structure of Repetition: Strategies of Informational Redundancy," 365–440. Cf. Suleiman, "Redundancy and the 'Readable' Text," 119–142; Anderson, "Double and Triple Stories, the Implied Reader, and Redundancy in Matthew," 71–89; and Burnett, "Prolegomenon to Reading Matthew's Eschatological Discourse: Redundancy and the Education of the Reader in Matthew," 91–109.

35. Sternberg, *Poetics*, 375–393.

36. See Luke 2:32 and Acts 13:47, where Isa. 49:6 is applied to Jesus and to the missionaries respectively (Conzelmann, *Acts*, 106, 212).

37. Parsons, *Departure of Jesus*, 91–93, 232–233 (esp. n. 151, recent bibliog.); Aletti, *L'art de raconter*, chap. 5, "En chemin vers Jérusalem. Lc 9,51–19,44," 111–131; Fitzmyer, *Luke I–IX*, 1.824–827.

38. Parsons, "Narrative Closure and Openness in the Plot of the Third Gospel: The Sense of an Ending in Luke 24:50–53," 201–223. The last chapter of Luke uses several analepses to recall and show fulfillment of earlier prophecies and promises from scripture or divine or human agents in the story. Cf. Parsons, *Departure of Jesus*, 69–93; Torgovnick, *Closure in the Novel*.

39. Parsons, "Closure and Openness," 205.

40. Ibid., 205–207 and n. 39.

41. Ibid., 208.

42. Ibid., 212–217.

43. Ibid., 219–220. See Lucian, *Hist.*, 52–54, 63–64 on interlacing events (συμπεριπλοκῇ τῶν πραγματῶν) as a leading narrative technique in writing history (Parsons, "Closure and Openness," 220).

44. Parsons, "Closure and Openness," 220.

45. Ibid., 220–221 incl. n. 104, citing Petersen, "When is the End Not the End?: Literary Reflections on the Ending of Mark's Narrative," 153: "The end of a text is not the end of the work when the narrator leaves unfinished business for the reader to complete, thoughtfully and imaginatively, not textually." Cf. Parsons, *Departure of Jesus*, 93–96; Tannehill, *Narrative Unity*, 2.353–357.

46. Tannehill, "Israel in Luke-Acts: A Tragic Story," 69–85; Tannehill, *Narrative Unity*, 2.345, 347–350.

47. See Culpepper, *Anatomy of the Fourth Gospel*, 79–84 on plotting, and his citation (p. 79) of Crane, "The Concept of Plot," in Scholes, ed., *Approaches to the Novel*, 233–243: " . . . the plot . . . is . . . not simply a means—a 'framework' or 'mere mechanism'—but rather the final end which everything in the work, if that is to be felt as a whole, must be made, directly or indirectly, to serve" (p. 241).

48. Cadbury, *The Making of Luke-Acts*, 321–324; Conzelmann, *Acts*, 227–228; Pesch, *Apostelgeschichte*, 2.311–313; Schneider, *Apostelgeschichte*, 2.411–414, 420–421.

49. Chrysostom, *Homilies on Acts*, 55, in Cadbury, *Making Luke-Acts*, 322.

50. See Schneider, *Apostelgeschichte*, 2.412–413, 421; Cadbury, *Making Luke-Acts*, 321–324; Roloff, *Die Apostelgeschichte*, 370–372, 375–376.

51. For introduction to reader-response criticism, see Suleiman and Crosman, *The Reader in the Text*; Tompkins, ed., *Reader-Response Criticism*; and their excellent annotated bibliog.; Freund, *The Return of the Reader*; Holub, *Reception Theory* for German counterparts. From a biblical perspective, see Fowler, "Who Is 'the Reader' in Reader Response Criticism?" 5–23; McKnight, *Post-Modern Use of the Bible* with bibliog.; McKnight, ed., *Semeia* 48 (*Reader Perspectives on the New Testament*); Moore, *Literary Criticism and the Gospels*, chap. 6, pp. 71–107, esp. bibliog. n. 2–3, pp. 71–72, and bibliog., pp. 185–221.

52. On readers actualizing codes, see Iser, "The Reading Process: A Phenomenological Approach," in Tompkins, ed., *Reader-Response*, 50–69 (cf. p. xv); and Iser, "Interaction between Text and Reader," in Suleiman and Crosman, eds., *Reader in the Text*, 106–119; McKnight, *Post-Modern Use*, 145–146, 153–158, 217–222, 235–241.

53. See esp. Iser, "Reading Process," and "Interaction." Cf. McKnight, *Post-Modern Use*, 115–166 on interdependence of structures, codes, and readers; and Sternberg, *Poetics*, chap. 6, "Gaps, Ambiguity, and the Reading Process," 186–229.

54. See McKnight, *Post-Modern Use*, 143–162, 165–166.

55. BAGD, 171.

56. Parsons, *Departure of Jesus*, 72–77; Tannehill, *Narrative Unity*, 1.299–301 also mentions the notion of "framing" from Uspensky, *A Poetics of Composition*.

57. Parsons, *Departure of Jesus*, 93–94.

58. Ibid., 194; cf. 194–198.

59. Ibid., 194–198.

60. See Tannehill, *Narrative Unity*, 2.349–353; Schneider, *Apostelgeschichte*, 2.418–420; Conzelmann, *Acts*, 227; and the debate in Tyson, *Luke-Acts and the Jewish People*.

61. Tannehill, *Narrative Unity*, 2.347–348.

62. Conzelmann, *Acts*, 227–228; Schneider, *Apostelgeschichte*, 2.411–413, 420; Pesch, *Apostelgeschichte*, 2.311–313.

63. Cited in Cadbury, *Making of Luke-Acts*, 322.

64. Cf. Thompson, *The Role of Disbelief in Mark*, 172–174; Magness, *Sense and Absence*, esp. 123–125.

4. The Prologue to Luke's Gospel: Narrative Questions

1. See Cadbury, *The Making of Luke-Acts*, 194–201; S. Brown, "The Role of the Prologues in Determining the Purpose of Luke-Acts," in *Perspectives on Luke-Acts*, 99–111; Fitzmyer, *The Gospel According to Luke (I–IX)*, 1.287–302 with bibliog.

2. W. Martin, *Recent Theories of Narrative*, 159; "Conventions are not a constraint on genuine communication; they make it possible." On p. 161 he says of Iser: "He holds that the writer does exercise control over the way readers perceive the text, through the use of mutually understood conventions, and to this extent he accepts the assumptions of the communication model." J. L. Austin's "speech-act" theory of language tries "to identify the conventions that make words meaningful in various situations" (p. 182).

Cf. Lanser, *The Narrative Act*, 60: "Fowler shares not only Weimann's understanding of the connection between ideology and technique but also his awareness of the social dimensions of literary discourse. As all writers belong to one or more linguistic communities, perspective is sociologically as well as psychologically conditioned. . . . " On p. 61 she adds, "Fowler also recognizes that writer and reader are limited by the conventions of literary communication and of language use which are operant at a given time and place." On p. 233 she remarks that texts are conventionally read against literary and cultural norms. Weimann, *Structure and Society in Literary History*, says: "Storytelling is an ancient convention, which, in contrast to the even older art of miming, has a nonmimetic time structure and a rhetoric distinctly its own" (p. 244). See p. 237. Cf. Mailloux, *Interpretive Conventions*.

3. Ricoeur, *Interpretation Theory*, 19.

4. See Alexander, "Luke's Preface in the Context of Greek Preface-Writing," 48–74.

5. Ricoeur, *Interpretation Theory*, 32–33 shows how genres are more inclusive than just for writing. They apply to discourse the categories of practice and work. Language is submitted to rules of craftsmanship [*technē*] to produce *works* of art and discourse. "And the style of a work is nothing else than the individual configuration of a singular product or work. The author here is not only the speaker, but also the maker of this work, which is his work" (p. 33).

6. Lucian, *A True Story*, LCL 1 (Cambridge, Mass.: Harvard University Press, 1961), 248–357, pp. 248–253. Cf. Cadbury, *Making of Luke-Acts*, 194; S. Brown, "Role of Prologues," 99–100.

7. Josephus, *Ag. Ap.*, 1.1; *Bel* 1 proem 1 § 3 LCL 2.2–3: "In these circumstances, I—Josephus, son of Matthias, a Hebrew by race, a native of Jerusalem and a priest, who at the opening of the war myself fought against the Romans and in the sequel was perforce an onlooker—propose to provide the subjects of the Roman Empire with a narrative of the facts. . . . " For fine recent assessments and applications of the research on prefaces in general and on those of Luke and Acts, see Bovon, *Das Evangelium nach Lukas*, 1.29–43; Nolland, *Luke 1–9:20*, 1.3–12; and Fitzmyer, *Luke I–IX*, 1.287–302.

8. See Scholes and Kellogg, *The Nature of Narrative*, 242–244.

9. See the criticisms by Sternberg, *The Poetics of Biblical Narrative*, 86–87, which however seem extreme and unwarranted in light of similar fluctuations in Luke's OT precedents like Ezra and 2 Maccabees. Also note Cadbury, *Making of Luke-Acts*, 223–224, on expected rhetorical contrast between prefaces and the rest of the works.

10. E.g., see Josephus, *Bel.* 6.2.1 § 108–110; 5.13.6 § 566.

11. See Kurz, "Narrative Approaches to Luke-Acts," 205 and nn. 33–34, and variations in Ezra between third-person (Ezra 1–7:26), first-person "I" (7:27–8:30), "we" (8:31–36), "I" (9:1–15), third-person (10:1–44). Tobit 1:3–3:7 uses first-person narration, the rest of the book third-person. The preface (2 Macc. 2:19–32) and ending (15:37c–39) of 2 Maccabees are in the first person, the rest the usual third-person omniscient narrator.

12. Cf. Josephus' nods as *histor* to possible skepticism of readers: "For my part, I have recounted each detail here told just as I found it in the sacred books. Nor let anyone marvel at the astonishing nature of the narrative or doubt that it was given to men of old, innocent of crime, to find a road of salvation through the sea itself, whether by the will of God [κατὰ βούλησιν θεοῦ] or maybe by accident [κατὰ ταὐτόματον]. . . . " After appealing to the parallel miracle in Alexander's life, Josephus ends with the typical *histor*'s comment: "However on these matters everyone is welcome to his own opinion [ὡς ἑκάστῳ δοκεῖ διαλαμβανέτω]" (Jos. *Ant.* 2.16.5, § 347–348, LCL 4.316–317). See *Ant.* 1.3.9, § 108, LCL 4.52–53 and

note "b" for other examples of similar formula in Josephus and Dionysius of Halicarnassus.

13. Josephus, *Bel.* 1 proem 6 § 18, LCL 2.10–11.

14. See Cadbury, *Making of Luke-Acts*, 346–347. Cf. Hemer, *The Book of Acts in the Setting of Hellenistic History*, 323–328; and Fitzmyer, *Luke I–IX*, 1.296–297 for the scholarly debate.

5. Narrators in Luke

1. See Cadbury, *The Making of Luke-Acts*, 12–110; Fitzmyer, *The Gospel According to Luke (I–IX)*, 1.63–106.

2. See the general introduction to plotting by Matera, "The Plot of Matthew's Gospel," 233–253, esp. 235–240 with literature.

3. See Tannehill, *The Narrative Unity of Luke-Acts*, 1.4–5, 295, 300–301; 2.5–7.

4. Scholes and Kellogg, *The Nature of Narrative*, 242–243.

5. Fitzmyer, *Luke I–IX*, 1.107–127; Horton, "Reflections on the Semitisms of Luke-Acts," in Talbert, ed. *Perspectives on Luke-Acts*, 1–23; Dawsey, *The Lukan Voice*, 18–32, esp. 27–32.

6. See Talbert, *Reading Luke*, 15–17.

7. Ibid.; Talbert, "Prophecies of Future Greatness: The Contribution of Greco-Roman Biographies to an Understanding of Luke 1:5–4:15," in Crenshaw and Sandmel, eds. *The Divine Helmsman*, 129–141.

8. See Tannehill, *Narrative Unity*, 1.53–55; Talbert, *Reading Luke*, 36–37.

9. For the gnoseological purposes of the Lukan introduction, see Aletti, *L'art de raconter Jésus Christ*, 67–85, esp. 79–80.

10. Nolland, *Luke 1–9.20*, 1.137–138; Fitzmyer, *Luke I–IX*, 1.453, 455–459.

11. Bovon, *Das Evangelium nach Lukas*, 1.169.

12. See chap. 3, "Plotting and Gaps."

13. See Ernst, *Das Evangelium nach Lukas*, 152–154.

14. See Kurz, "Luke 3:23–38 and Greco-Roman and Biblical Genealogies," in Talbert, *Luke-Acts*, 169–187.

15. On framing, see Rhoads and Michie, *Mark as Story*, 51, and ref. p. 149 n. 25. Cf. the Markan interpolation technique in Kee, *Community of the New Age*, 54–56.

16. Cf. the survey in Praeder, "Jesus-Paul, Peter-Paul, and Jesus-Peter Parallelisms in Luke-Acts: A History of Reader Response," 23–39.

17. See Aletti, *L'art de raconter*, 39–61; Ernst, *Evangelium nach Lukas*, 168–169; Fitzmyer, *Luke I–IX*, 1.529; Kodell, "Luke's Gospel in a Nutshell (Lk 4:16–30)," 16–18.

18. On focalization as the perspective from which a narrative is perceived, see Genette, *Narrative Discourse*, 185–194, esp. 189; Rimmon-Kenan, *Narrative Fiction*, 71–85, esp. 71; Bal, "The Narrating and the Focalizing: A Theory of the

Agents in Narrative," 234–237, 247–249, esp. 235. However, a standard glossary of literary terms uses only "point of view," not "focalization": Abrams, *Glossary*, 144–148.

19. On telling and showing points of view in Hellenistic and Semitic forms of narration, see F. Martin, *Narrative Parallels to the New Testament*, 10–11.

20. For a brief introduction to intertextuality, see Abrams, *A Glossary of Literary Terms*, 247. A novel that vividly illustrates intertextuality is Eco, *The Name of the Rose*, with its key symbol of the labyrinthine library. See Eco, *Reflections on the Name of the Rose*, 20: "Thus I rediscovered what writers have always known . . . : books always speak of other books, and every story tells a story that has already been told."

21. See Fitzmyer, *Luke I–IX*, 1.660 on the Lukan emphasis on fame about Jesus in Luke 7:17, as at Luke 4:37 (1.547) and 5:15 (1.575). Cf. the theme in Acts of the spread of the word (e.g., Acts 6:7, 12:24, 13:49, 19:20, and the ending of Acts [28:31]).

22. For opinions about how the two versions are related, see Fitzmyer, *Luke I–IX*, 1.684–686; Nolland, *Luke 1–9:20*, 1.352; and Marshall, *The Gospel of Luke*, 305–307.

23. On this refrain, see Tannehill, *Narrative Unity*, 1.94–96; Marshall, *Luke*, 314; Fitzmyer, *Luke I–IX*, 1.692.

24. See Nolland, *Luke 1–9:20*, 1.365; Tannehill, *Narrative Unity*, 1.137–139, 210; Talbert, *Reading Luke*, 91–93; Fitzmyer, *Luke I–IX*, 1.696–697.

25. See Fitzmyer, *Luke I–IX*, 1.67, 166, esp. 770–771.

26. Moessner, *Lord of the Banquet*, esp. 1–44 *Forschungsbericht*, and 290–307. Cf. Fitzmyer, *Luke I–IX*, 1.823, esp. 825–826 and bibliog. 1.830–832; cf. 1.166–170; Aletti, *L'art de raconter*, 112–123.

27. Moore, "Are the Gospels Unified Narratives?" 443–458.

28. Moessner, *Lord of the Banquet*, esp. 290–296, finds much more of an actual travel narrative than this (grounded in Deuteronomistic History).

29. Cf. Moessner, *Lord of the Banquet*, 66, 78 n. 99; Fitzmyer, *Luke I–IX*, 1.827–828.

30. The manuscripts are almost equally divided whether there were seventy or seventy-two disciples. Both numbers find support in the list of nations in Genesis 10 (seventy in Hebrew, and seventy-two in LXX) and in the Moses story of the elders filled with Moses' spirit (Num. 11:16–17, 24–25, plus Eldad and Medad in Num. 11:26). See *TCGNT*, 150–151; Marshall, *Luke*, 414–415; Fitzmyer, *The Gospel According to Luke (X–XXIV)*, 2.845–846.

31. Fitzmyer, *Luke X–XXIV*, 2.1152–1153.

32. Fitzmyer, *Luke I–IX*, 1.241–243.

33. Tiede, *Prophecy and History in Luke-Acts*, chap. 3, "Weeping for Jerusalem," 65–96, 143–148.

34. See Fitzmyer, *Luke I–IX*, 1.167–168; Aletti, *L'art de raconter*, 112–116.

35. See Aletti, *L'art de raconter*, 112–116.

36. See Talbert, *Reading Luke*, 185–196; Tannehill, *Narrative Unity*, 1.187–199.

37. Johnson, *The Literary Function of Possessions in Luke-Acts*, 48–49, 119–121.

38. This pattern of the narrator's foreshadowing what is to come (prolepses), and referring back to what has already happened (analepses), plays an important role in consolidating the protracted Luke-Acts narratives and accentuating their main plot line from among many smaller episodes. Cf. Aletti, *L'art de raconter*, 26–29, 71–72, 182–183.

39. See Carroll, *Response to the End of History*, 103–119.

40. See Kurz, "Acts 3:19–26 as a Test of the Role of Eschatology in Lukan Christology," 309–323; Carroll, *Response to the End*, 107–114.

41. Johnson, *Literary Function*, 48–49, 119–121.

42. Ibid.

43. See Tannehill, *Narrative Unity*, 1.60, 263–264; Fitzmyer, *Luke X–XXIV*, 2.1374.

44. Fitzmyer, *Luke X–XXIV*, 2.1377–1378; Marshall, *Luke*, 789.

45. Kurz, *Farewell Addresses in the New Testament*, 54–55. Fitzmyer, *Luke X–XXIV*, 2.1384, 1452 refers to "the hour" as a salvation-history designation.

46. Kurz, "Luke 22:14–38 and Greco-Roman and Biblical Farewell Addresses," 251–268; Kurz, *Farewell Addresses*, 52–70.

47. On the textual question of Luke 22:19–20, see *TCGNT*, 173–177; Fitzmyer, *Luke X–XXIV*, 2.1387–1388; Kurz, *Farewell Addresses*, 57–59.

48. Kurz, *Farewell Addresses*, 59; Fitzmyer, *Luke X–XXIV*, 2.1395.

49. On elements of the farewell genre, see Kurz, "Luke 22:14–38," 253–263.

50. Plato, *Phaedo*, 115c–116a; see Kurz, *Farewell Addresses*, 69.

51. Cf. Talbert, *Reading Luke*, 212–214; Beck, " 'Imitatio Christi' and the Lucan Passion Narrative," in Horbury and McNeil, eds., *Suffering and Martyrdom in the New Testament*, 28–47; Neyrey, *The Passion According to Luke*, chap. 2, "Jesus in the Garden (Lk 22:39–46)," 49–68; Kurz, "Narrative Models for Imitation in Luke-Acts," in Meeks, Balch, and Ferguson, eds., *Greeks, Romans, and Christians*, 171–189, esp. 185–186.

52. On the textual problem, see Neyrey, *Passion*, 55–57 with bibliog. notes, 198 n. 1, p. 200; *TCGNT*, 177; Fitzmyer, *Luke X–XXIV*, 2.1443–1444; Marshall, *Luke*, 831–832.

53. Sternberg, *The Poetics of Biblical Narrative*, 52–53, cf. 137, 175; Berlin, *Poetics and Interpretation of Biblical Narrative*, "The Term *Hinneh*," 62–63, 149 n. 37, bibliog.

54. Cf. Rhoads and Michie, *Mark as Story*, 51, 149 n. 25; Donahue, *Are You the Christ?*, 58–63.

55. Fitzmyer, *Luke X–XXIV*, 2.1466; Marshall, *Luke*, 846–847.

56. Luke 1:1, "to order a narrative" (ἀνατάξασθαι διήγησιν); 1:3, "to write for you in order" (καθεξῆς σοι γράψαι).

57. Note the juxtaposition of "the king and governor" finding Paul innocent in Acts 26:30–31, as well as Jesus' prophecy in Luke 21:12 that his disciples will be led before "kings and governors" for his name's sake.

58. Cf. Tannehill, *Narrative Unity*, 1.197; Talbert, *Reading Luke*, 219–225; Fitzmyer, *Luke X–XXIV*, 2.1520.

59. See Neyrey, *Passion*, 108–128, n. 207–210.

60. Many scholars doubt the authenticity of this verse because it is missing in important early manuscripts from disparate geographical regions. But internal evidence linking it to Stephen's similar statement of forgiveness in Acts 7:60, as well as to references back to it in the speeches of Acts 3:17, 13:27, and 17:30, strongly argue for its Lukan origin. See the authenticity debate over Luke 23:34a in Fitzmyer, *Luke X–XXIV*, 2.1503–1504; Talbert, *Reading Luke*, 219–220; esp. Tannehill, *Narrative Unity*, 1.272 n. 126; Marshall, *Luke*, 867–868. Even if it should not be original to Luke, most second- and third-century Fathers and the second-century four-Gospel harmony, Tatian's Diatesseron, attest the reading as present by the time of the canonization of the NT.

61. This distinction between people and leaders continues in Acts. Thousands of the people repent and believe in Jesus at Peter's speeches (Acts 2:37–41, 3:19–26, 4:4), but the leaders continue to persecute the apostles (Acts 4–5). See Johnson, *Literary Function*, 115–119, and his *Writings*, 220–221.

62. See Neyrey, "The Absence of Jesus' Emotions—the Lukan Redaction of Lk. 22, 39–46," 153–171; Neyrey, *Passion*, 49–68.

63. Cf. Fitzmyer, *Luke X–XXIV*, 2.1520–1521; Tannehill, *Narrative Unity*, 1.271–274.

64. See treatment of "and behold" earlier, p. 62 (and by Sternberg and Berlin, cited in n. 53 of this chapter).

65. Cf. Fitzmyer, *Luke X–XXIV*, 2.1543.

66. Against the majority opinion classically expressed by R. E. Brown, *The Virginal Conception and Bodily Resurrection of Jesus*, 108–111, that the first appearance(s) occurred in Galilee.

67. On the Markan ending, see esp. Magness, *Sense and Absence*.

68. On the Emmaus scene, see esp. Dillon, *From Eye-Witnesses to Ministers of the Word*.

69. Cf. Aletti, *L'art de raconter*, 185, 187–188; Tannehill, *Narrative Unity*, 1.282–284 (including the irony that results); Fitzmyer, *Luke X–XXIV*, 2.1563. On the "theological passive," see Zerwick, *Biblical Greek*, 76 § 236.

70. Cf. esp. R. E. Brown, *Virginal Conception and Bodily Resurrection*, 69–129.

71. Cf. Aletti, *L'art de raconter,* 184–190; Aristotle, *Poetics,* 11.4–10, 1452a–52b on plotted recognition (ἀναγνώρισις); 16, 1454b–55a on kinds of recognition; Ernst, *Lukas,* 658; Tannehill, *Narrative Unity,* 1.279–285.

72. Cf. Ernst, *Lukas,* 657–658; Tannehill, *Narrative Unity,* 1.285–289.

73. Parsons, *The Departure of Jesus in Luke-Acts,* 93–96; Aletti, *L'art de raconter,* 182–184.

74. Parsons, *Departure of Jesus,* 112.

6. Narrators in Acts

1. Conzelmann, *Acts of the Apostles,* xxxviii; Haenchen, *The Acts of the Apostles,* 35–36, 81–82; on the source question and recent scholarship, see 82–132. Cf. Schneider, *Die Apostelgeschichte,* 1.103–108; Pesch, *Die Apostelgeschichte,* 1.51–53.

2. Kurz, "Luke 22:14–38 and Greco-Roman and Biblical Farewell Addresses," 251–268, esp. 251–253, 267–268.

3. See Schneider, *Apostelgeschichte,* 1.95–108 and bibliog. The classic is Wilckens, *Die Missionsreden der Apostelgeschichte.* On the *prosopopoeia* as the rhetorical practice of wording speeches according to the supposed speaker and occasion, see Kurz, "Hellenistic Rhetoric in the Christological Proof of Luke-Acts," 186; Cadbury, *The Making of Luke-Acts,* 185–190; Johnson, *The Writings of the New Testament,* 237–238; and Aune, *The New Testament in Its Literary Environment,* 31, 125–128.

4. Tannehill, *The Narrative Unity of Luke-Acts,* 2.5–6.

5. On "showing" and "telling," see F. Martin, *Narrative Parallels to the New Testament,* 10–11.

6. Parsons, *The Departure of Jesus in Luke-Acts,* 177–178, citing Walworth, "The Narrator of Acts," 37–38; Tannehill, *Narrative Unity,* 2.9; Conzelmann, *Acts,* 6.

7. The Revised New American Bible consistently refrains from capitalizing *holy* in *Holy Spirit* which I find a historicist conceit that does not do justice to the canonical nature of the text. Even in the writer's time, the Holy Spirit was considered divine and would have been capitalized if the language had had the distinction between capital and small letters at that time.

8. See Tannehill, *Narrative Unity,* 2.14–17; cf. 1.257–261.

9. Haenchen, *Acts,* 143–144, esp. n. 9; Tannehill, *Narrative Unity,* 2.17–18 amends the consensus: Acts 1:8 outlines the Christian mission, but only partly the plot of Acts.

10. See Johnson, *Writings,* 213, with a list of passages in Luke and Acts; Tannehill, *Narrative Unity,* 2.19–20.

11. Scholars have noted how the plot in Acts alternates between vivid scenes showing particular events and generalizing summary and transition passages that

place those events in a broader historical context. By thus linking individual stories together, they provide a sense of general plot movement rather than merely juxtaposed episodes. See Tannehill, *Narrative Unity*, 2.43–44. Cf. Dibelius, *Studies in the Acts of the Apostles;* Cadbury, "The Summaries in Acts," in Foakes Jackson and Lake, eds., *The Beginnings of Christianity*, 5.392–402; Schneider, *Apostelgeschichte*, 1.105–108.

12. Other well-known examples of these summaries are the following: Acts 2:42–47, which generalizes the Pentecost event into a movement of church growth in Jerusalem and provides a transition to the next episode of the healing of the lame man; Acts 4:32–35 similarly generalizes about further church growth and life after that healing and its consequent confrontation with Jewish leaders, and with the information about Barnabas in 4:36–37 provides a transition to the Ananias and Sapphira episode.

13. Schneider, *Apostelgeschichte*, 1.215–216; Pesch, *Apostelgeschichte*, 1.87; both rely on G. Lohfink, *Die Sammlung Israels*, 71–72.

14. Cf. Kurz, "Luke 22:14–38," 258; Kurz, *Farewell Addresses in the New Testament*, 16, esp. 67; Schneider, *Apostelgeschichte*, 1.216.

15. Aletti, *L'art de raconter Jésus Christ*, 190–197.

16. Tannehill, *Narrative Unity*, 2.26–27; Lohse, "Die Bedeutung des Pfingstberichtes im Rahmen des lukanischen Geschichtswerkes," 422–436. Cf. Pesch, *Apostelgeschichte*, 1.102; Conzelmann, *Acts*, 13.

17. See Cadbury, *Making Luke-Acts*, 184–190; Schneider, *Apostelgeschichte*, 1.95–108 and bibliog. We will devote a special chapter to comparing the effects of the Lukan narrator of Acts with a narrator within the story of Acts, using the test case of the three narratives of Paul's call, one by the narrator in Acts 9 and two by Paul himself in Acts 22 and 26. For simplicity's sake in analyzing Acts 2, we shall simply refer to Peter speaking, without having to reiterate constantly that it is the Lukan narrator who shows him doing so.

18. Aletti, *L'art de raconter*, 190–197.

19. Cf. Pesch, *Apostelgeschichte*, 1.117, 119–120.

20. See esp. Tannehill, *Narrative Unity*, 1.29–33.

21. See Hamm, "Acts 3, 1–10: The Healing of the Temple Beggar as Lucan Theology," 311; Lake and Cadbury, *Beginnings of Christianity*, 4.31.

22. Kurz, "Hellenistic Rhetoric," 176–178; Grimaldi, *Studies in the Philosophy of Aristotle's Rhetoric*, 110–113; for a contemporary application of this insight in relation to Acts 2, see Kurz, *Following Jesus: A Disciple's Guide to Luke and Acts*, 102–103.

23. Johnson, *The Literary Function of Possessions in Luke-Acts*, 119–121.

24. This and other references back to ignorance as leaving room for repentance in Acts 13:27 and 17:30, joined with the parallel prayer for forgiveness by Stephen in Acts 7:60, seem strong internal evidence that that textually disputed verse,

Luke 23:34, is original. Jesus' prayer for forgiveness of those who had him killed opens the way here and in Acts 2 for their forgiveness, as Stephen's prayer for his killers, among whom the narrator goes out of his way to mention Saul (Acts 8:1), lays the groundwork for Saul's forgiveness. Cf. Tannehill, *Narrative Unity*, 1.272, 2.101; Marshall, *The Gospel of Luke*, 867–868.

25. For how the Johannine prologue provides implied readers information needed to understand the narrative, especially its ironies, see Culpepper, *Anatomy of the Fourth Gospel*, 18–20.

26. Johnson, *Literary Function*, 119–121.

27. Cf. Conzelmann, *Acts*, 35; Haenchen, *Acts*, 226–227; Schneider, *Apostelgeschichte*, 1.357–358. For the *pesher* type of applying of scripture to current events as one of several adaptations of biblical narratives and prophecies popularly called "midrashic," see Harrington and Horgan, "Palestinian Adaptations of Biblical Narratives and Prophecies," in Kraft and Nickelsburg, eds., *Early Judaism and Its Modern Interpreters*, 239–258 with bibliog., esp. Horgan pp. 247–255, and the classic essays of Miller, "Targum, Midrash and the Use of the Old Testament in the New Testament," 29–82, and Bloch, "Midrash," and "Methodological Note for the Study of Rabbinic Literature," in Green, ed., *Approaches to Ancient Judaism*, 29–50, 51–75.

28. Johnson, *Literary Function*, 183–190; Conzelmann, *Acts*, 36, 23–24; Pesch, *Apostelgeschichte*, 1.181–182, 131; Schneider, *Apostelgeschichte*, 1.365.

29. Kurz, "Narrative Models for Imitation in Luke-Acts," in Meeks, Balch, and Ferguson, eds., *Greeks, Romans, and Christians*, esp. 171 n. 2; 174 n. 13; 174–176, 187–188. Cf. Tannehill, *Narrative Unity*, 2.78–79.

30. Kurz, "Hellenistic Rhetoric," *passim.*

31. Kurz, "Narrative Models," 187–188.

32. Tannehill, *Narrative Unity*, 2.66–67.

33. Ibid., 2.94; Schneider, *Apostelgeschichte*, 1.437–439.

34. Tannehill, *Narrative Unity*, 2.101, 1.272.

35. Cf. Schneider, *Apostelgeschichte*, 1.487; Tannehill, *Narrative Unity*, 2.103–105.

36. Haenchen, *Acts*, 304 (vs. Schneider, *Apostelgeschichte*, 1.492–493). Cf. Tannehill, *Narrative Unity*, 2.106–107; Conzelmann, *Acts*, 65–66.

37. On *exempla*, see Kurz, "Narrative Models." Cf. Haenchen, *Acts*, 304; Schneider, *Apostelgeschichte*, 1.492–493.

38. Cf. Abrams, *A Glossary of Literary Terms*, 145: "omniscient point of view."

39. Cf. Ong, *Orality and Literacy*, 119: even financial accounts were "audited"—i.e., the numbers were checked by reading them aloud—as late as the twelfth century in England. Cf. Nelson, "From 'Listen, Lordings' to 'Dear Reader,'" 110–124.

40. Schneider, *Apostelgeschichte*, 1.503–504; Pesch, *Apostelgeschichte*, 1.292; Kurz, *The Acts of the Apostles*, 47.

41. On Qumran *pesharim* and messianic reading of the Hebrew Bible, see Horgan, "The Bible Explained (Prophecies)," in Kraft and Nickelsburg, eds., *Early Judaism and Its Modern Interpreters*, 247–253; and Fitzmyer, *The Dead Sea Scrolls*.

42. Cf. Tannehill, *Narrative Unity*, 2.114.

43. Paul's account in Gal. 1:18–24 is hard to reconcile with this report (e.g., see Conzelmann, *Acts*, 75), but this is simply an analysis of what the narrative says and how it says it.

44. Cf. Tannehill, *Narrative Unity*, 2.124; Schneider, *Apostelgeschichte*, 2.40–41.

45. On redundancy, information theory, and Luke-Acts, see the fine treatment and bibliog. notes in Tannehill, *Narrative Unity*, 2.74–77.

46. Aune, *The New Testament in Its Literary Environment*, 134–135; Dionysius, *Roman Antiquities*, 1.48.1: "There are different accounts given of the same events by some others, which I look upon as less probable than this. But let every reader judge as he thinks proper" (LCL 1.155); Herodotus 2.123; 5.45; Josephus, *Ant.* 1.108 (see LCL 4.52–53 n. b); 2.348; 3.81: "Of these happenings each of my readers may think as he will [ὡς βούλεται φρονείτω]" (LCL 4.356–357); Lucian, *Hist.*, 60.

47. Bassler, *Divine Impartiality*.

48. Cf. Pesch, *Apostelgeschichte*, 1.344; Schneider, *Apostelgeschichte*, 2.78–79.

49. Kurz, *Acts*, 11, 30.

50. The narrator exemplifies in Acts 11 what is meant by the promise in Luke 1:3–4 to give assurance through narrative, by showing the assurance Peter gives by his story within the story, or imbedded narrative. When circumcised believers challenged Peter for eating with the uncircumcised, Peter's answer was simply a narrative of what happened step by step (καθεξῆς, Acts 11:4, cf. Luke 1:3). Cf. Tannehill, *Narrative Unity*, 2.143–144; on the enactment-report sequence, see Sternberg, *The Poetics of Biblical Narrative*, 375–378, 380–382.

51. Similar repetitions with varying points of view affect the story of Paul's conversion and call in Acts 9, 22, and 26.

52. Cf. Tannehill, *Narrative Unity*, 2.146–147.

53. Schneider, *Apostelgeschichte*, 2.91–92; Tannehill, *Narrative Unity*, 2.124; cf. Conzelmann, *Acts*, 88–89, excursus on "Christian."

54. See *UBSGNT*[3], textual apparatus p. 464; and *TCGNT*, 398–400. Besides the evidence of the framing device at 11:30 and 12:25, the awareness (to which many variants give evidence) both of the problem and of the probably correct information, namely, the presence of Barnabas, Saul (13:1), and John Mark (13:5) immediately thereafter in *Antioch*, as well as the fact that John Mark's home is

ordinarily in *Jerusalem* (12:12, 13:13), also argue that before the textual corruption this is what the narrative was trying to say.

55. The narrator further intertwines the Barnabas and Saul plot lines with those of Peter by the presence in both of John Mark. In 12:12, Peter goes to the home of John Mark's mother in Jerusalem after his escape from prison. In 12:25, Barnabas and Saul take John Mark with them from Jerusalem to Antioch, and in 13:5 they take him as their assistant on their mission from Antioch to Cyprus. In 13:13 John Mark abandons Barnabas and Saul and returns to Jerusalem. Finally, after the Jerusalem Council where Barnabas, Saul, and Peter all played major roles, Barnabas and Paul returned to Antioch where they disagreed about taking Mark on their next missionary trip. This resulted in their separation, with Barnabas taking Mark (Col. 4:10 informs us they were cousins), and Paul taking Silas (15:35–41), who was also from Jerusalem and a leader in that church (15:22, 32–33).

56. Tannehill, *Narrative Unity*, 2.159–161; Schneider, *Apostelgeschichte*, 2.119.

57. Tannehill, *Narrative Unity*, 2.160, 164–165, 170–172. On the identity of structure between Acts missionary speeches, see Richard, *Acts 6:1–8:4*, 13.

58. Cf. Abrams, *Glossary*, 93; Duke, *Irony in the Fourth Gospel*, 7–27; Culpepper, *Anatomy*, 165–169.

59. The flesh-and-blood Paul's own account in 1 Cor. 15:1–11 does not make this distinction but includes himself at the end of the list of resurrection witnesses. Cf. Conzelmann, *Acts*, 105; Haenchen, *Acts*, 410–411.

60. In Acts 18:6 and at the climactic final scene in 28:28, Paul will repeat this turn from resisting Jews to Gentiles, which thus proves to be a major motif for the narrative.

61. Cf. Tannehill, *Narrative Unity*, 2.178–180; Kurz, *Acts*, 12, 66, 83–84; Pervo, *Profit with Delight*, 64–65.

62. There is a widespread current tendency to treat all such details as novelistic, yet Paul himself says he had been stoned once and shipwrecked three times, all of which are normally fatal (2 Cor. 11:25). On the use of traditional *topoi* to portray actual events, see Aune, *Literary Environment*, 129–130.

63. Peter's recognition of James as head of the Jerusalem church seems implied in Acts 12:17 by his having his escape reported to James. Cf. Roloff, *Die Apostelgeschichte*, 190–191.

64. Cf. Pesch, *Apostelgeschichte*, 2.80–81; Lake, "The Apostolic Council of Jerusalem," Additional Note 16, in *Beginnings*, 5.195–212, esp. 204–209; Schneider, *Apostelgeschichte*, 2.189–192, bibliog. 2.169–171; Conzelmann, *Acts*, 118–119.

65. For what he calls an enactment-report sequence, see Sternberg, *Poetics*, 375–378, 380–382. This relates to the practice of oral supplementation and

authentication of letters by messengers: see Dahl, "Letter," 538–541, esp. 538–539; Tannehill, *Narrative Unity*, 2.192–193; J. L. White, *Light from Ancient Letters*, esp. 215–216.

66. Cf. Schneider, *Apostelgeschichte*, 2.185–186.

67. Nestle-Aland[26] 367, UBSGNT[3] 478, TCGNT 439.

68. His apparent lack of concern may be due to his probable retrospective awareness that the rift between Mark and Paul was eventually healed, as both the undisputed Pauline letters (Philemon 24) and the disputed letters (Col. 4:10, 2 Tim. 4:11) testify to contemporary readers.

69. Tannehill, *Narrative Unity*, 2.195–196.

70. Cf. Wehnert, *Die Wir-Passagen der Apostelgeschichte*, 130–131.

71. Pesch, *Apostelgeschichte*, 2.97; Tannehill, *Narrative Unity*, 2.190 with n. 23; cf. Schneider, *Apostelgeschichte*, 2.200–201.

72. Cf. Aune, *Literary Environment*, 123–124; Tannehill, *Narrative Unity*, 2.246–247.

73. Cf. Tannehill, *Narrative Unity*, 2.210–220; Schubert, "The Place of the Areopagus Speech in the Composition of Acts," in Rylaarsdam, ed., *Transitions in Biblical Scholarship*, 235–261; Conzelmann, *Acts*, 140.

74. Cf. Conzelmann, *Acts*, 152.

75. Cf. Tannehill, *Narrative Unity*, 2.222; Pesch, *Apostelgeschichte*, 2.148–149; Schneider, *Apostelgeschichte*, 2.250–251.

76. Haenchen, *Acts*, 542–546; Schneider, *Apostelgeschichte*, 2.255–256; Conzelmann, *Acts*, 155; Tannehill, *Narrative Unity*, 2.227; Pesch, *Apostelgeschichte*, 2.155–156.

77. Cf. Tannehill, *Narrative Unity*, 2.230–231. Roloff, *Apostelgeschichte*, 237–238, 274, prefers not to refer to a "second" and "third" journey, but to the epoch of major Pauline mission.

78. With Pesch, *Apostelgeschichte*, 2.166, 1.87; vs. Schneider, *Apostelgeschichte*, 2.265; Conzelmann, *Acts*, 160.

79. Tannehill, *Narrative Unity*, 2.236–237.

80. The narrator's interpretation that the Jewish exorcists' attempts to expel demons in the name of Jesus, in whom they did not believe, was magic, is corroborated by papyri with magic formulae that show the use in exorcisms of a syncretistic mixture of names of gods and goddesses, including biblical names for God. See the examples of the exorcism in the Paris Magical Papyrus in Barrett, *The New Testament Background*, 31–35, and that in Kee, *The Origins of Christianity*, 85–86.

81. Cf. Tannehill, *Narrative Unity*, 2.243; Schneider, *Apostelgeschichte*, 2.274–275.

82. Kurz, "Hellenistic Rhetoric," 186; Cadbury, *Making Luke-Acts*, 185–190; Johnson, *Writings*, 237–238; Aune, *Literary Environment*, 31, 125–128.

83. Cf. Tannehill, *Narrative Unity*, 2.228–229.

84. Some scholars find these unprepared alternations between "we" and "they" narrators a sign of insufficiently redacted use of sources and a deficiency in the narrative. See the nuanced discussion in Walworth, "Narrator of Acts," 34–35.

85. Tannehill, *Narrative Unity*, 2.248–249.

86. Cf. Kurz, *Farewell Addresses*, 33–51, esp. 33–34.

87. Ibid., esp. 121–123; cf. Kurz, "The Beloved Disciple and Implied Readers," 100–107.

88. Cf. Tannehill, *Narrative Unity*, 2.262–267.

89. On "evangelist" and the link to earlier Philip episodes, see Schneider, *Apostelgeschichte*, 2.304.

90. As introducing mention of other prophets, see Schneider, *Apostelgeschichte*, 2.304.

91. Tannehill, *Narrative Unity*, 2.262–267.

92. It is a Lukan pattern to prepare for a return from a first- to third-person narrator by distinguishing Paul from the "we" group. Cf. Walworth, "Narrator of Acts," 35–36.

93. At Philippi, however, Paul and Silas escape from jail with God's help, which is unlike his later imprisonments or that of Jesus. The fact that Silas accompanies Paul in prison parallels the imprisonment not of Jesus but of Peter and John who are jailed together in Acts 4, and the escape of Paul and Silas parallels the deliverance of the apostles from prison in Acts 5.

94. Cf. Aune, *Literary Environment*, 127.

95. Cf. Tannehill, *Narrative Unity*, 2.241–242.

96. Ibid., 2.295–296; cf. pp. 310–313 regarding differing accounts by Festus and the narrator; Sternberg, *Poetics*, 390–440.

97. Kurz, "Hellenistic Rhetoric," 185; cf. Veltman, "The Defense Speeches of Paul in Acts," in Talbert, ed., *Perspectives on Luke-Acts*, 243–256; Neyrey, "The Forensic Defense Speech and Paul's Trial Speeches in Acts 22–26: Form and Function," in Talbert, *Luke-Acts*, 210–224.

98. Cf. Tannehill, *Narrative Unity*, 2.304.

99. Cf. Ibid., 2.306.

100. Cf. Schneider, *Apostelgeschichte*, 2.374–375; O'Toole, *The Christological Climax of Paul's Defense (Ac 22:1–26:32)*, 65–66, 71–78; Tannehill, *Narrative Unity*, 2.116–123, 275–278, 283, 321–325. On Lukan symbolic use of light, see also Hamm, "Sight to the Blind: Vision as Metaphor in Luke," 457–477.

101. On retrospective changes of perspective in autobiography, see W. Martin, *Recent Theories of Narrative*, 76–78. The collapsing of a process into its initiating moment may actually correspond to a similar contraction in Paul's own autobiographical statements in an apologetic setting in Galatians 1–2. It is quite

possible that Paul himself, because of his apologetic situation in Galatians, collapsed a process with discrete steps into his initial experience. If so, the closer similarities of Galatians 1–2 to Acts 26 than to Acts 9 and 22 would find partial explanation.

102. Cf. Kurz, "The Function of Christological Proof from Prophecy for Luke and Justin," 114–125, esp. 122–123; Kurz, "Hellenistic Rhetoric."

103. Malherbe, " 'Not in a Corner': Early Christian Apologetic in Acts 26:26," 193–210.

104. Conzelmann, Acts, 216–217.

105. On focalization through characters (here the "we" narrator), see Tannehill, Narrative Unity, 2.246–249, 28–29; Lanser, The Narrative Act, 141–142. Cf. Rimmon-Kenan, Narrative Fiction, 71–85.

106. See esp. Tannehill, Narrative Unity, 2.353–357 and his references.

107. The narrator of the Gospel of Luke calls his narrative by the Greek general term for any narrative, διήγησις, rather than using the names of more specific genres of narrative like history or biography. Thus the terms extradiegetic and intradiegetic are particularly appropriate to Lukan terminology, despite their awkwardness in English. Cf. Rimmon-Kenan, Narrative Fiction, 91–95, 103; Abrams, A Glossary of Literary Terms, 145, avoids the terms.

7. Narrative Claims of "We" in Acts

1. Praeder, "The Problem of First Person Narration in Acts," 216. Her main criticisms are directed toward Plümacher, "Wirklichkeitserfahrung und Geschichtsschreibung bei Lukas: Erwägungen zu den Wir-Stücken der Apostelgeschichte," 2–22; and esp. Robbins, "By Land and By Sea: The We-Passages and Ancient Sea Voyages," in Talbert, ed. Perspectives on Luke-Acts, 215–242.

2. Praeder, "First Person Narration." Cf. criticisms of Robbins by Walworth, "The Narrator of Acts," 35–36, n. 35; Hemer, The Book of Acts in the Setting of Hellenistic History, 317–319, and his "First Person Narrative in Acts 27–28," 79–109; Kurz, "Narrative Approaches to Luke-Acts," 195–220; Wehnert, Die Wir-Passagen der Apostelgeschichte, 114–117, 123; and Fitzmyer, Luke the Theologian, 17–22.

3. Praeder, "First Person Narration," 214 (emphasis mine).

4. See bibliog. in ibid.; Hemer, Book of Acts; Wehnert, Wir-Passagen; Pesch, Die Apostelgeschichte, 1.47 n. 37; Schneider, Die Apostelgeschichte, 1.89–95.

5. E.g., Berg, "Reading In/to Mark," 190–191 (cf. 187), doubts that she as Jew can be a NT implied reader.

6. Tannehill, The Narrative Unity of Luke-Acts, 2.246–247. Tannehill goes further to claim that readers are invited to participate as companions of Paul (p. 247). Such invitation to identify with characters or even observers in a narrative is a separate issue needing further investigation (p. 247, esp. n. 5.). It is related to

whether the narrative invites participation through depicting some characters as models for reader imitation.

7. Ibid., 2.248–249.

8. Ibid., 2.264.

9. Ibid., n. 5.

10. Cf. Kurz, "Narrative Approaches," 218, esp. n. 67 and references there to Nestle-Aland[26], 402.

11. Translation is from Lake and Cadbury in Foakes Jackson and Lake, ed., *The Beginnings of Christianity*, 4.325. The Greek variations from Codex Vaticanus are cited in Ropes, in Foakes Jackson and Lake, eds., *The Beginnings of Christianity*, 3.241.

12. So also Pesch, *Die Apostelgeschichte*, 2.288, and Schneider, *Die Apostelgeschichte*, 2.383. Cf. Conzelmann, *Acts of the Apostles*, 215.

13. Also Schneider, *Apostelgeschichte*, 2.388 and n. 8.

14. So also Pesch, *Apostelgeschichte*, 2.288–289.

15. Walworth, "Narrator of Acts," 34 and n. 33 citing Genette, *Narrative Discourse*, 246.

16. Walworth, "Narrator of Acts," 34.

17. Schneider, *Apostelgeschichte*, 2.396–397; cf. Tannehill, *Narrative Unity*, 2.334–336, but I disagree with Tannehill's suggestion that this was an *actual* Eucharist.

18. Tannehill, *Narrative Unity*, 2.335, his translation.

19. Warnecke, *Die tatsächliche Romfahrt des Apostels Paulus*, challenges the almost universal contemporary understanding that Malta is the Melitē (Μελίτη) of Acts 28:1. He gives impressive evidence that the West Greek Island of Cephallenia near Ithaca and the mainland city of Nicopolis fit all the information in Acts about the storm and about where Paul was shipwrecked.

20. See Tannehill, *Narrative Unity*, 2.340–341 and Pervo, *Profit with Delight*, 65. Tannehill also stresses that this scene deliberately presents the natives' perspective, not the implied author's (or narrator's).

21. On humor in Acts, see Pervo, *Profit with Delight*, 58–59, esp. in this episode, p. 65; Kurz, *Acts*, 12. Cf. Tannehill, *Narrative Unity*, 2.340–341.

22. See Schneider, *Apostelgeschichte*, 2.199.

23. See Wehnert, *Wir-Passagen*. Through an analysis of actants in Acts 16, Wehnert argues that Luke names only chief representatives of any group (e.g., Jesus alone, not the Twelve [Luke 18:31–19:28], or Paul and Silas, not Timothy [Acts 17:10–14]), though the context shows that the Twelve and Timothy were part of those respective groups (p. 131).

This observation works for Acts 15:40–16:1, where the narrator keeps third-person singular verbal forms even after Paul has brought Silas along as a companion. It is true that Luke sometimes names a group through the main character

Jesus (thus one for thirteen in Luke 18–19), and Acts 15:40–16:1 uses the (third-person) singular verb even when both Paul and Silas are implied, but changes to the (third-person) plural in 16:4 after adding Timothy to the named group in 16:3 (pp. 130–132). But few would accept that Timothy is included where only Paul and Silas are named (two as chief representatives for only three), especially in the third-person prison account in 16:19–40. Cf. Schneider, *Apostelgeschichte*, 2.201.

24. Cf. Conzelmann, *Acts*, 127: "Haenchen believes that for the ancient reader the 'we' would have pointed to Silas and Timothy. But these two were with Paul for a long time without the narrative shifting into the first person. 'We' rather gives the impression that at this point the narrator has become Paul."

Wehnert, *Wir-Passagen*, argues that the "we" in 16:10–17 adds no other characters to those previously (and later) mentioned as "they" in 16:4–8 (18–40) (pp. 132–133). Because Wehnert accepts no new person under "we," and because 16:17 separates Paul from "us," Wehnert identifies "us" as Silas and Timothy, identical with Sil(v)a(nu)s and Timothy in the same Macedonian setting in 1 Thess. 1:1 (pp. 132–134). Wehnert therefore identifies the speaker in the "we" as Silas, since Silas is with Paul the main representative of the group of three, and since Timothy plays a totally subordinate role in 16:10–17:14, never being named after 16:4. With most readers I would see the narrator as an unnamed new person besides Silas and Timothy, since they have already been treated in the third person, as Conzelmann notes above. I would further argue that Timothy is not present at all in the exorcism and Paul and Silas's arrest in 16:18–40, even though he is probably still included in the "we" passage including Lydia's conversion in 16:10–15. I grant Wehnert that the context seems to demand Timothy's unmentioned presence in 17:10–13, because he is mentioned in 17:14–15. All this indicates how frequently difficult it is to know whom the anonymous "we" includes.

25. But some scholars limit the separate group to the Asians Tychicus and Trophimus, e.g., Conzelmann, *Acts*, 168: "(so most exegetes)"; Schneider, *Apostelgeschichte*, 2.282; Praeder, "First Person Narration," 197.

26. So also holds Wehnert, *Wir-Passagen*, 132–134.

27. Sternberg, *The Poetics of Biblical Narrative*, 58–59, 159–163, and *passim*.

28. Cf. Walworth, "Narrator of Acts," 35–36.

29. Cf. Praeder, "First Person Narration," 196–206.

30. With Tannehill, *Narrative Unity*, 2.246 against most redaction critics cited by Conzelmann, *Acts*, 168: "Either the whole company went on ahead to Troas, or only the Asians (so most exegetes)." Cf. Praeder, "First Person Narration," 197; Schneider, *Apostelgeschichte*, 2.282.

31. Cf. the report in Bovon, *Das Evangelium nach Lukas*, 1.37–38 and nn. 48–51; Cadbury, "Commentary on the Preface of Luke," App. C., *The Beginnings of Christianity*, 2.489–510, pp. 501–502 with references to Josephus. Bovon, n. 51,

refers to Jos., *Vit.*, 357 and *Ag. Ap.*, 1.10. 53–55. See esp. Jos., *Ag. Ap.*, 1.10.53–55, LCL 1.184–185.

32. Cadbury, "Commentary on Preface," 502; A. J. B. Higgins, "The Preface to Luke and the Kerygma in Acts," in W. W. Gasque, ed., *Apostolic History and the Gospel* (FS F. F. Bruce) (Exeter: Paternoster Press, 1970), 78–91, as cited in Bovon, *Lukas*, 1.37 n. 48.

The "we" passages seem to point to the same meaning of παρηκολουθηκότι in Luke 1:3 as does Jos., *Ag. Ap.*, 1.10.53–55. In the latter, Josephus claims, " . . . it is the duty of one who promises to present his readers with actual facts first to obtain an exact knowledge of them himself, either through having been in close touch with the events [ἢ παρηκολουθηκότα τοῖς γεγονόσιν], or by inquiry from those who knew them. That duty I consider myself to have amply fulfilled in both my works. In my *Antiquities*, as I said, I have given a translation of our sacred books. . . . My qualification as historian of the war was that I had been an actor [αὐτουργὸς] in many, and an eyewitness [αὐτόπτης] of most, of the events . . . " (*Ag. Ap.*, 1.10.53–55, LCL 1.184–185). As Cadbury points out, "παρηκολουθηκότα τοῖς γεγονόσιν seems . . . to refer directly to Josephus' own presence and participation at the events recorded by him in his Jewish War" (Cadbury, "Commentary on Preface," 502.) The "we" passages lend weight to a similar implication for παρηκολουθηκότι in Luke 1:3 that the narrator was present at events so described.

33. Fitzmyer, *The Gospel According to Luke (I–IX)*, 1.47–51; Fitzmyer, *Luke the Theologian*, chap. 1, "The Authorship of Luke-Acts Reconsidered," 1–26.

34. Fitzmyer, *Luke I–IX*, 1.48–49; Fitzmyer, *Luke the Theologian*, 3–7.

35. Fitzmyer, *Luke the Theologian*, 9–11. In fact, a recent published dissertation (Wehnert, *Wir-Passagen*) argues for Silas as the narrator behind the "we" passages.

36. Fitzmyer, *Luke the Theologian*, 7–11.

37. See esp. Pervo, *Profit with Delight*, 51–54 with 155–157 (nn. 176–206).

38. Praeder, "First Person Narration," 214. The quoted phrases in this section are from her, though the emphases are mine.

39. In the Philippi instance, however, the parallel between Paul and Silas imprisoned and miraculously freed parallels rather Peter and John imprisoned and freed in the first part of Acts, not the solitary imprisonment and final suffering of Jesus in the Gospel.

40. Robbins, "By Land and By Sea"; on the discussion see the first two notes of this chapter.

8. Influence of Variant Narrators on Repeated Acts Narratives

1. Other well-known repetitions are the Peter-Cornelius incident (Acts 10–11) and the apostolic decree (Acts 15:20, 29; 21:25); cf. Tannehill, *The Narrative*

Unity of Luke-Acts, 2.191–192 and 130 with nn. 5–6, his citations of R. Barthes, "L'analyse structurale du récit à propos d'Actes X–XI," 58 (1970): *Recherches de Science religieuse* 17–37, pp. 33–36.

2. See Kurz, "Hellenistic Rhetoric in the Christological Proof of Luke-Acts," 185–186.

3. On narrators and points of view, see Abrams, *A Glossary of Literary Terms,* 144–148 with ref.; Rhoads and Michie, *Mark as Story,* 35–44, 146–148 (notes), esp. bibliog. nn. 1–2, 10, 14.

4. Cf. Conzelmann, *Acts of the Apostles,* 72–73; Schneider, *Die Apostelgeschichte,* 2.21–24.

5. Cf. Chatman, *Story and Discourse,* 155–157: Where there is a conflict between the ideology of the narrator and of a character, the narrator's point of view (unless unreliable) "tends to override the character's" (156). Rimmon-Kenan, *Narrative Fiction,* 81 notes how "the norms of the text" as provided by the dominant perspective of the extradiegetic narrator subordinate other ideologies within the text. They transform other evaluating subjects like the narrator Paul in Acts 22 "into objects of evaluation. . . . Put differently, the ideology of the narrator-focalizer is usually taken as authoritative, and all other ideologies in the text are evaluated from this 'higher' position." Sheeley, "The Narrator in the Gospels: Developing a Model," 221, proposes the taxonomies of Rimmon-Kenan, here extra- or intradiegetic, for narrative level, as an inclusive approach to study of NT narrators. Cf. W. Martin, *Recent Theories of Narrative,* 185.

6. W. Martin, *Recent Theories,* 74: "History and much realistic fiction also share certain linguistic conventions: the narrator never speaks in his own voice but simply records events, giving readers the impression that no subjective judgment or identifiable person has shaped the story being told." Cf. F. Martin, *Narrative Parallels to the New Testament,* 10–11; Abrams, *Glossary,* 145–146, 23–24.

7. By "free indirect speech" (or discourse), I mean a narrator's indirect quotation of what a chracter says but in the narrator's third-person paraphrase, not in the character's own words. See the explanation and examples in Tannehill, *Narrative Unity,* 2.106–107, 248–249; Sternberg, *The Poetics of Biblical Narrative,* 52–53 (in Hebrew Scripture); Haacker, "Einige Fälle von 'erlebter Rede' im Neuen Testament," 70–77.

8. For fellow travelers not both seeing and hearing, cf. Maximus of Tyre 9 (15 Dübner) 7d–f: "In this place sailors often saw a young man with yellow hair leaping in golden armor. Some by no means saw him, but heard him singing the song of victory; others both saw and heard" (οἱ δὲ εἶδον μέν οὐδαμῶς, ἤκουσαν δὲ παιωνίζοντος. οἱ δὲ καὶ εἶδον καὶ ἤκουσαν.); cited by Conzelmann, *Acts,* 71.

9. For double visions see Wikenhauser, "Doppelträume," 100–111; *Herm. Vis.,* 3.1.2; Dionysius, *Roman Antiquities,* 1.57.4; Josephus, *Ant.,* 11.327, 333–

334; Valerius Maximus 1.7.3; Apuleius, *Met.*, 11.27, etc. The double dream motif is found in fiction also (Conzelmann, *Acts*, 72). Cf. Pervo, *Profit With Delight*, 73 and references 164 n. 85.

10. Cf. (on Acts 10–11) Tannehill, *Narrative Unity*, 2.130; Funk, *The Poetics of Biblical Narrative*, 153–156.

11. Compare Jer. 50:25=27:25 LXX; Ps.-Clem. *Recog.* 3.49: Simon has become a "choice vessel for the wicked one" *(vas electionis maligno)*; cited by Conzelmann, *Acts*, 72.

12. On his major theme of the relation between God's omniscience and the narrator's, see Sternberg, *Poetics*, 12–13, 87–99, and frequently. On foreshadowing, see the treatment of Luke 1–2 as "Previews of Salvation" in Tannehill, *Narrative Unity*, 1.15–44.

13. On intertextuality within a deconstructionist perspective, see Funk, *Poetics*, 293–294 and, more radically, Moore, *Literary Criticism and the Gospels*, 133–134. My use of the term, esp. regarding Lukan allusions to the OT, addresses that phenomenon without the almost nihilistic suppositions of much deconstruction.

14. On ancient *prosopopoeia*, see Kurz, "Hellenistic Rhetoric," 185–186 and ancient sources cited there. Cf. Johnson, *The Writings of the New Testament*, 201. Theon's meaning of *prosopopoeia* differs from other ancient rhetoricians like Hermogenes, who applies *ethopoeia* to writing speeches for persons and *prosopopoeia* to writing speeches for things treated as persons. This kind of personification of inanimate or abstract beings is the modern meaning for *prosopopoeia* that Abrams gives (*Glossary*, 67).

15. Cf. Kurz, "Rhetoric," 186; Johnson, *Writings*, 237–238; Aune, *The New Testament in Its Literary Environment*, 31, 125. This presumes with most contemporary scholars that the author of Acts is responsible for the wording of the speeches in Acts as we now have them, without prejudice to questions of what oral or written traditions, sources, or information he may have used to fashion those speeches.

16. Cf. Schneider, *Apostelgeschichte*, 2.25.

17. On unreliable narrators, mostly in a contemporary setting, see Booth, *The Rhetoric of Fiction*, 158–159; Chatman, *Story and Discourse*, 148–149; Rimmon-Kenan, *Narrative Fiction*, 100–103; Abrams, *Glossary*, 147; cf. Funk, *Poetics*, 29, 34.

18. E.g., the change from Acts 9, "to the synagogues," to Acts 22, "brethren," maintains the character of an autobiographical account (Conzelmann, *Acts*, 186–187).

19. See W. Martin, *Recent Theories*, 76. Two variables in autobiography cause change of perspective: "The significance of the events may change when they are viewed in retrospect; and the self that describes the events may have changed since they were first experienced. . . . In narrative, truth is time-dependent."

20. Cf. Acts 26:11 "I punished. . . . "

21. The term "blaspheme" in Acts 26:11 ("I punished them in an attempt to force them to blaspheme [βλασφημεῖν]") is consistent with this Jewish point of view, despite contrary first impressions. Pliny in his letter to Trajan uses this term for what he tried to get accused Christians to do, namely to blaspheme Christ (maledicere Christo). Cited by Conzelmann, Acts, 210 from Pliny, Ep., 10.96.5: "He who maintains that he is not a Christian must offer sacrifices and maledicere Christo . . . quorum nihil posse cogi dicuntur qui sunt re vera Christiani. . . . "

22. On autobiographical apology in Acts 22, see Conzelmann, Acts, 186–187.

23. The fact that the perspective of Acts 26, which includes Paul's commission in his first experience of the risen Jesus, is that of Paul's own letters should not distract from this study of the differences within Acts of the points of view of variant narrators. In the context of Acts, the narrative by the omniscient extradiegetic narrator in Acts 9 is the standard against which intradiegetic versions of the same event are measured, not historical inferences from Paul's letters, which are not part of the Lukan corpus and narrative world.

The similarity of perspective between Acts 26 and Galatians raises an interesting question, however. Is it possible that Paul himself may have combined earlier and later steps in his conversion process in his narrative in Galatians because of the autobiographical apology in which he was engaged there? If so, this would suggest a very different explanation to the inconsistencies between Acts and Galatians from that of the majority view.

24. See Schneider, Apostelgeschichte, 2.322.

9. Implicit Commentary in Luke-Acts

1. Culpepper, Anatomy of the Fourth Gospel, chap. 6, "Implicit Commentary," 149–202.

2. See Praeder, "Jesus-Paul, Peter-Paul, and Jesus-Peter Parallelisms in Luke-Acts: A History of Reader Response," 23–39 with bibliog.

3. The three days are debated, since in Luke the Markan "after three days" for the resurrection is changed to "on the third day": cf. Fitzmyer, The Gospel According to Luke (I–IX), 1.441 and Nolland, Luke 1–9:20, 1.130 against Laurentin, Jésus au temple, 101–102; Dupont, "L'Évangile (Lc 2,41–52): Jésus à douze ans," 25–43, esp. 42; and Elliott, "Does Luke 2:41–52 Anticipate the Resurrection?" 87–89. On the metaphor and symbolism in Luke 5:1–11, see Fitzmyer, Luke I–IX, 1.568–569. On eucharistic symbolism in Acts 27:35, see Tannehill, The Narrative Unity of Luke-Acts, 2:334–335 (I see it as more symbolic of than an actual Eucharist, with Schneider, Die Apostelgeschichte, 2.396–397).

4. Culpepper, Anatomy, 167; see the distinction between stable and unstable irony, and between verbal and dramatic irony in "Irony," in Abrams, A Glossary

of *Literary Terms*, 91–95. Cf. the deconstructive challenge to this notion in Moore, *Literary Criticism and the Gospels*, 159–170.

5. Abrams, *Glossary*, 92; or as pure paradox undercutting all irony, see Moore, *Literary Criticism*, 159–170.

6. Culpepper, *Anatomy*, 165–180; Tannehill, *Narrative Unity*, 1.282–284; cf. Rhoads and Michie, *Mark as Story*, 61–62.

7. E.g., see Tannehill, *Narrative Unity*, 1.194 and *passim*.

8. Ibid., 1.282–284, 288–289.

9. Cf. Ibid., 2.101, 103.

10. Cf. Ibid., 1.214; Bovon, *Das Evangelium nach Lukas*, 1.426–427.

11. Cf. also Luke 10:22, "no one knows who the Son is except the Father, or who the Father is except the Son . . . "; 19:3, Zacchaeus sought to see who Jesus was; 20:2, leaders ask, "Who gave you this authority?"; and Acts 9:5; 22:8; and 26:15, where Saul asks Jesus, "Who are you, Lord?"

12. Cf. Tannehill, *Narrative Unity*, 1.192.

13. On how the Temple was destroyed because the people did not recognize Jesus (in Acts 6 and Luke 19) see Tannehill, ibid., 2.169; Neyrey, *The Passion According to Luke*, 108–128.

14. Tannehill, *Narrative Unity*, 1.194.

15. On recognition see Aristotle's *Poetics*, 10–11, 1452a–52b, and 16, 1454b–55a. Cf. Culbertson, *The Poetics of Revelation*, 15–20, 33–54 (in Greek writings), 137–174 (in Mark and John), 175–185; p. 21 n. 19 refers to Sternberg, *The Poetics of Biblical Narrative*, 177, and his discussion of how recognition is essential to Hebrew narrative.

16. Cf. Tannehill, *Narrative Unity*, 2.33–37; Aune, *The New Testament in Its Literary Environment*, 124–128.

17. Cf. Tannehill, *Narrative Unity*, 2.169.

18. Cf. Ibid., 2.37.

19. Schneider, *Apostelgeschichte*, 1.319–320; cf. Conzelmann, *Acts of the Apostles*, 28; Pesch, *Die Apostelgeschichte*, 1.153.

20. Cf. Tannehill, *Narrative Unity*, 1.125–127, 198–199.

21. Johnson, *The Literary Function of Possessions in Luke-Acts*, 70–78.

22. See Carroll, *Response to the End of History*, 103–104, 107–114, 117–119.

23. Johnson, *Literary Function*, 70–78.

24. Cf. Culbertson, *Poetics of Revelation*, 9, 11.

25. Tannehill, *Narrative Unity*, 1.282–284.

26. Ibid., 2.101.

27. Ibid., 1.30. The most recent assessment of the Lukan use of reversal strategies is York, *The Last Shall Be First*. Especially helpful is his treatment of Greco-Roman perceptions of the form in the first century, pp. 173–182, as a corrective to excessive reliance on the Aristotelian notion.

28. Cf. Tannehill, *Narrative Unity*, 2.102–103.

29. Ibid., 2.146; cf. Pesch, *Apostelgeschichte*, 2.351; Schneider, *Apostelgeschichte*, 2.88–89.

30. Tannehill, *Narrative Unity*, 2.102–105, 146–147.

31. On Gamaliel see Tannehill, ibid., 2.67; Conzelmann, *Acts*, 43. On Caiaphas see Culpepper, *Anatomy*, 177–179.

32. Cf. Garrett, *The Demise of the Devil*, 89–99, esp. 108; Pervo, *Profit with Delight*, 63–64; Conzelmann, *Acts*, 163–164; Schneider, *Apostelgeschichte*, 2.270.

33. Dawsey, *The Lukan Voice*, esp. 15–40.

34. Ibid., plus the appendices on the different language used by Jesus and the narrator, 157–183.

35. Ibid., 43–122.

36. Moore, *Literary Criticism*, 33, cf. 30–34.

37. The religious nature of Luke and Acts, written in the tradition of biblical narratives like Samuel-Kings and 1–2 Maccabees (in all of which the narrator faithfully represents the authors' positions), further argues against the narrator of Luke being unreliable. See Tannehill, *Narrative Unity*, 1.6–7.

38. This may contribute to the reasons why Dawsey argues against the unity of Luke and Acts in "The Literary Unity of Luke-Acts: Questions of Style—A Task for Literary Critics," 48–66. However, others agree with him in doubting the unity of Luke-Acts. See the recent Parsons, "Christian Origins and Narrative Openings: The Sense of a Beginning in Acts 1–5," 403–422, esp. 420 n. 1, which alludes to the forthcoming M. C. Parsons and R. I. Pervo, *Rethinking the Unity of "Luke–Acts"* (Minneapolis: Fortress Press).

39. Thus the speeches of Acts are closer to narrator's style in Luke than the sayings of Jesus in the Gospel because they are Lukan creations (using *prosopopoeia*) as distinguished from sayings-source material. See Aune, *Literary Environment*, 125–128.

40. Dawsey, *Lukan Voice*, 43–102, see esp. 71, 101–102.

41. Tannehill, *Narrative Unity*, 2.35–36 links ignorance to the Aristotelian theme of recognition (*Poetics* 1450a) and ignorance (ἄγνοια 1453a–54a); cf. Tannehill, 2.57, 169.

42. Tannehill notes the difficulties but argues cogently for the verse in his *Narrative Unity*, 1.272, esp. n. 126. So does Marshall, *The Gospel of Luke*, 867–868. Some who argue for the exemplary nature of Jesus' death in Luke also tend to accept the authenticity of Luke 23:34: Ernst, *Das Evangelium nach Lukas*, 634–635; and Kurz, "Narrative Models for Imitation in Luke-Acts," in Meeks, Balch, and Ferguson, eds., *Greeks, Romans, and Christians*, 186–187. For strong arguments against the verse and a synopsis of the argument, see esp. *TCGNT*, 180 and Fitzmyer, *The Gospel According to Luke (X–XXIV)*, 2.1503–1504.

43. On reader-elevating, character-elevating, and evenhanded communication of information and reading positions, see esp. Sternberg, *Poetics*, 163–175. Applied to Luke 4:22, cf. Tannehill, *Narrative Unity*, 1.68; Nolland, *Luke 1–9:20*, 1.199.

44. Fitzmyer, *Luke I–IX*, 1.814, and Zerwick, *Biblical Greek Illustrated by Examples*, 76 § 236.

45. Cf. Fitzmyer, *Luke X–XXIV*, 2.873; Aune, *Literary Environment*, 55–56.

46. *Phaedo*, 115c–116a, as in Hamilton and Cairnes, *The Collected Dialogues of Plato*, 95–96; cf. Kurz, *Farewell Addresses in the New Testament*, 69, and Kurz, "Luke 22:14–38 and Greco-Roman and Biblical Farewell Addresses," 253–255, 257–258.

47. Cf. Dillon, *From Eye-Witnesses to Ministers of the Word*, 19–20, 146–147, 150–151 esp. n. 232, esp. 195–197.

48. Cf. Tannehill, *Narrative Unity*, 2.85–87, 91–92; Sternberg, *Poetics*, 268–270 on foreshadowing through "analogical organization."

49. See Garrett, *Demise of the Devil*, passim, esp. 103–109, 113 n. 4.

50. Cf. Pervo, *Profit with Delight*, 64–65.

51. In mocking the Jewish sons of Sceva in Acts 19:13–20, the narrator ridicules them not for Jewish practices but for trying to use Jesus' name magically in exorcisms. See Garrett, *Demise of the Devil*, 89–99; Pervo, *Profit with Delight*, 63.

52. For a recent comparative philosophical treatment of Acts 17, see Balch, "The Areopagus Speech: An Appeal to the Stoic Historian Posidonius against Later Stoics and the Epicureans," in Meeks, Balch, and Ferguson, eds., *Greeks, Romans, and Christians*, 52–79.

53. Cf. Tannehill, *Narrative Unity*, 2.327, 342–343; Conzelmann, *Acts*, 212; Roloff, *Die Apostelgeschichte*, 355.

54. This polemic against not only barbarians but Greco-Roman philosophers and rulers confirms that the intended audience for Luke-Acts is not Greco-Roman non-Christians. Cf. Haenchen, *Acts*, 24 on Johannes Weiss; 37 on B. S. Easton.

55. Cf. Tannehill, "Rejection by Jews and Turning to Gentiles: The Pattern of Paul's Mission in Acts," in Tyson, ed., *Luke-Acts and the Jewish People*, 96–101.

56. There is significant debate whether this final citation marks a complete Lukan despair of any further Christian mission to Jews or not. For a recent series of essays by many of the main participants in this controversy, see Tyson, ed., *Luke-Acts and the Jewish People*, featuring Jacob Jervell, David L. Tiede, David P. Moessner, Jack T. Sanders, Marilyn Salmon, Robert C. Tannehill, Michael J. Cook, Joseph B. Tyson, and their bibliog. notes discussing most of the publications in the dispute.

57. Tannehill, *Narrative Unity*. 2.346–353, esp. 348.

58. See the classics, Lindars, *New Testament Apologetic*; Dupont, "L'utilisation apologétique de l'Ancien Testament dans les discours des Actes,"

Etudes sur les Actes des Apôtres, 245–282 (reprinted from *ETL* 29 (1953): 298–327), translated (but without notes) as "Apologetic Use of the Old Testament in the Speeches of Acts," *The Salvation of the Gentiles*, 129–159.

10. Luke and Acts as Canonical

1. Powell, *What is Narrative Criticism?*, 85.

2. Keegan, *Interpreting the Bible*, 132–134, 138–140; Gamble, *The New Testament Canon*, 75–80; J. A. Sanders, "Adaptable for Life: The Nature and Function of the Canon," in his *From Sacred Story to Sacred Text*, 9–39.

3. Gasque, *A History of the Interpretation of the Acts of the Apostles*, 348–349; Johnson, *The Writings of the New Testament*, 203–204.

4. On a "third volume," cf. Quinn, "The Last Volume of Luke: The Relation of Luke-Acts to the Pastoral Epistles," in Talbert, ed., *Perspectives on Luke-Acts*, 62–75; Wilson, *Luke and the Pastoral Epistles*, 139–140 discusses the pastorals as "third volume" of the Lukan trilogy as one explanation of his theory that Luke wrote the pastorals.

On Lukan sources and composition, see Fitzmyer, *The Gospel According to Luke (I–IX)*, 1.63–106. It is also standard practice to compare the information in Acts with that in the Pauline letters; e.g., Fitzmeyer, *The Gospel According to Luke (I–IX)*, 1.27–29.

5. See F. Martin, "Literary Theory, Philosophy of History and Exegesis," 575–604, esp. 587–592, 595–599, 601–604. On *Sachkritik*, see the classical treatment by Bultmann, "The Problem of Hermeneutics," in his *Essays Philosophical and Theological*, esp. 257–259; and Donahue, "The Changing Shape of New Testament Theology," 319 with refs.

6. Cf. Montague, "Hermeneutics and the Teaching of Scripture," in G. Martin, ed., *Scripture and the Charismatic Renewal*, 77–95, nn. 123–126 (slightly revised presidential address of the Catholic Biblical Association from *CBQ* 41 (1979): 1–17), esp. 83–84. Cf. also Keegan, *Interpreting the Bible*, 137–149.

7. Dahl, "The Particularity of the Pauline Epistles as a Problem in the Ancient Church," in van Unnik, ed., *Neotestamentica et Patristica*, 261–271.

8. Cf. Childs, *The New Testament as Canon*, 278–281.

9. Contrast the paradigm for letting the scripture change the reader in Montague, "Hermeneutics," 90–94 with refs. 125–126.

10. Cf. Hagen, Harrington, Osborne, and Burgess, *The Bible in the Churches*.

11. Cf. Kurz, "Narrative Approaches to Luke-Acts," 195; Crossan, " 'Ruth Amid the Alien Corn': Perspectives and Methods in Contemporary Biblical Criticism," in Polzin and Rothman, eds., *The Biblical Mosaic*, 199–210; Donahue, "Changing Shape," 314–335, esp. 327–335.

12. Moore, *Literary Criticism and the Gospels*, 7–12 and chaps. 3, 4, 8, criticizes this holism, but his deconstructive alternative causes as serious problems for the needs of the church and believers as those for which historical criticism has come under attack.

13. In response to criticism of biblical critics for not fully plunging into the latest trends of literary criticism by Moore, *Literary Criticism, passim*. On criticism of traditional and orally based literature, see respectively Weimann, *Structure and Society in Literary History*, expanded ed., esp. 234–266; and Ong, *Orality and Literacy*, 165–170; Kurz, "Narrative Approaches," 197–200.

14. Cf. Kurz, "Narrative Models for Imitation in Luke-Acts," in Meeks, Balch, and Ferguson, eds., *Greeks, Romans, and Christians*, 171–189.

15. Ibid.

16. Cf. esp. Fish, *Is There a Text in this Class?*; Keegan, *Interpreting the Bible*, 132–134, 138–140; Gamble, *New Testament Canon*, 75–80; Sanders, "Adaptable for Life," 9–39.

17. Keegan, *Interpreting the Bible*, 132–134, 138–140; cf. Berg, "Reading In/to Mark," esp. her abstract (187) and 190–191, 196–197; and Powell, *What is Narrative Criticism?*, 88–89.

18. Cf. Kurz, "Narrative Models."

19. E.g., ecumenical treatments of Peter and of Mary in the New Testament have been perceived as quite helpful. See, for instance, R. E. Brown, Donfried, Fitzmyer, and Reumann, *Mary in the New Testament*.

20. Johnson, *Decision Making in the Church*.

21. E.g., Cassidy, *Politics and Society*; Moxnes, *The Economy of the Kingdom*; Pilgrim, *Good News to the Poor*; Kilgallen, "Social Development and the Lucan Works," 21–47; Kilgallen, " 'Peace' in the Gospel of Luke and Acts of Apostles," 55–79. Cf. the overview by Donahue, "Two Decades of Research on the Rich and the Poor in Luke-Acts," in D. A. Knight and P. J. Peters, eds., *Justice and the Holy*, 129–144.

22. Cf. Childs, "The Canonical Shape of the Prophetic Literature," in Mays and Achtemeier, eds., *Interpreting the Prophets*, 41–49, esp. 48. In each seminar on NT narratives that I currently teach, I have been inviting graduate students to join in the search for and attempt to refine some methodological ways of implementing this canonical stance.

11. Epilogue: Literary Criticism, Canon, and Orality

1. See Fitzmyer, *The Gospel According to Luke (I–IX)*, 1.47–51; Fitzmyer, *Luke the Theologian*, 1–26 and the works cited.

2. For an excellent overview from a Christian perspective and a good starting point, see McKnight, *Post-Modern Use of the Bible*.

3. Cf. Abrams, *A Glossary of Literary Terms*, 92 with examples.

4. Weimann, *Structure and Society in Literary History*, esp. chap. 6, "Structure and History in Narrative Perspective: The Problem of Point of View Reconsidered," 234–266.

5. Ibid., 252, and n. 17 citing W. P. Ker, *Epic and Romance: Essays on Medieval Literature* (London: Macmillan, 1908), 21.

6. Weimann, *Structure and Society*, 252.

7. Ibid., 253.

8. Johnson, *The Writings of the New Testament*, 204. In this regard Luke-Acts is similar to 1 Maccabees, which continued the biblical history to the time of the Maccabees.

9. See Ricoeur, *Interpretation Theory*, 44: "This dialectic may also be expressed as that of the tradition as such, understood as the reception of historically transmitted cultural heritages. A tradition raises no philosophical problem as long as we live and dwell within it in the naiveté of the first certainty. Tradition only becomes problematic when this first naiveté is lost. Then we have to retrieve its meaning through and beyond estrangement [as since the Enlightenment]. . . . Interpretation, philosophically understood, is nothing else than an attempt to make estrangement and distanciation productive." Cf. Ricoeur, "The Hermeneutical Function of Distanciation," 129–141.

10. See the classic treatment of narrative as having a beginning, middle, and end in Aristotle's *Poetics* (50b26) and in Paul Ricoeur's application of Aristotle to contemporary narrative in his *Time and Narrative*, vol. 1, part 1, chap. 2, "Emplotment: A Reading of Aristotle's *Poetics*," 31–51, esp. 38–39.

11. Thus, Luke 1:1: "a narrative of the events that have been fulfilled among us" (RNAB). Cf. Fitzmyer, *Luke I–IX*, 1.293–294.

12. E.g., see "*Dei Verbum*, The Dogmatic Constitution on Divine Revelation," in Flannery, ed., *Vatican Council II*, 750–765.

13. Johnson, *Writings*, 86–141 treats the experience and tradition behind the NT writings.

14. Cf. "The Infancy Story of Thomas," in Hennecke, *New Testament Apocrypha*, 1.388–399, § 4.1, p. 1.393.

15. Cf. Kurz, "Narrative Approaches to Luke-Acts," 197–198 with bibliog. cited in n. 10, vs. Moore, *Literary Criticism and the Gospels*, 150–151. Scholars in fields other than scripture find deconstruction problematic to philosophy as well as to faith. Cf. Abrams, *Glossary*, 203–207 with bibliog. See articles in Rajnath, ed., *Deconstruction*, esp. Abrams, "Construing and Deconstructing," 68–92; and Krieger, "From Theory to Thematics: the Ideological Underside of Recent Theory," 10–31; cf. p. 4 in Rajnath's introduction: "As against the New Criticism, deconstruction, with its dissociations of language from reality and the emphasis on pure temporality, expresses by implication faith in 'the disappearance of God.'"

16. Cf. Abrams, *Glossary*, 239–241; Pratt, *Toward a Speech Act Theory of Literary Discourse*; Reese, *Experiencing the Good News*.

17. On codes and readers, see Iser, "The Reading Process: A Phenomenological Approach," in Tompkins, ed., *Reader-Response Criticism*, 50–69 (cf. xiv–xv); and Iser, "Interaction between Text and Reader," in Suleiman and Crosman, eds., *The Reader in the Text*, 106–119.

18. The phrase recalls common charges in the popular media of academic thought control on behalf of various "politically correct" ideologies. For a Jewish awareness of Christian hesitancy to use deconstruction on the NT, see Berg, "Reading In/to Mark," 190–192.

19. Wink, *The Bible in Human Transformation*.

20. Cf. Keegan, *Interpreting the Bible*, 73–81. See chap. 4, "Readers and Gaps," esp. n. 51. Porter, "Why Hasn't Reader-Response Criticism Caught on in New Testament Studies?" 278–292, insists on the primacy of the contemporary readers in reader-response. That is not how NT scholars have tended to use it, for which he criticizes them.

21. Following esp. the approach of Iser, "Phenomenological Approach," and "Interaction between Text and Reader."

22. Cf. Greenwood, "Poststructuralism and Biblical Studies: Frank Kermode's *The Genesis of Secrecy*," in R. T. France and D. Wenham, eds., *Gospel Perspectives*, 263–288; Gardner, *In Defence of the Imagination*, chap. 5, "Narratives and Fictions," 111–137; Poythress, "Philosophical Roots of Phenomenological and Structuralist Literary Criticism," 165–171; Seung, *Structuralism and Hermeneutics*; Kurz, "Narrative Approaches," 197–199.

23. E.g., Moore, "Postmodernism and Biblical Studies," 36–41.

24. A. Bloom, *The Closing of the American Mind*.

25. Ong, *Orality and Literacy*, 119.

26. Kelber, *The Oral and the Written Gospel*. See, for example, Ong, *Orality and Literacy*.

27. Cf. Ong, *Orality and Literacy*, 78–116.

28. Ong, "A Writer's Audience Is Always a Fiction," in his *Interfaces of the Word*, 53–81.

29. Ricoeur, *Interpretation Theory*, 27 remarks that writing fixes not the event but the "said" of speaking. It inscribes the noema and meaning of the speech event: *sagen* has become *Aus-sage*, e-nunciation.

30. Ricoeur, *Interpretation Theory*, 29–30.

31. Ibid., 28.

32. Cf. Moore, *Literary Criticism*, 84–88 with bibliog.; Ong, "Text as Interpretation: Mark and After," 7–26; and the rest of *Semeia* 39.

33. Ricoeur, "Distanciation," 129–141.

34. Cf. Ong, *Orality and Literacy*, 178–179.

35. Ibid., 74–75.

36. Cf. Nelson, "From 'Listen, Lordings,' to 'Dear Reader,' " 110–124; see n. 32 above.

37. Cf. Ong, *Orality and Literacy*, 165–170; Kurz, "Narrative Approaches," 197–200.

38. Ricoeur, "Distanciation," 130–134, 141; cf. Ricoeur, *Interpretation Theory*, 26–30, 36–43.

39. Ricoeur, "Distanciation," 130–134, 141; Ricoeur, *Interpretation Theory*, 35–36.

40. Thus Paul's letters, for example, escape the "scandal of particularity." Cf. Dahl, "The Particularity of the Pauline Epistles as a Problem in the Ancient Church," in van Unnik, ed., *Neotestamentica et Patristica*, 261–271; Kurz, "Inspiration and the Origins of the New Testament," in G. Martin, ed., *Scripture and the Charismatic Renewal*, 51–52.

41. See de la Potterie, "Reading Holy Scripture 'In the Spirit': Is the Patristic Way of Reading the Bible Still Possible Today?" 308–325, esp. 315: "The *sensus moralis* has as its object the moral and religious life of the Christian. This is the sense that Scripture takes on for his spiritual life and for his exterior action *(quid agas).*"

42. See Ong, *Orality and Literacy*, chap. 3, "Some Psychodynamics of Orality," 31–78; chap. 4, "Writing Restructures Consciousness," 78–116.

43. See Fitzmyer, *Luke I–IX*, 1.292–293.

44. Cf. n. 40 above.

45. An analogous effect would occur if collected letter fragments were rearranged into a larger letter, as many claim for 2 Corinthians. In such a case, readers of 2 Corinthians are not dealing with an actual letter of Paul from a single life setting *(Sitz im Leben)* but with an artificial compilation (a pseudo-letter) somewhat removed from the original *Sitz im Leben* of each of the underlying letter fragments.

46. Cf. Kurz, "Narrative Models for Imitation in Luke-Acts," in Meeks, Balch, and Ferguson, eds., *Greeks, Romans, and Christians*, 171–189.

Select Bibliography

Abrams, M. H. "Construing and Deconstructing." In *Deconstruction: A Critique*, edited by Rajnath, 68–92. London: Macmillan Press, 1989.

———. *A Glossary of Literary Terms*. 5th ed. New York: Holt, Rinehart and Winston, 1988.

———. "How to Do Things with Texts." *Partisan Review* 46 (1979): 566–588.

Aletti, Jean-Noël. *L'art de raconter Jésus Christ: L'écriture narrative de l'évangile de Luc*. Parole de Dieu. Paris: Éditions Du Seuil, 1989.

Alexander, Loveday. "Luke's Preface in the Context of Greek Preface-Writing." *NovT* 28 (1986):48–74.

Alter, Robert. *The Art of Biblical Narrative*. New York: Basic, 1981.

———. "Sacred History and the Beginnings of Prose Fiction." *Poetics Today* 1, no. 3 (1980): 143–162.

Alter, Robert, and Frank Kermode, eds. *The Literary Guide to the Bible*. Cambridge, Mass.: Harvard University Press, Belknap, 1987.

Anderson, Janice Capel. "Double and Triple Stories, the Implied Reader, and Redundancy in Matthew." *Semeia* 31 (1985): 71–89. In Issue: Reader Response Approaches to Biblical and Secular Texts. Edited by Robert Detweiler.

Auerbach, Erich. *Mimesis: The Representation of Reality in Western Literature*. Translated by Willard Trask. Garden City, N.Y.: Doubleday, 1957.

Aune, David E. *The New Testament in Its Literary Environment*. Library of Early Christianity. Philadelphia: Westminster Press, 1987.

Austin, J. L. *How to Do Things with Words*. 2d ed. Edited by J. O. Urmson and Marina Sbisà. Cambridge, Mass.: Harvard University Press, 1975.

Bal, Mieke. "The Narrating and the Focalizing: A Theory of the Agents in Narrative." *Style* 17 (Spring 1983): 234–269.

Balch, David L. "Acts as Hellenistic Historiography." In *SBLSP 1985*, edited by Kent Harold Richards, 429–432. Atlanta: Scholars Press, 1985.

———. "The Areopagus Speech: An Appeal to the Stoic Historian Posidonius Against Later Stoics and the Epicureans." In *Greeks, Romans, and Christians:*

Essays in Honor of Abraham J. Malherbe, edited by David L. Balch, Everett Ferguson, and Wayne A. Meeks, 52–79. Minneapolis: Fortress Press, 1990.

———. "Comparing Literary Patterns in Luke and Lucian." *Perkins Journal* 40 (April 1987): 39–42.

Balthasar, Hans Urs von. "God is His Own Exegete." *Communio International Catholic Review* 13 (Winter 1986): 280–287.

Barnouw, Dagmar. "Critics in the Act of Reading." Review Article. *Poetics Today* 1, no. 4 (1980): 213–222.

Barrett, C. K., ed. *The New Testament Background: Selected Documents.* 1956. Reprint. New York: Harper and Row, 1961.

Bassler, Jouette M. *Divine Impartiality: Paul and a Theological Axiom.* SBLDS 59. Chico, Calif.: Scholars Press, 1982.

Bauer, Walter. *A Greek-English Lexicon of the New Testament and Other Early Christian Literature.* 2d ed., rev. and aug. Translated and adapted by William F. Arndt, F. Wilber Gingrich, and Frederick W. Danker. Chicago: University of Chicago Press, 1979.

Beardslee, William A. *Literary Criticism of the New Testament.* Guides to Biblical Scholarship, New Testament Series. Philadelphia: Fortress Press, 1970.

Beck, Brian E. " 'Imitatio Christi' and the Lucan Passion Narrative." In *Suffering and Martyrdom in the New Testament: Studies Presented to G. M. Styler by the Cambridge New Testament Seminar,* edited by William Horbury and Brian McNeil, 28–47. Cambridge: Cambridge University Press, 1981.

Berg, Temma F. "Reading In/to Mark." *Semeia* 48 (1989): 187–206. In Issue: Reader Perspectives on the New Testament. Edited by Edgar V. McKnight.

Berger, Klaus. "Hellenistische Gattungen im Neuen Testament." In *Aufstieg und Niedergang der römischen Welt: Geschichte und Kultur Roms im Spiegel der neueren Forschung,* vol. 2.25, edited by Hildegard Temporini and Wolfgang Haase, 1031–1432. Berlin/New York: Walter de Gruyter, 1984.

Berlin, Adele. *Poetics and Interpretation of Biblical Narrative.* Bible and Literature Series 9. Sheffield: Almond Press, 1983.

Best, Ernest. "Mark's Narrative Technique." *Journal for the Study of New Testament* 37 (1989): 43–58.

Betz, Hans Dieter, ed. *The Bible as Document of the University.* Polebridge Books 3. Chico, Calif.: Scholars Press, 1981.

Black, C. C. "Rhetorical Criticism and Biblical Interpretation." *Expository Times* 100 (1988–89): 304–307.

Bleich, David. *Subjective Criticism.* Baltimore: Johns Hopkins University Press, 1981.

Bloch, Renée. "Methodological Note for the Study of Rabbinic Literature." Translated by William Scott Green with William J. Sullivan. In *Approaches to*

Ancient Judaism: Theory and Practice, edited by William Scott Green, 51–75. Brown Judaic Studies 1. Missoula, Mont.: Scholars Press, 1978.

―――. "Midrash." Translated by Mary Howard Callaway. In *Approaches to Ancient Judaism: Theory and Practice*, edited by William Scott Green, 29–50. Brown Judaic Studies 1. Missoula, Mont.: Scholars Press, 1978.

Bloom, Allan. *The Closing of the American Mind*. New York: Simon and Schuster, 1987.

Bloom, Edward, ed. "In Defense of Authors and Readers." Summary of Conference Discussions. Speakers Wayne C. Booth and Wolfgang Iser. *Novel* 11 (1977): 5–25.

Booth, Wayne C. *The Company We Keep: An Ethics of Fiction*. Berkeley: University of California Press, 1988.

―――. *Critical Understanding: The Powers and Limits of Pluralism*. Chicago: University of Chicago Press, 1979.

―――. *The Rhetoric of Fiction*. 2d ed. Chicago: University of Chicago Press, 1983.

Bösen, W. *Jesusmahl, Eucharistisches Mahl, Endzeitmahl, Ein Beitrag zur Theologie des Lukas*. Stuttgarter Bibel Studien 97. Stuttgart: Katholisches Bibelwerk, 1980.

Bovon, François. *Das Evangelium Nach Lukas: 1. Teilband, Lk. 1,1-9,50*. Evangelisch-Katholischer Kommentar zum Neuen Testament, 3,1. Zürich, Neukirchen-Vluyn: Benziger Verlag, Neukirchener Verlag, 1989.

―――. *Luke the Theologian: Thirty-three Years of Research (1950–1983)*. Allison Park, Pa.: Pickwick Press, 1987.

Brehm, Alan. "The Significance of the Summaries for Interpreting Acts." *Southwestern Journal of Theology* 33 (Fall 1990): 29–40.

Brown, Raymond E. *The Birth of the Messiah: A Commentary on the Infancy Narratives in Matthew and Luke*. Garden City, N.Y.: Doubleday, 1977.

―――. *The Virginal Conception and Bodily Resurrection of Jesus*. New York: Paulist Press, 1973.

Brown, Raymond E., and Raymond F. Collins. "Canonicity." In *The New Jerome Biblical Commentary*, edited by Raymond E. Brown, Joseph A. Fitzmyer, and Roland E. Murphy, 1034–1054. Englewood Cliffs, N.J.: Prentice Hall, 1990.

Brown, Raymond E., Joseph A. Fitzmyer, and Roland E. Murphy, eds. *The New Jerome Biblical Commentary*. Englewood Cliffs, N.J.: Prentice Hall, 1990.

Brown, Raymond E., Karl P. Donfried, Joseph A. Fitzmyer, and John Reumann, eds. *Mary in the New Testament: A Collaborative Assessment by Protestant and Roman Catholic Scholars*. Philadelphia: Fortress Press; New York: Paulist Press, 1978.

Brown, Schuyler. "The Role of the Prologues in Determining the Purpose of Luke-Acts." In *Perspectives on Luke-Acts*, edited by Charles H. Talbert, 99–111. Perspectives in Religious Studies: Special Studies Series 5. Danville, Va.: Association of Baptist Professors of Religion, 1978.

Bultmann, Rudolf. "The Problem of Hermeneutics." In his *Essays Philosophical and Theological*. London: SCM Press, 1955.

Burnett, Fred W. "Prolegomenon to Reading Matthew's Eschatological Discourse: Redundancy and the Education of the Reader in Matthew." *Semeia* 31 (1985): 91–109. In Issue: Reader Response Approaches to Biblical and Secular Texts. Edited by Robert Detweiler.

Cadbury, Henry J. "Commentary on the Preface of Luke." Appendix C. In *The Beginnings of Christianity*, Part 1: *The Acts of the Apostles*. Vol. 2: *Prologomena II: Criticism*. 1922. Reprint. Edited by F. J. Foakes Jackson and Kirsopp Lake, 489–510. Grand Rapids, Mich.: Baker Book House, 1979.

———. *The Making of Luke-Acts*. 1927. Reprint. London: SPCK, 1968.

———. "The Summaries in Acts." In *The Beginnings of Christianity*, Part 1: *The Acts of the Apostles*. Vol. 5: *Additional Notes to the Commentary*. 1933. Reprint. Edited by F. J. Foakes Jackson and Kirsopp Lake, vol. edited by Kirsopp Lake and Henry J. Cadbury, 392–402. Grand Rapids, Mich.: Baker Book House, 1979.

Carroll, John T. *Response to the End of History: Eschatology and Situation in Luke-Acts*. SBLDS 92. Atlanta, Ga.: Scholars Press, 1988.

Carson, D. A., and H. G. M. Williamson, eds. *It is Written: Scripture Citing Scripture: Essays in Honour of Barnabas Lindars, SSF*. New York: Cambridge University Press, 1988.

Cassidy, Richard J. *Jesus, Politics, and Society: A Study of Luke's Gospel*. Maryknoll, N.Y.: Orbis Books, 1978.

———. *Society and Politics in the Acts of the Apostles*. Maryknoll, N.Y.: Orbis Books, 1987.

Chance, J. Bradley. *Jerusalem, the Temple, and the New Age in Luke-Acts*. Macon, Ga.: Mercer University Press, 1988.

Charlesworth, James H., ed. *Apocalyptic Literature and Testaments*. Vol. 1 of *The Old Testament Pseudepigrapha*. Garden City, N.Y.: Doubleday, 1983.

———, ed. *Expansions of the "Old Testament" and Legends, Wisdom and Philosophical Literature, Prayers, Psalms and Odes, Fragments of Lost Judaeo-Hellenistic Works*. Vol. 2 of *The Old Testament Pseudepigrapha*. Garden City, N.Y.: Doubleday, 1985.

Chatman, Seymour. *Coming to Terms: The Rhetoric of Narrative in Fiction and Film*. Ithaca, N.Y.: Cornell University Press, 1990.

———. *Story and Discourse: Narrative Structure in Fiction and Film*. Ithaca, N.Y.: Cornell University Press, 1978.

Childs, Brevard S. "The Canonical Shape of the Prophetic Literature." In *Interpreting the Prophets*, edited by James Luther Mays and Paul J. Achtemeier. Philadelphia: Fortress Press, 1987.

————. *Introduction to the Old Testament as Scripture*. Philadelphia: Fortress Press, 1979.

————. *The New Testament as Canon: An Introduction*. Philadelphia: Fortress Press, 1984.

Cohn, Dorrit. *Transparent Mind: Narrative Modes for Presenting Consciousness in Fiction*. Princeton: Princeton University Press, 1978.

Collins, Raymond F. "Inspiration." In *The New Jerome Biblical Commentary*, edited by Raymond E. Brown, Joseph A. Fitzmyer, and Roland E. Murphy, 1023–1033. Englewood Cliffs, N.J.: Prentice Hall, 1990.

Combrink, H. J. B. "Multiple Meaning and/or Multiple Interpretation of a Text." *Neotestamentica* 18 (1984): 26–37.

————. "Readings, Readers and Authors: An Orientation." *Neotestamentica* 22, no. 2 (1988): 189–203. In Issue: Readings and Readers of Luke 12:35–48. Edited by Pieter G. R. De Villiers.

Communio International Catholic Review 13 (Winter 1986). Special issue "On the Reading of Scripture."

Conzelmann, Hans. *Acts of the Apostles. A Commentary on the Acts of the Apostles*. Translated by James Limburg, A. Thomas Kraabel, and Donald H. Juel. Edited by Eldon Jay Epp and Christopher R. Matthews. Hermeneia. Philadelphia: Fortress Press, 1987.

————. *The Theology of Luke*. Translated by Geoffrey Buswell. New York: Harper and Row, 1961.

Crane, R. S. "The Concept of Plot." In *Approaches to the Novel*, 2d rev. ed., edited by Robert Scholes, 233–243. San Francisco: Chandler Publishing Co., 1966.

Cranford, Lorin L., ed. "Studies in Acts." *Southwestern Journal of Theology* 33 (Fall 1990): 5–51.

Crim, Keith R., ed. *Interpreter's Dictionary of the Bible: Supplementary Volume*. OT ed. Lloyd Richard Bailey; Sr. NT ed. Victor Paul Furnish. Nashville: Abingdon Press, 1976.

Crosman, Inge. "Annotated Bibliography of Audience-Oriented Criticism." In *The Reader in the Text: Essays on Audience and Interpretation*, edited by Susan R. Suleiman and Inge Crosman, 401–424. Princeton: Princeton University Press, 1980.

Crossan, John Dominic. " 'Ruth Amid the Alien Corn': Perspectives and Methods in Contemporary Biblical Criticism." In *The Biblical Mosaic: Changing Perspectives*, edited by Robert Polzin and Eugene Rothman, 199–210. Philadelphia: Fortress Press; Chico, Calif.: Scholars Press, 1982.

Culbertson, Diana. *The Poetics of Revelation: Recognition and the Narrative Tradition.* Studies in American Biblical Hermeneutics. Macon, Ga.: Mercer University Press, 1989.

Culler, Jonathon. *On Deconstruction: Theory and Criticism After Structuralism.* Ithaca, N.Y.: Cornell University Press, 1983.

————. *Structuralist Poetics: Structuralism, Linguistics and the Study of Literature.* Ithaca, N.Y.: Cornell University Press, 1976.

Cullmann, Oscar. "The Infancy Story of Thomas." In Edgar Hennecke, *New Testament Apocrypha.* Vol. 1: *Gospels and Related Writings,* edited by Wilhelm Schneemelcher and R. McL. Wilson, 1:388–399. Philadelphia: Westminster Press, 1963.

Culpepper, R. Alan. *Anatomy of the Fourth Gospel: A Study in Literary Design.* Foundations and Facets. Philadelphia: Fortress Press, 1983.

Dahl, Nils A. "Letter." In *IDB Sup,* edited by Keith R. Crim, 538–541. Nashville: Abingdon Press, 1976.

————. "The Particularity of the Pauline Epistles as a Problem in the Ancient Church." In *Neotestamentica et Patristica, FS O. Cullman,* edited by W. C. van Unnik, 261–271. NovT Supplements 6. Leiden: Brill, 1962.

Danto, Arthur C. *Analytical Philosophy of History.* Cambridge: Cambridge University Press, 1968.

————. *Narration and Knowledge.* New York: Columbia University Press, 1985.

Davies, John Gordon. "Subjectivity and Objectivity in Biblical Exegesis." *Bulletin of the John Rylands University Library of Manchester* 66 (1983): 44–53.

Dawsey, James M. "The Literary Unity of Luke-Acts: Questions of Style—A Task for Literary Critics." *NTS* 35 (1989): 48–66.

————. *The Lukan Voice: Confusion and Irony in the Gospel of Luke.* Macon, Ga.: Mercer University Press, 1986.

"Dei Verbum, The Dogmatic Constitution on Divine Revelation." In *Vatican Council II: The Conciliar and Post Conciliar Documents,* edited by Austin Flannery, 750–765. Northport, N.Y.: Costello Publishing Company, 1975.

Detweiler, R. ed. *Semeia* 31 (1985). Issue: Reader Response Approaches to Biblical and Secular Texts.

De Villiers, Pieter G. R., ed. *Neotestamentica* 22, no. 2 (1988). Special Issue: Readings and Readers of Luke 12:35–48.

Dibelius, Martin. *Studies in the Acts of the Apostles.* Edited by Heinrich Greeven. London: SCM, 1956.

Dillon, Richard J. *From Eye-Witnesses to Ministers of the Word: Tradition and Composition in Luke 24.* Analecta Biblica 82. Rome: Biblical Institute Press, 1978.

Donahue, John R. *Are You the Christ? The Trial Narrative in the Gospel of Mark.* SBLDS 10. Missoula, Mont.: Scholars Press, 1973.

———. "The Changing Shape of New Testament Theology." *TS* 50 (June 1989): 314–335.

———. "Two Decades of Research on the Rich and the Poor in Luke-Acts." In *Justice and the Holy: Essays in Honor of Walter Harrelson*, edited by Douglas A. Knight and Peter J. Peters, 129–144. Scholars Press Homage Series. Atlanta: Scholars Press, 1989.

Dormeyer, Detlev. *Evangelium als literarisch und theologische Gattung*. Erträge der Forschung 263. Darmstadt: Wissenschaftliche Buchgesellschaft, 1989.

———. "Das Verhältnis von 'wilder' und historisch-kritischer Exegese als methodologisches und didaktisches Problem." *Jahrbuch der Religionspädogogik* 3 (1987): 111–127.

Draisma, Sipke, ed. *Intertextuality in Biblical Writings: Essays in Honour of Bas Van Iersel*. Kampen, Netherlands: J. H. Kok, 1989.

Du Plooy, Gerhard P. V. "The Author in Luke-Acts." *Scriptura: Journal of Bible and Theology in Southern Africa* 32 (March 1990): 28–35.

Duke, Paul D. *Irony in the Fourth Gospel*. Atlanta: John Knox Press, 1985.

Dupont, Jacques. "Apologetic Use of the Old Testament in the Speeches of Acts." In *The Salvation of the Gentiles: Essays on the Acts of the Apostles*, translated by John R. Keating, 129–159. New York: Paulist Press, 1979.

———. "L'Évangile (Lc 2,41–52): Jésus à douze ans." *AsSeign* 14 (1961): 25–43.

———. *The Salvation of the Gentiles: Essays on the Acts of the Apostles*. Translated by John R. Keating. New York: Paulist Press, 1979.

———. "L'utilisation apologétique de l'Ancien Testament dans les discours des Actes." In *Etudes sur les Actes Des Apôtres*, 245–282. Lectio Divina 45. Paris: Editions de Cerf, 1967.

Eagleton, Terry. *Literary Theory: An Introduction*. Minneapolis: University of Minnesota Press, 1983.

Eco, Umberto. *The Name of the Rose*. Translated by William Weaver. New York: Warner Books, 1984.

———. *Reflections on the Name of the Rose*. Translated by William Weaver. London: Secker & Warburg, 1985.

Elliott, J. K. "Does Luke 2:41–52 Anticipate the Resurrection?" *Expository Times* 83 (1971–72): 87–89.

Epp, Eldon Jay, and George W. MacRae, eds. *The New Testament and Its Modern Interpreters*. The Bible and Its Modern Interpreters 3. Philadelphia: Fortress Press; Atlanta: Scholars Press, 1989.

Ernst, Josef. *Das Evangelium nach Lukas*. Regensburger Neues Testament. Regensburg: Verlag Friedrich Pustet, 1977.

Farmer, William R. *The Synoptic Problem: A Critical Analysis*. Rev. ed. no. 2. Dillsboro, N.C.: Western North Carolina Press, 1976.

————., ed. "Critical Responses to Joseph B. Tyson's *The Death of Jesus in Luke-Acts.*" *Perkins Journal* 40 (April 1987): 33–50.

Fish, Stanley. *Is There a Text in This Class? The Authority of Interpretative Communities.* Cambridge, Mass.: Harvard University Press, 1980.

Fishbane, Michael. *Biblical Interpretation in Ancient Israel.* Oxford: Oxford University Press, Clarendon, 1985.

————. "Inner Biblical Exegesis: Types and Strategies of Interpretation in Ancient Israel." In *Midrash and Literature,* edited by Geoffrey N. Hartman and Sanford Budick, 19–37. New Haven: Yale University Press, 1986.

Fitzmyer, Joseph A. *The Dead Sea Scrolls: Major Publications and Tools for Study: With an Addendum (January 1977).* Rev. ed. no. 2. SBL Sources for Biblical Study. Missoula, Mont.: Scholars Press, 1977.

————. *The Gospel According to Luke (I–IX). Introduction, Translation, and Notes.* Anchor Bible 28. Garden City, N.Y.: Doubleday, 1981.

————. *The Gospel According to Luke (X–XXIV). Introduction, Translation, and Notes.* Anchor Bible 28A. Garden City, N.Y.: Doubleday, 1985.

————. "Historical Criticism: Its Role in Biblical Interpretation and Church Life." *TS* 50 (1989): 244–259.

————. *Luke the Theologian: Aspects of His Teaching.* New York: Paulist Press, 1989.

Flannery, Austin, ed. *Vatican Council II: The Conciliar and Post Conciliar Documents.* Northport, N.Y.: Costello Publishing Company, 1975.

Foakes Jackson, F. J., and Kirsopp Lake, eds. *The Beginnings of Christianity.* Part 1: *The Acts of the Apostles.* Vol. 3: *The Text of Acts.* 1925. Reprint. Edited by James Hardy Ropes. Grand Rapids, Mich.: Baker Book House, 1979.

————, eds. *The Beginnings of Christianity.* Part 1: *The Acts of the Apostles.* Vol. 4: *English Translation and Commentary.* 1932. Reprint. Edited by Kirsopp Lake and Henry J. Cadbury. Grand Rapids, Mich.: Baker Book House, 1979.

Fiore, Benjamin. *The Function of Personal Example in the Socratic and Pastoral Epistles.* Analecta Biblica 105. Rome: Biblical Institute Press, 1986.

Foley, John Miles. *Oral-formulaic Theory and Research: An Introduction and Annotated Bibliography.* New York: Garland Press, 1985.

Forbes, Christopher. "Paul's Boasting and Hellenistic Rhetoric." *NTS* 32 (1986): 1–30.

Fornara, Charles William. *The Nature of History in Ancient Greece and Rome.* EIDOS Studies in Classical Kinds. Berkeley: University of California Press, 1983.

Fowler, Robert M. *Loaves and Fishes: The Function of the Feeding Stories in the Gospel of Mark.* SBLDS 54. Chico, Calif.: Scholars Press, 1981.

———. "Postmodern Biblical Criticism." *Forum: Foundations & Facets* 5 (September 1989): 3–30.

———. "Who is 'the Reader' in Reader Response Criticism?" *Semeia* 31 (1985): 5–23. In Issue: Reader Response Approaches to Biblical and Secular Texts. Edited by Robert Detweiler.

Frei, Hans W. *The Eclipse of Biblical Narrative: A Study in Eighteenth and Nineteenth Century Hermeneutics*. New Haven: Yale University Press, 1974.

———. *The Identity of Jesus Christ: The Hermeneutical Bases of Dogmatic Theology*. Philadelphia: Fortress Press, 1975.

Frend, W. H. C. *Martyrdom and Persecution in the Early Church: A Study of a Conflict from the Maccabees to Donatus*. Garden City, N.Y.: Doubleday, Anchor, 1967.

Freund, Elizabeth. *The Return of the Reader: Reader-Response Criticism*. New Accents. New York: Methuen, 1987.

Frye, Northrop. *Anatomy of Criticism: Four Essays*. Princeton: Princeton University Press, 1971.

———. *The Great Code: The Bible and Literature*. San Diego: Harcourt Brace Jovanovich, Harvest/HBJ, 1983.

Funk, Robert W. *The Poetics of Biblical Narrative*. Foundations & Facets. Literary Facets. Sonoma, Calif.: Polebridge Press, 1988.

Gamble, Harry Y. "The Canon of the New Testament." In *The New Testament and Its Modern Interpreters*, edited by Eldon Jay Epp and George W. MacRae, 201–243. The Bible and Its Modern Interpreters 3. Philadelphia: Fortress Press; Atlanta: Scholars Press, 1989.

———. *The New Testament Canon: Its Making and Meaning*. Guides to Biblical Scholarship, New Testament Series. Philadelphia: Fortress Press, 1985.

Gardner, Helen. *In Defence of the Imagination*. Charles Eliot Norton Lectures: 1979–1980. Cambridge, Mass.: Harvard University Press, 1982.

Garrett, Susan R. *The Demise of the Devil: Magic and the Demonic in Luke's Writings*. Minneapolis: Fortress Press, 1989.

Gasque, W. Ward. *A History of the Interpretation of the Acts of the Apostles*. Peabody, Mass.: Hendrickson Publishers, 1989.

Gaventa, Beverly Roberts. "Galatians 1 and 2: Autobiography as Paradigm." *NovT* 28 (1986): 309–326.

———. "Toward a Theology of Acts: Reading and Rereading." *Interpretation* 42 (April 1988): 146–147.

Genette, Gérard. *Narrative Discourse: An Essay in Method*. Translated by Jane E. Lewin. Ithaca, N.Y.: Cornell University Press, 1980.

Goppelt, Leonhard. *Typos: The Typological Interpretation of the Old Testament in the New.* Translated by Donald H. Madvig. Grand Rapids, Mich.: William B. Eerdmans, 1982.

Graham, William A. *Beyond the Written Word: Oral Aspects of Scripture in the History of Religion.* Cambridge: Cambridge University Press, 1988.

Green, Garrett, ed. *Scriptural Authority and Narrative Interpretation. Essays on the Occasion of the Sixty-fifth Birthday of Hans W. Frei.* Philadelphia: Fortress Press, 1987.

Green, William Scott, ed. *Approaches to Ancient Judaism: Theory and Practice.* Brown Judaic Studies 1. Missoula, Mont.: Scholars Press, 1978.

Greenwood, D. S. "Poststructuralism and Biblical Studies: Frank Kermode's *The Genesis of Secrecy.*" In *Gospel Perspectives: Studies in Midrash and Historiography,* vol. 3, edited by R. T. France and David Wenham, 3:263–288. Sheffield: JSOT Press, 1983.

Grimaldi, William. *Studies in the Philosophy of Aristotle's Rhetoric.* Hermes Einzelschriften 25. Wiesbaden: Franz Steiner GMBH, 1972.

Guelich, Robert A. *Mark 1–8:26.* Word Biblical Commentary 34A. Dallas, Tex.: Word Books, 1989.

Güttgemanns, Erhardt. *Candid Questions Concerning Gospel Form Criticism: A Methodological Sketch of the Fundamental Problematics of Form and Redaction Criticism.* Translated by William G. Doty. Pittsburgh: Pickwick Press, 1979.

Haacker, Klaus. "Einige Fälle von 'erlebter Rede' im Neuen Testament." *Nov T* 12 (1970): 70–77.

Haenchen, Ernst. *The Acts of the Apostles: A Commentary.* Translated from 14th German ed. (1965). Philadelphia: Westminster Press, 1971.

Hagen, Kenneth, Daniel J. Harrington, Grant R. Osborne, and Joseph A. Burgess. *The Bible in the Churches: How Different Christians Interpret the Scriptures.* New York: Paulist Press, 1985.

Hamilton, Edith, and Huntington Cairns, eds. *The Collected Dialogues of Plato.* Bollingen Series 71. Princeton: Princeton University Press, 1961.

Hamm, Dennis. "Acts 3,1–10: The Healing of the Temple Beggar as Lucan Theology." *Bib* 67 (1986): 305–319.

———— "Sight to the Blind: Vision as Metaphor in Luke." *Bib* 67 (1986): 457–477.

Harrington, Daniel J., and Maurya P. Horgan. "Palestinian Adaptations of Biblical Narratives and Prophecies." In *Early Judaism and Its Modern Interpreters,* edited by Robert A. Kraft and George W. E. Nickelsburg, 239–258. The Bible and Its Modern Interpreters 2. Philadelphia: Fortress Press; Atlanta: Scholars Press, 1986.

Hartman, Geoffrey H., and Sanford Budick, eds. *Midrash and Literature.* New Haven: Yale University Press, 1986.

Heil, John Paul. "Reader-response and the Irony of Jesus Before the Sanhedrin in Luke 22:66–71." *CBQ* 51 (April 1989): 271–282.

Hemer, Colin J. *The Book of Acts in the Setting of Hellenistic History.* Edited by Conrad H. Gempf. Wissenschaftliche Untersuchungen zum Neuen Testament 49. Tübingen: J. C. B. Mohr (Paul Siebeck), 1989.

———. "First Person Narrative in Acts 27–28." *Tyndale Bulletin* 36 (1985): 79–109.

Hengel, Martin. *Acts and the History of Earliest Christianity.* Translated by John Bowden. Philadelphia: Fortress Press, 1979.

———. *The Charismatic Leader and His Followers.* Translated by James Grieg. New York: Crossroad, 1981.

———. *Judaism and Hellenism: Studies in Their Encounter in Palestine During the Early Hellenistic Period.* 2 vols. Translated by John Bowden. London: SCM Press, 1974.

Hennecke, Edgar. *New Testament Apocrypha.* Vol. 1: *Gospels and Related Writings.* Edited by Wilhelm Schneemelcher and R. McL. Wilson. Philadelphia: Westminster Press, 1963.

———. *New Testament Apocrypha.* Vol. 2: *Writings Related to the Apostles: Apocalypses and Related Subjects.* Edited by Wilhelm Schneemelcher and R. McL. Wilson. Philadelphia: Westminster Press, 1965.

Hirsch, E. D., Jr. "Current Issues in Theory of Interpretation." *Journal of Religion* 55 (1975): 298–312.

———. *Validity in Interpretation.* New Haven: Yale University Press, 1967.

Holub, Robert C. *Reception Theory: A Critical Introduction.* New Accents. New York: Methuen, 1984.

Horgan, Maurya P. "The Bible Explained (prophecies)." In *Early Judaism and Its Modern Interpreters,* edited by Robert A. Kraft and George W. E. Nickelsburg, 247–253. The Bible and Its Modern Interpreters 2. Philadelphia: Fortress Press, Atlanta: Scholars Press, 1986.

Horton, Fred L. "Reflections on the Semitisms of Luke-Acts." In *Perspectives on Luke-Acts,* edited by Charles H. Talbert, 1–23. Perspectives in Religious Studies: Special Studies Series 5. Danville, Va.: Association of Baptist Professors of Religion, 1978.

Hunter, J. H. "Deconstruction and Biblical Texts: Introduction and Critique." *Neotestamentica* 21 (1987): 125–140.

Ingarden, Roman. *The Cognition of the Literary Work of Art.* Translated by Ruth Ann Crowley and Kenneth R. Olson. Northwestern Studies in Phenomenology and Existential Philosophy. Evanston: Northwestern University Press, 1973.

Iser, Wolfgang. *The Act of Reading: A Theory of Aesthetic Response.* Baltimore: Johns Hopkins University Press, 1978.

———. *The Implied Reader: Patterns of Communication in Prose Fiction from Bunyan to Beckett.* Baltimore: Johns Hopkins University Press, 1974.

———. "Interaction Between Text and Reader." In *The Reader in the Text: Essays on Audience and Interpretation*, edited by Susan R. Suleiman and Inge Crosman, 106–119. Princeton: Princeton University Press, 1980.

———. "The Reading Process: A Phenomenological Approach." 1972. Reprinted in *Reader-Response Criticism: From Formalism to Post-Structuralism*, edited by Jane P. Tompkins, 50–69. Baltimore: Johns Hopkins University Press, 1980.

Jauss, Hans Robert. "Levels of Identification of Hero and Audience." Translated by Benjamin Bennett and Helga Bennett. *New Literary History* 5 (1974): 283–317.

———. *Toward an Aesthetic of Reception*. Translated by Timothy Bahti. Theory and History of Literature 2. Minneapolis: University of Minnesota Press, 1982.

Jeanrond, Werner G. *Text and Interpretation as Categories of Theological Thinking*. Translated by Thomas J. Wilson. New York: Crossroad, 1988.

Jervell, Jacob. *Luke and the People of God*. Minneapolis: Augsburg Publishing House, 1972.

———. *The Unknown Paul: Essays on Luke-Acts and Early Christian History*. Minneapolis: Augsburg Publishing House, 1984.

Johnson, Luke Timothy. *Decision Making in the Church: A Biblical Model*. Philadelphia: Fortress Press, 1983.

———. *The Literary Function of Possessions in Luke-Acts*. SBLDS 39. Missoula, Mont.: Scholars Press, 1977.

———. "On Finding the Lukan Community: A Cautious Cautionary Essay." *SBLSP* 1 (1979): 87–100.

———. *The Writings of the New Testament: An Interpretation*. Philadelphia: Fortress Press, 1986.

Juel, Donald. *Messianic Exegesis: Christological Interpretation of the Old Testament in Early Christianity*. Philadelphia: Fortress Press, 1988.

Kahl, Brigitte. *Armenevangelium und Heidenevangelium: "Sola Scriptura" und die ökumenische Traditionsproblematik im Lichte von Väterkonflikt und Väterkonsens bei Lukas*. Berlin: Evangelische Verlagsanstalt, 1987.

Kee, Howard Clark. *Community of the New Age: Studies in Mark's Gospel*. Philadelphia: Westminster Press, 1977.

———. *Good News to the Ends of the Earth: The Theology of Acts*. Philadelphia: Trinity Press International, 1990.

———. *The Origins of Christianity: Sources and Documents*. Englewood Cliffs, N.J.: Prentice-Hall, 1973.

Keegan, Terence J. *Interpreting the Bible: A Popular Introduction to Biblical Hermeneutics*. New York: Paulist Press, 1985.

Kelber, Werner H. "Markus und die mündliche Tradition." *Linguistica Biblica* 45 (1979): 55–58.

———. "Narrative as Interpretation and Interpretation of Narrative: Hermeneutical Reflections on the Gospels." *Semeia* 39 (1987): 107–134. In Issue: Orality, Aurality and Biblical Narrative. Edited by Lou H. Silberman.

———. *The Oral and the Written Gospel: The Hermeneutics of Speaking and Writing in the Synoptic Tradition, Mark, Paul, and Q.* Philadelphia: Fortress Press, 1983.

Kennedy, George A. *New Testament Interpretation Through Rhetorical Criticism.* Studies in Religion. Chapel Hill, N.C.: University of North Carolina Press, 1984.

Kermode, Frank. *The Genesis of Secrecy: On the Interpretation of Narrative.* Cambridge, Mass.: Harvard University Press, 1979.

———. *The Sense of an Ending: Studies in the Theory of Fiction.* Oxford: Oxford University Press, 1968.

Kilgallen, John J. " 'Peace' in the Gospel of Luke and Acts of Apostles." *Studia Missionalia* 38 (1989): 55–79. Special Issue: Peace and Religions.

———. "Social Development and the Lucan Works." *Studia Missionalia* 39 (1990): 21–47. Special Issue: Human Rights and Religions.

Kinneavy, James L. *Greek Rhetorical Origins of Christian Faith.* New York: Oxford University Press, 1987.

Kodell, Jerome. "Luke's Gospel in a Nutshell (Lk 4:16–30)." *BTB* 13 (1983): 16–18.

Kort, Wesley A. *Story, Text, and Scripture: Literary Interests in Biblical Narrative.* University Park, Pa.: Pennsylvania University Press, 1988.

Kraft, Robert A., and George W. E. Nickelsburg, eds. *Early Judaism and Its Modern Interpreters.* The Bible and Its Modern Interpreters 2. Philadelphia: Fortress Press; Atlanta: Scholars Press, 1986.

Krentz, Edgar. *The Historical-Critical Method.* Guides to Biblical Scholarship, Old Testament Series. Philadelphia: Fortress Press, 1978.

Krieger, Murray. "From Theory to Thematics: The Ideological Underside of Recent Theory." In *Deconstruction: A Critique,* edited by Rajnath, 10–31. London: Macmillan Press, 1989.

Kuenzli, Robert E., ed. "Interview: Wolfgang Iser." Interviewers Norman Holland, Wayne Booth, and Stanley Fish. *Diacritics* 10 (June 1980): 57–86.

Kurz, William S. "Acts 3:19–26 as a Test of the Role of Eschatology in Lukan Christology." In *SBLSP 1977,* edited by Paul J. Achtemeier, 309–323. Missoula, Mont.: Scholars Press, 1977.

———. *The Acts of the Apostles.* Collegeville Bible Commentary 5. Collegeville, Minn.: Liturgical Press, 1983.

————. "The Beloved Disciple and Implied Readers." *BTB* 19 (July 1989): 100–107.

————. *Farewell Addresses in the New Testament.* Zacchaeus Studies: New Testament. A Michael Glazier Book. Collegeville, Minn.: Liturgical Press, 1990.

————. *Following Jesus: A Disciple's Guide to Luke and Acts.* Ann Arbor, Mich.: Servant Books, 1984.

————. "The Function of Christological Proof from Prophecy for Luke and Justin." Ph.D. diss., Yale University, 1976, microfilm.

————. "Hellenistic Rhetoric in the Christological Proof of Luke-Acts." *CBQ* 42 (April 1980): 171–195.

————. "Inspiration and the Origins of the New Testament." In *Scripture and the Charismatic Renewal: Proceedings of the Milwaukee Symposium December 1–3, 1978,* edited by George Martin, 29–58, 121–123. Ann Arbor, Mich.: Servant Books, 1979.

————. "Luke 22:14–38 and Greco-Roman and Biblical Farewell Addresses." *JBL* 104 (1985): 251–268.

————. "Luke 3:23–38 and Greco-Roman and Biblical Genealogies." In *Luke-Acts: New Perspectives from the Society of Biblical Literature Seminar,* edited by Charles H. Talbert, 169–187. New York: Crossroad, 1984.

————. "Narrative Approaches to Luke-Acts." *Bib* 68 (1987): 195–220.

————. "Narrative Models for Imitation in Luke-Acts." In *Greeks, Romans, and Christians: Essays in Honor of Abraham J. Malherbe,* edited by Wayne A. Meeks, David L. Balch, and Everett Ferguson, 171–189. Minneapolis: Fortress Press, 1990.

Lake, Kirsopp. "The Apostolic Council of Jerusalem." Additional Note 16. In *The Beginnings of Christianity.* Part 1: *The Acts of the Apostles.* Vol. 5: *Additional Notes to the Commentary.* 1933. Reprint. Edited by Kirsopp Lake and Henry J. Cadbury, 195–212. Grand Rapids, Mich.: Baker Book House, 1979.

Lake, Kirsopp, and Henry J. Cadbury, eds. *Additional Notes to the Commentary.* 1933. Reprint. Vol. 5 of *The Beginnings of Christianity.* Part 1: *The Acts of the Apostles,* edited by F. J. Foakes Jackson and Kirsopp Lake. Grand Rapids, Mich.: Baker Book House, 1979.

Lambrecht, Jan. "Rhetorical Criticism and the New Testament." *Bijdragen, Tidschrift voor Filosofie en Theologie* 50, no. 3 (1989): 239–253.

Lanser, Susan Sniader. *The Narrative Act: Point of View in Prose Fiction.* Princeton: Princeton University Press, 1981.

Lategan, Bernard C. "Coming to Grips with the Reader in Biblical Literature." *Semeia* 48 (1989): 3–17. In Issue: Reader Perspectives on the New Testament. Edited by Edgar V. McKnight.

————. "Current Issues in the Hermeneutical Debate." *Neotestamentica* 18 (1984): 1–17.

Lategan, Bernard C., and Willem S. Vorster. *Text and Reality: Aspects of Reference in Biblical Texts.* Atlanta: Scholars Press, 1985.

Laurentin, René. *Comment réconcilier l'exégèse et la foi.* Paris: OEIL, 1984.

————. *Jésus au temple: Mystère de Pâques et foi de Marie en Luc 2.48–50.* Etudes bibliques. Paris: Gabalda, 1966.

————. *Structure et théologie de Luc I–II.* Paris: Gabalda, 1957.

Lindars, Barnabas. *New Testament Apologetic: The Doctrinal Significance of the Old Testament Quotations.* Philadelphia: Westminster Press, 1961.

Lohfink, Gerhard. *Die Sammlung Israels: Eine Untersuchung zur lukanischen Ekklesiologie.* Studien zum Alten und Neuen Testament 39. Munich: Kösel-Verlag, 1975.

Lohse, Eduard. "Die Bedeutung des Pfingstberichtes im Rahmen des lukanischen Geschichtswerkes." *EvT* 13 (1953): 422–436.

Lord, Albert B. "The Gospels as Oral Traditional Literature." In *The Relationships Among the Gospels: An Interdisciplinary Dialogue,* edited by William O. Walker, 33–91. San Antonio: Trinity University Press, 1978.

Lotman, J. M. "Point of View in a Text." Chapter 8 of his *Struktura Khudozhestvennogo Teksta* (1970). Reprint translated by L. M. O'Toole. *New Literary History* 6 (1974–75): 339–352.

Luedemann, Gerd. *Early Christianity According to the Traditions in Acts.* Philadelphia: Fortress Press, 1988.

McDonnell, Kilian, and George T. Montague. *Christian Initiation and Baptism in the Holy Spirit: Evidence from the First Eight Centuries.* A Michael Glazier Book. Collegeville, Minn.: Liturgical Press, 1991.

Mack, Burton L. *Rhetoric and the New Testament.* Guides to Biblical Scholarship, New Testament Series. Minneapolis: Fortress Press, 1990.

McKnight, Edgar V. *The Bible and the Reader: An Introduction to Literary Criticism.* Philadelphia: Fortress Press, 1985.

————. *Post-Modern Use of the Bible: The Emergence of Reader-Oriented Criticism.* Nashville: Abingdon Press, 1988.

————, ed. *Semeia* 48 (1989). Issue: Reader Perspectives on the New Testament.

Maddox, Robert. *The Purpose of Luke-Acts.* Göttingen: Vandenhoeck & Ruprecht, 1982.

Magness, J. Lee. *Sense and Absence: Structure and Suspension in the Ending of Mark's Gospel.* Semeia Studies. Atlanta, Ga.: Scholars Press, 1986.

Mailloux, Stephen. *Interpretive Conventions: The Reader in the Study of American Fiction.* Ithaca, N.Y.: Cornell University Press, 1982.

————. "Reader-Response Criticism?" *Genre* 10 (1977): 413–431.

Malherbe, Abraham J. "Epistolary Theory and Rhetoric." *Ohio Journal of Religious Studies* 5 (1977): 3–77.

———. *Moral Exhortation: A Greco-Roman Sourcebook.* Library of Early Christianity 4. Philadelphia: Westminster Press, 1986.

———. " 'Not in a Corner': Early Christian Apologetic in Acts 26:26." *Sec Cent* (1985–86): 193–210.

———. *Paul and the Popular Philosophers.* Minneapolis: Fortress Press, 1989.

———. *Paul and the Thessalonians: The Philosophic Tradition of Pastoral Care.* Philadelphia: Fortress Press, 1987.

Marshall, I. Howard. *The Gospel of Luke: A Commentary on the Greek Text.* The New International Greek Testament Commentary 3. Grand Rapids, Mich.: William B. Eerdmans, 1978.

Martin, Francis. "Literary Theory, Philosophy of History and Exegesis." *The Thomist* 52 (October 1988): 575–604.

———, ed. *Narrative Parallels to the New Testament.* SBL Resources for Biblical Study 22. Atlanta: Scholars Press, 1988.

Martin, George, ed. *Scripture and the Charismatic Renewal: Proceedings of the Milwaukee Symposium December 1–3, 1978.* Ann Arbor, Mich.: Servant Books, 1979.

Martin, James P. "Toward a Post-Critical Paradigm." *NTS* 33 (1987): 370–385.

Martin, Wallace. *Recent Theories of Narrative.* Ithaca, N.Y.: Cornell University Press, 1986.

Matera, Frank J. "The Plot of Matthew's Gospel." *CBQ* 40 (April 1987): 233–253.

Metzger, Bruce M. *A Textual Commentary on the Greek New Testament.* London and New York: United Bible Societies, 1971.

Miller, Merrill P. "Targum, Midrash and the Use of the Old Testament in the New Testament." *JSJ* 2 (1971): 29–82.

Mills, Watson E. *A Bibliography of the Periodical Literature on the Acts of the Apostles 1962–1984.* NovT Supplements 58. Leiden: E. J. Brill, 1986.

Mitchell, W. J. T., ed. *On Narrative.* Chicago: University of Chicago Press, 1981.

Moessner, David P. *Lord of the Banquet: The Literary and Theological Significance of the Lukan Travel Narrative.* Minneapolis: Fortress Press, 1989.

Montague, George T. "Hermeneutics and the Teaching of Scripture." In *Scripture and the Charismatic Renewal: Proceedings of the Milwaukee Symposium December 1–3, 1978,* edited by George Martin, 75–95, notes pp. 123–126. Ann Arbor, Mich.: Servant Books, 1979.

Moore, Stephen D. "Are the Gospels Unified Narratives?" *SBLSP* 1987 (1987): 443–458. Atlanta: Scholars Press.

———. *Literary Criticism and the Gospels. The Theoretical Challenge.* New Haven: Yale University Press, 1989.

———. "Narrative Commentaries on the Bible: Context, Roots, and Prospects." *Forum* 3 (1987) 29–62.

———. "Postmodernism and Biblical Studies." *Forum* 5 (September 1989): 36–41. Special Issue: Literary Criticism.

Moxnes, Halvor. *The Economy of the Kingdom: Social Conflict and Economic Relations in Luke's Gospel.* Overtures to Biblical Theology. Philadelphia: Fortress Press, 1988.

Nelson, William. "From 'Listen, Lordings' to 'Dear Reader.'" *University of Toronto Quarterly* (1976–77): 110–124.

Neuhaus, Richard John, ed. *Biblical Interpretation in Crisis: The Ratzinger Conference on Bible and Church.* Papers by Joseph Cardinal Ratzinger, Raymond E. Brown, William H. Lazareth, and George Lindbeck. Encounter Series. Grand Rapids, Mich.: William B. Eerdmans, 1989.

Neyrey, Jerome. "The Absence of Jesus' Emotions—the Lukan Redaction of Lk. 22,39–46." *Bib* 61 (1980): 153–171.

———. "The Forensic Defense Speech and Paul's Trial Speeches in Acts 22–26: Form and Function." In *Luke-Acts: New Perspectives from the Society of Biblical Literature Seminar,* edited by Charles H. Talbert, 210–224. New York: Crossroad, 1984.

———. *The Passion According to Luke: A Redaction Study of Luke's Soteriology.* Theological Inquiries. New York: Paulist Press, 1985.

Nolland, John. *Luke 1–9:20.* Word Biblical Commentary 35A. Dallas, Tex.: Word Books, 1989.

O'Toole, Robert F. *The Christological Climax of Paul's Defense (Ac 22:1–26:32).* Analecta Biblica 78. Rome: Biblical Institute Press, 1978.

Ong, Walter J. *Interfaces of the Word: Studies in the Evolution of Consciousness and Culture.* Ithaca, N.Y.: Cornell University Press, 1977.

———. *Orality and Literacy: The Technologizing of the Word.* New Accents. New York: Methuen, 1982.

———. *The Presence of the Word: Some Prolegomena for Cultural and Religious History.* New York: Simon and Schuster, 1967.

———. "Text as Interpretation: Mark and After." *Semeia* 39 (1987): 7–26. In Issue: Orality, Aurality and Biblical Narrative. Edited by Lou H. Silberman.

———. "A Writer's Audience is Always a Fiction." Chapter 8 in his *Interfaces of the Word: Studies in the Evolution of Consciousness and Culture,* 53–81. Ithaca, N.Y.: Cornell University Press, 1977.

Osiek, Carolyn. "The New Handmaid: The Bible and the Social Sciences." *TS* 50 (1989): 260–278.

Parsons, Mikeal. "Christian Origins and Narrative Openings: The Sense of a Beginning in Acts 1–5." *ReExp* 87 (1990): 403–422.

———. *The Departure of Jesus in Luke-Acts: The Ascension Narratives in Con-*

text. Journal for the Study of the New Testament Supplement Series 21. Sheffield, England: JSOT Press, 1987.

———. "Narrative Closure and Openness in the Plot of the Third Gospel: The Sense of an Ending in Luke 24:50–53." *SBLSP* (1986): 201–223.

Perelman, Chaim and Lucie Olbrechts-Tyteca. *The New Rhetoric: A Treatise on Argumentation.* Translated by John Wilkinson and Purcell Weaver. Notre Dame, Ind.: University of Notre Dame Press, 1969.

———. *Realm of Rhetoric.* Translated by William Kluback. With an introduction by Carroll C. Arnold. Notre Dame, Ind.: University of Notre Dame Press, 1982.

Perkins, Pheme. "Crisis in Jerusalem? Narrative Criticism in New Testament Studies." *TS* 50, no. 2 (1989): 296–313.

Perry, Menakhem. "Literary Dynamics: How the Order of a Text Creates Its Meanings [With an Analysis of Faulkner's 'A Rose for Emily']." *Poetics Today* 1, nos. 1–2 (1979): 35–64, 311–361.

Pervo, Richard I. *Profit with Delight: The Literary Genre of the Acts of the Apostles.* Philadelphia: Fortress Press, 1987.

Pesch, Rudolf. *Die Apostelgeschichte. 1. Teilband: Apg 1–12.* Evangelisch-Katholischer Kommentar zum Neuen Testament 5.1. Zürich/Köln/Neukirchen-Vluyn: Einsiedeln/Benziger/Neukirchener Verlag, 1986.

———. *Die Apostelgeschichte. 2. Teilband: Apg 13–28.* Evangelisch-Katholischer Kommentar zum Neuen Testament 5.2. Zürich/Köln/Neukirchen-Vluyn: Einsiedeln/Benziger/Neukirchener Verlag, 1986.

Petersen, Norman R. *Literary Criticism for New Testament Critics.* Guides to Biblical Scholarship, New Testament Series. Philadelphia: Fortress Press, 1978.

———. "Literary Criticism in Biblical Studies." In *Orientation by Disorientation: Studies in Literary Criticism and Biblical Literary Criticism,* edited by Richard A. Spencer, 25–50. Pittsburgh: Pickwick Press, 1980.

———. "The Reader in the Gospel." *Neotestamentica* 18 (1984): 38–51.

———. *Rediscovering Paul: Philemon and the Sociology of Paul's Narrative World.* Philadelphia: Fortress Press, 1985.

———. "When is the End not the End?: Literary Reflections on the Ending of Mark's Narrative." *Interpretation* 34 (1980): 151–166.

Pilgrim, Walter E. *Good News to the Poor: Wealth and Poverty in Luke-Acts.* New York: Paulist Press, 1981.

Plümacher, Eckhard. "Wirklichkeitserfahrung und Geschichtsschreibung bei Lukas: Erwägungen zu den Wir-Stücken der Apostelgeschichte." *ZNW* 68 (1977): 2–22.

Poland, Lynn M. *Literary Criticism and Biblical Hermeneutics: A Critique of Formalist Approaches.* American Academy of Religion Academy Series, 48. Chico, Calif.: Scholars Press, 1985.

Popper, Karl R. *The Poverty of Historicism*. New York: Harper and Row, Harper Torchbooks, 1964.

Porter, Stanley E. "Thucydides 1.22.1 and Speeches in Acts: Is There a Thucydidean View?" *NovT* 32 (April 1990): 121–142.

———. "Why Hasn't Reader-Response Criticism Caught on in New Testament Studies?" *Journal of Literature & Theology* 4 (November 1990): 278–292.

Potterie, Ignace de la. "Reading Holy Scripture 'In the Spirit': Is the Patristic Way of Reading the Bible Still Possible Today?" *Communio International Catholic Review* 13 (Winter 1986): 308–325. Special Issue: On the Reading of Scripture.

Powell, Mark Allen. *The Bible and Modern Literary Criticism: A Critical Assessment and Annotated Bibliography*. Westport, Conn.: Greenwood Press, 1992.

———. "The Bible and Modern Literary Criticism." *American Theological Library Association: Proceedings* 43 (1989): 78–94.

———. "Types of Readers and Their Relevance for Biblical Hermeneutics." *Trinity Seminary Review* 12 (Fall 1990): 67–76.

———. *What is Narrative Criticism?* Guides to Biblical Scholarship, New Testament Series. Minneapolis: Fortress Press, 1990.

Poythress, Vern S. "Philosophical Roots of Phenomenological and Structuralist Literary Criticism." *WTJ* 41 (1978–79): 165–171.

Praeder, Susan Marie. "Jesus-Paul, Peter-Paul, and Jesus-Peter Parallelisms in Luke-Acts: A History of Reader Response." In *SBLSP* 1984, 23–39. Chico, Calif.: Scholars Press, 1984.

———. "The Narrative Voyage: An Analysis and Interpretation of Acts 27–28." Ph.D. diss., Graduate Theological Union, 1980.

———. "The Problem of First Person Narration in Acts." *NovT* 29 (July 1987): 193–218.

Pratt, Mary Louise. *Toward a Speech Act Theory of Literary Discourse*. Bloomington: Indiana University Press, 1977.

Prickett, Stephen. "The Status of Biblical Narrative." *Pacifica* 2 (1989): 26–46.

———. *Words and the Word: Language, Poetics and Biblical Interpretation*. Cambridge: Cambridge University Press, 1986.

Quinn, Jerome D. "The Last Volume of Luke: The Relation of Luke-Acts to the Pastoral Epistles." In *Perspectives on Luke-Acts*, edited by Charles H. Talbert, 62–75. Perspectives in Religious Studies: Special Studies Series 5. Danville, Va.: Association of Baptist Professors of Religion, 1978.

Rajnath, ed. *Deconstruction: A Critique*. London: Macmillan Press, 1989.

Reese, James M. *Experiencing the Good News: The New Testament as Communication*. Good News Studies 10. Wilmington, Del.: Michael Glazier, 1984.

Resseguie, James L. "Reader-response Criticism and the Synoptic Gospels." *Journal of the American Academy of Religion* 52 (1984): 302–324.

Rhoads, David. "Narrative Criticism and the Gospel of Mark." *Journal of the American Academy of Religion* 50 (1982): 411–434.

Rhoads, David, and Donald Michie. *Mark as Story: An Introduction to the Narrative of a Gospel.* Philadelphia: Fortress Press, 1982.

Richard, Earl. *Acts 6:1–8:4: The Author's Method of Composition.* SBLDS 41. Missoula, Mont.: Scholars Press, 1978.

———, ed. *New Views on Luke and Acts.* A Michael Glazier Book. Collegeville, Minn.: Liturgical Press, 1990.

Ricoeur, Paul. *The Conflict of Interpretation: Essays in Hermeneutics.* Edited by Don Ihde. Northwestern University Studies in Phenomenology and Existential Philosophy. Evanston: Northwestern University Press, 1974.

———. *Essays on Biblical Interpretation.* Philadelphia: Fortress Press, 1980.

———. "The Hermeneutical Function of Distanciation." *Philosophy Today* 17 (1973): 129–141.

———. *History and Truth.* Translated and introduced by Charles Kelbley. Northwestern University Studies on Phenomenology and Existential Philosophy. Evanston: Northwestern University Press, 1965.

———. *Interpretation Theory: Discourse and the Surplus of Meaning.* Fort Worth: Texas Christian University Press, 1976.

———. *The Rule of Metaphor: Multi-disciplinary Studies of the Creation of Meaning in Language.* Translated by Robert Czerny, Kathleen McLaughlin, and John Costello. Toronto: University of Toronto Press, 1977.

———. *Time and Narrative.* 2 vols. Translated by Kathleen McLaughlin and David Pellauer. Chicago: University of Chicago Press, 1984–85.

———. *Time and Narrative.* Translated by Kathleen Blamey and David Pellauer. Vol. 3. Chicago: University of Chicago Press, 1988.

Rimmon-Kenan, Shlomith. *Narrative Fiction: Contemporary Poetics.* New Accents. New York: Methuen, 1983.

Robbins, Vernon K. "By Land and by Sea: The We-Passages and Ancient Sea Voyages." In *Perspectives on Luke-Acts,* edited by Charles H. Talbert, 215–242. Perspectives in Religious Studies: Special Studies Series 5. Danville, Va.: Association of Baptist Professors of Religion, 1978.

Roloff, Jürgen. *Die Apostelgeschichte.* 17th ed., no. 1 new version. Das Neue Testament Deutsch 5. Göttingen: Vandenhoeck & Ruprecht, 1981.

Rorty, Richard, J. B. Schneewind, and Quentin Skinner, eds. *Philosophy in History: Essays on the Historiography of History.* Cambridge: Cambridge University Press, 1984.

Ruthrof, Horst. *The Reader's Construction of Narrative.* Boston: Routledge and Kegan Paul, 1981.

Sacks, Kenneth S. "Rhetorical Approaches to Greek History Writing in the Hellenistic Period." In *SBLSP 1984,* 123–133. Chico, Calif.: Scholars Press, 1984.

Said, Edward W. *Beginnings: Intention and Method.* New York: Basic, 1975.

Sanders, E. P., ed. *Aspects of Judaism in the Greco-Roman Period.* Vol. 2 of *Jewish and Christian Self-definition.* Philadelphia: Fortress Press, 1981.

———, ed. *Self-definition in the Greco-Roman World.* Vol. 3 of *Jewish and Christian Self-definition.* Philadelphia: Fortress Press, 1982.

———, ed. *The Shaping of Christianity in the Second and Third Centuries.* Vol. 1 of *Jewish and Christian Self-definition.* Philadelphia: Fortress Press, 1980.

Sanders, James A. "Adaptable for Life: The Nature and Function of Canon." 1972. Reprinted in his *From Sacred Story to Sacred Text,* 9–39. Philadelphia: Fortress Press, 1987.

———. *Canon and Community: A Guide to Canonical Criticism.* Guides to Biblical Scholarship, Old Testament Series. Philadelphia: Fortress Press, 1984.

———. *From Sacred Story to Sacred Text.* Philadelphia: Fortress Press, 1987.

———. "Hermeneutics." In *IDBSup,* 402–407. Nashville: Abingdon Press, 1976.

Scheub, Harold. "Oral Narrative Process and the Use of Models." *New Literary History* 6 (1974–75): 353–377.

Schmidt, Daryl. "The Historiography of Acts: Deuteronomistic or Hellenistic?" In *SBLSP* 1985, edited by Kent Harold Richards, 417–427. Atlanta: Scholars Press, 1985.

———. "Tyson's Approach to the Literary Death of Luke's Jesus." *Perkins Journal* 40 (April 1987): 33–38.

Schneider, Gerhard. *Die Apostelgeschichte. I. Teil: Kommentar Zu Kap. 1,1-8,40.* Edited by Alfred Wikenhauser, Anton Vögtle, and Rudolf Schnackenburg. Herders Theologischer Kommentar zum Neuen Testament 5.1. Freiburg: Herder, 1980.

———. *Die Apostelgeschichte. II. Teil: Kommentar Zu Kap. 9,1-28,31.* Edited by Alfred Wikenhauser, Anton Vögtle, and Rudolf Schnackenburg. Herders Theogischer Kommentar zum Neuen Testament 5.2. Freiburg: Herder, 1982.

Scholes, Robert, and Robert Kellogg. *The Nature of Narrative.* New York: Oxford University Press, 1966.

Schubert, Paul. "The Place of the Areopagus Speech in the Composition of Acts." In *Transitions in Biblical Scholarship,* edited by J. Court Rylaarsdam, 235–261. Chicago: University of Chicago Press, 1968.

Schuler, Philip L. "Questions of an Holistic Approach to Luke-Acts." *Perkins Journal* 40 (April 1987): 43–47.

Schwartz, Regina M., ed. *The Book and the Text: The Bible and Literary Theory.* Cambridge, Mass.: Basil Blackwell, 1990.

Searle, John R. *Speech Acts: An Essay in the Philosophy of Language.* Cambridge: Cambridge University Press, 1969.

Seung, T. K. *Structuralism and Hermeneutics.* New York: Columbia University Press, 1982.

Sheeley, Steven M. "Narrative Asides and Narrative Authority in Luke-Acts." *BTB* 18 (July 1988): 102–107.

———. "The Narrator in the Gospels: Developing a Model." *Perspectives in Religious Studies* 16 (Fall 1989): 213–223.

Sheppard, Gerald T. "Canonization: Hearing the Voice of the Same God Through Historically Dissimilar Situations." *Interpretation* 36 (January 1982): 21–33.

Silberman, Lou H., ed. *Semeia* 39 (1978). Issue: Orality, Aurality and Biblical Narrative.

Smith, D. Moody. *John*. 2d. rev. and enlarged ed. Proclamation Commentaries. Philadelphia: Fortress Press, 1986.

Smith, David L., ed. "The Book of Acts." *Didaskalia* 2 (October 1990): 5–43.

Smith, Dennis E., ed. *Semeia* 52 (1991). Issue: How Gospels Begin.

Soards, Marion L. *The Passion According to Luke: The Special Material of Luke-Acts*. Journal for the Study of the Old Testament Supplement Series. Sheffield: JSOT Press, 1987.

Starr, Raymond J. "Reading Aloud: Lectores and Roman Reading." *Classical Journal* 86 (April-May 1991): 337–343.

Stegemann, Wolfgang. *Zwischen Synagoge und Obrigkeit: Zur historischen Situation der lukanischen Christen*. Forschungen zur Religion und Literatur des Alten und Neuen Testaments 152. Göttingen: Vandenhoeck & Ruprecht, 1991.

Steiner, George. " 'Critic'/'Reader' " *New Literary History* 10 (1979): 423–452.

Stendahl, Krister. "Contemporary Biblical Theology." In *IDB* (1962) vol. 1, 418–432.

Sternberg, Meir. *The Poetics of Biblical Narrative: Ideological Literature and the Drama of Reading*. Indiana Literary Biblical Series. Bloomington: Indiana University Press, 1985.

Sternberg, Meir, and Menakhem Perry. "The King Through Ironic Eyes: Biblical Narrative and the Literary Reading Process." *Poetics Today* 7 (1986): 275–322.

Stuhlmacher, Peter. *Historical Criticism and Theological Interpretation of Scripture: Towards a Hermeneutics of Consent*. Translated by Roy A. Harrisville. Philadelphia: Fortress Press, 1977.

———. *Vom Verstehen des Neuen Testament: Eine Hermeneutik*. 2d ed. Grundrisse zum Neuen Testament. Göttingen: Vandenhoeck & Ruprecht, 1986.

Suleiman, Susan R. "Redundancy and the 'Readable' Text." *Poetics Today* 1 (1980): 119–142.

Suleiman, Susan R., and Inge Crosman, eds. *The Reader in the Text: Essays on Audience and Interpretation*. Princeton: Princeton University Press, 1980.

Talbert, Charles H. "Prophecies of Future Greatness: The Contribution of Greco-Roman Biographies to an Understanding of Luke 1:5–4:15." In *The Divine*

Helmsman: Studies on God's Control of Human Events, Presented to Lou H. Silberman, edited by James L. Crenshaw and Samuel Sandmel, 129–141. New York: Ktav Publishing House, 1980.

——. *Reading Luke: A Literary and Theological Commentary on the Third Gospel.* New York: Crossroad, 1982.

——, ed. *Luke-Acts: New Perspectives from the Society of Biblical Literature Seminar.* New York: Crossroad, 1984.

——, ed. *Perspectives on Luke-Acts.* Perspectives in Religious Studies: Special Studies Series 5. Danville, Va.: Association of Baptist Professors of Religion, 1978.

Tannehill, Robert C. "Israel in Luke-Acts: A Tragic Story." *JBL* 104 (1985): 69–85.

——. *The Narrative Unity of Luke-Acts: A Literary Interpretation.* Vol. 1: *The Gospel According to Luke.* Foundations and Facets. Minneapolis: Fortress Press, 1986.

——. *The Narrative Unity of Luke-Acts: A Literary Interpretation.* Vol. 2: *The Acts of the Apostles.* Foundations and Facets. Minneapolis: Fortress Press, 1990.

——. "Rejection by Jews and Turning to Gentiles: The Pattern of Paul's Mission in Acts." In *Luke-Acts and the Jewish People: Eight Critical Perspectives,* edited by Joseph B. Tyson, 96–101. Minneapolis: Augsburg Publishing House, 1988.

Theological Studies 50 (June 1989). Special Issue: Biblical Scholarship.

Thiemann, Ronald F. *Revelation and Theology: The Gospel as Narrated Promise.* Notre Dame, Ind.: University of Notre Dame Press, 1985.

Thiselton, Anthony C. *The Two Horizons: New Testament Hermeneutics and Philosophical Description with Special Reference to Heidegger, Bultmann, Gadamer, and Wittgenstein.* Grand Rapids, Mich.: William B. Eerdmans, 1977.

Thompson, Mary R. *The Role of Disbelief in Mark: A New Approach to the Second Gospel.* New York: Paulist Press, 1989.

Tiede, David L. *Prophecy and History in Luke-Acts.* Philadelphia: Fortress Press, 1980.

Todorov, Tzvetan. *The Fantastic: A Structural Approach to a Literary Genre.* Translated by Richard Howard. Ithaca, N.Y.: Cornell University Press, 1975.

——. *The Poetics of Prose.* Translated by Richard Howard. Ithaca, N.Y.: Cornell University Press, 1977.

——. *Theories of the Symbol.* Translated by Catherine Porter. Ithaca, N.Y.: Cornell University Press, 1982.

Tompkins, Jane P., ed. *Reader-Response Criticism: From Formalism to Post-Structuralism.* Baltimore: Johns Hopkins University Press, 1980.

Torgovnick, Marianna. *Closure in the Novel.* Princeton: Princeton University Press, 1981.

Trible, Phyllis. *God and the Rhetoric of Sexuality.* Overtures to Biblical Theology. Philadelphia: Fortress Press, 1978.

Trompf, G. W. *The Idea of Historical Recurrence in Western Thought: From Antiquity to the Reformation.* Berkeley: University of California Press, 1979.

Tyson, Joseph B. "Source Criticism of the Gospel of Luke." In *Perspectives on Luke-Acts,* edited by Charles H. Talbert, 24–39. Perspectives in Religious Studies: Special Studies Series 5. Danville, Va.: Association of Baptist Professors of Religion, 1978.

————, ed. *Luke-Acts and the Jewish People: Eight Critical Perspectives.* Minneapolis: Augsburg Publishing House, 1988.

Uspensky, Boris, *A Poetics of Composition: The Structure of the Artistic Text and Typology of a Compositional Form.* Translated by Valentina Zavarin and Susan Wittig. Berkeley: University of California Press, 1973.

Valdés, Mario J., and Owen J. Miller. *Interpretation of Narrative.* Toronto: University of Toronto Press, 1978.

Vanhoozer, Kevin J. *Biblical Narrative in the Philosophy of Paul Ricoeur: A Study in Hermeneutics and Theology.* New York: Cambridge University Press, 1990.

Vanhoye, A., ed. *L'Apôtre Paul: Personalité, style et concêption du ministère.* Bibliotheca Ephemeridum Theologicarum Lovaniensium. Leuven: Leuven University Press, 1986.

Veltman, Fred. "The Defense Speeches of Paul in Acts." In *Perspectives on Luke-Acts,* edited by Charles H. Talbert, 243–256. Perspectives in Religious Studies: Special Studies Series 5. Danville, Va.: Association of Baptist Professors of Religion, 1978.

Wagner, Günter, ed. *An Exegetical Bibliography of the New Testament: Luke and Acts.* Macon, Ga.: Mercer University Press, 1985.

Wall, Robert. "The Acts of the Apostles in Canonical Context." *BTB* 18 (1988): 16–24.

Wallace, Martin. *Recent Theories of Narrative.* Ithaca, N.Y.: Cornell University Press, 1986.

Walworth, Allen James. "The Narrator of Acts." Ph.D. dissertation, Southern Baptist Theological Seminary, 1985.

Warnecke, Heinz. *Die tatsächliche Romfahrt des Apostels Paulus.* Stuttgarter Bibelstudien 127. Stuttgart: Verlag Katholisches Bibelwerk, 1987.

Warner, Martin, ed. *The Bible as Rhetoric: Studies in Biblical Persuasion and Credibility.* Warwick Studies in Philosophy and Literature. New York: Routledge, 1990.

Watson, D. F. "The New Testament and Greco-Roman Rhetoric: A Bibliography." *Journal of the Evangelical Theological Society* 31 (1988): 465–472.

Wehnert, Jürgen. *Die Wir-Passagen der Apostelgeschichte. Ein lukanisches Stilmittel aus jüdischer Tradition.* Göttinger theologische Arbeiten 40. Göttingen: Vandenhoeck & Ruprecht, 1989.

Weimann, Robert. *Structure and Society in Literary History: Studies in the History and Theory of Historical Criticism.* Charlottesville, Va.: University Press of Virginia, 1976.

————. *Structure and Society in Literary History: Studies in the History and Theory of Historical Criticism.* Expanded ed. Baltimore: Johns Hopkins University Press, 1984.

White, Hayden. *Metahistory: The Historical Imagination in Nineteenth-Century Europe.* Baltimore: Johns Hopkins University Press, 1973.

White, Hugh C., ed. *Semeia* 41 (1988). Issue: Speech Act Theory and Biblical Criticism.

White, John L. *Light from Ancient Letters.* Foundations and Facets. Philadelphia: Fortress Press, 1986.

————. "New Testament Epistolary Literature in the Framework of Ancient Epistolography." In *Aufstieg und Niedergang der römischen Welt: Geschichte und Kultur Roms im Spiegel der neueren Forschung,* vol. 2.25, edited by Hildegard Temporini and Wolfgang Haase, 1730–1756. Berlin/New York: Walter de Gruyter, 1984.

Wikenhauser, Alfred. "Doppelträume." *Bib* 29 (1948): 100–111.

Wilckens, Ulrich. *Die Missionsreden der Apostelgeschichte: Form- und traditionsgeschichtliche Untersuchung.* 3d ed. Wissenschaftliche Monographien zum Alten und Neuen Testament 5. Neukirchen-Vluyn: Neukirchener Verlag, 1974.

Wildhaber, Bruno, O.Cist. *Paganism populaire et prédication apostolique: D'après l'exégèse de quelques séquences des Actes. Eléments pour une théologique lucanienne de la mission.* Genève: Éditions Labor et Fides, 1987.

Wiles, Maurice. "Scriptural Authority and Theological Construction: The Limitations of Narrative Interpretation." in *Scriptural Authority and Narrative Interpretation,* edited by Garrett Green, 42–58. Philadelphia: Fortress Press, 1987.

Wilson, Stephen G. *Luke and the Pastoral Epistles.* London: SPCK, 1979.

Wink, Walter. *The Bible in Human Transformation: Toward a New Paradigm for Biblical Study.* Philadelphia: Fortress Press, 1973.

Wuellner, Wilhelm. "Where is Rhetorical Criticism Taking Us?" *CBQ* 49 (July 1987): 448–453.

Yoder, John H[oward]. *The Politics of Jesus.* Grand Rapids, Mich.: William B. Eerdmans, 1972.

York, John O. *The Last Shall Be First: The Rhetoric of Reversal in Luke.* Journal for the Study of the New Testament Supplement Series 46. Sheffield: JSOT Press, 1991.

Zerwick, Maximilian. *Biblical Greek: Illustrated by Examples.* Translated and edited by Joseph Smith. Scripta Pontificii Instituti Biblici 114. Rome: Pontifical Biblical Institute, 1963.

Zerwick, Maximilian, and Mary Gosvenor. *A Grammatical Analysis of the Greek New Testament.* Unabridged, rev. ed. in one vol. Rome: Biblical Institute Press, 1981.

Index of Scripture and Other Ancient Writings

Primary treatments appear in bold print.

247

Index of Subjects and Names

Primary treatments appear in bold print.

255